Watching Race

Watching Race

Television and the Struggle
for "Blackness"

Herman Gray

University of Minnesota Press

Minneapolis / London

Chapter 7 was previously published, in slightly different form, as "Recodings: Possibilities and Limitations in commercial Television Representations of African American Culture," *Quarterly Review of Film and Video* 13, nos. 1–3 (Fall 1991): 117–30. Reprinted with permission of Harwood Academic Publishers.

Published by the University of Minnesota Press
111 Third Avenue South, Suite 290, Minnesota, MN 55401-2520
http://www.upress.umn.edu
Printed in the United States of America on acid-free paper

Second printing 1998

Library of Congress Cataloging-in-Publication Data

Gray, Herman.
    Watching race : television and the struggle for "Blackness" /
Herman Gray.
        p.   cm.
    Includes bibliographical references and index.
    ISBN 0-8166-2250-7 (hc)
    ISBN 0-8166-2251-5 (pb)
    1. Afro-Americans in television.   I. Title.
PN1992.8.A34G73   1995
791.45'6520396073—dc20   94-31783

The University of Minnesota is an
equal-opportunity educator and employer.

In memory of Lucille Dudly, my grandmother, who passed away while I was writing this book, and for Maya, my niece

Contents

CONTENTS

Acknowledgments

During the Clarence Thomas confirmation hearings and again after a PBS broadcast featuring Cornel West and Sister Souljah, a very dear friend and colleague, Hardy Frye, would often invite me out for a drink in order to discuss these (and other) media events that focused so squarely on blacks. Hardy would invariably begin our conversation with, "Gray, you are the media expert, explain this shit to me." Now, I should explain that Hardy is a professor of sociology with a long and respected history as a scholar, teacher, writer, and, most important, political activist. Frye cut his political teeth in SNCC's Mississippi voter registration campaigns during the "freedom summers" in the 1960s. But something about the new conditions of black political discourse—the facts that television figured so prominently, that cultural matters occupied such a central place, and that little of it seemed to have a direct and measurable impact on the material lives and circumstances of large numbers of poor and disenfranchised blacks—seemed deeply puzzling and troubling to him.

My conversations with Hardy (and other friends as well) about these matters seemed to accelerate as more and more debates, controversies, and spectacles appeared in the media in the form of controversies about gansta rap, the Los Angeles riots, and the Whoopi Goldberg Friars Club roast, the humor on HBO's *Russell Simmons' Def Comedy Jam,* and the antics of comedian Martin Lawrence on network television. Hardy's rich political history and the practical organizational and political concerns that underwrite them did not help him make sense of increasingly troubling representations of and claims on blackness in commercial media and popular culture.

Hardy's impatience with the disturbing spectacles and frustrating (often naive) cultural politics is emblematic, for he is certainly not alone in his frustration and impatience with the turn toward media and culture and what seems like an increasing disconnection from the immediacy, urgency, and materiality of social transformation. This frustration stems not so much from a desire to return to the direct organizing campaigns of the 1960s as, perhaps, from the fact that the politics of media and culture and the struggles over representation that occur there seem to take up so much space, transforming everything into matters of spin, image, and discourse. The preoccupation with cultural politics appears to displace and gloss over any connection to the material circumstances and conditions of people's everyday lives, translating the difficult and messy work of political organization and struggle for social transformation and social justice into an endless analysis of consumer commodities, role models, and images.

Along with Hardy, I've had countless conversations and provocative exchanges with friends, colleagues, and students about media and cultural politics. This book is an extension of many of these conversations. In thinking through the issues explored here, I have had a great deal of help. I am grateful to the many colleagues and friends whose support, encouragement, and community made the completion of this book possible.

I owe a special debt of gratitude to Rosa Linda Fregoso, my companion, confidante, and intellectual partner. A fine film scholar in her own right, Rosa Linda has a critical understanding of cultural politics, representation, and feminism that helped me to make sense of both the power and the subtleties of the influence of media and popular culture in everyday life. In return I, along with her son Sergio, have tried to impress upon her the power and fun of the small screen. My thanks also to Xochitl for help with all the names, titles, and plot lines of various television episodes and to Sergio for turning me on to those amazing commercials for Sega Genesis. (Hey Serge, Sega!) Thanks to my parents, Lillie and Frank; to my sisters, Anne and Shirley; and to my niece, Maya, for being there for me.

In the course of writing this book I have formed many new friendships and deepened old ones. Clyde Taylor, Tommy Lott, and I talked about black cultural politics many a Sunday afternoon in Boston. Melvin Oliver was an especially gracious host and earnest sponsor during my year at UCLA. George Lipsitz has been an important supporter and intellecual influence over the years, and never more so than in the writing of this book. Robin D. G. Kelley, Horace Newcomb, and Lawrence Grossberg provided careful readings and critical comments on the manuscript. My editor, Janaki Bakhle, at the University of Minnesota Press was patient, encouraging, and determined in shepherding this project through to the end.

Kimberle Crenshaw, Valerie Smith, Teshome Gabriel, Richard Yarbrough, Ella Taylor, and Arthe Anthony provided a welcoming and stimulating community during a year's stay in Los Angeles. Sharon Baker and Earl Williams opened their home to me and were enormously helpful while I was establishing contacts within the television industry.

My thanks also to those who have studied and created forms of television and popular culture, and were willing to talk with me about that: Marlon Riggs, Vivian Kleiman, Patricia Turner, Clark White, Kobena Mercer, Sally Steenland, Stanley Robertson, Susan Fales, Dolores Morris, Kellie Goode, Phyllis Vinson-Tucker, Harvey Lehman, Marla Gibbs, Frank Dawson, Elliot Butler Evans, David Scott, Hamid Naficy, John Brown Childs, Richard Allen, Cynthia Martin, Kristal Brent Zook, Jimmie Reeves, Richard Campbell, Manthia Diawara, William Bielby, Hardy T. Frye, Tricia Rose, David Wellman, Sandra Ball-Rokeach, B. Ruby Rich, Lourdes Portillo, Saidya Hartman, Gilbert McCauley, Marti Taylor, Edward Guerrero, and Alvina Quintana. I learned a lot from watching a lot of television with Jeffrey Mitchell, Travis Dixon, and Kim Richards, all students at UCLA.

The University of California Office of the President provided the U.C. President's Postdoctoral Fellowship that enabled me to take a year's leave from teaching. A Faculty Research Grant from the University of California, Santa Cruz, Division of Social Science, also enabled me to complete the research and writing of this book. Special thanks go to Claudia Mitchell Kernan and Patricia, Jan, and Sandra at the Center for African American Studies at UCLA as well as the administrative staff in the UCLA Department of Sociology. The staff at the Instructional Media Lab at Powell Library, UCLA, went beyond the call of duty to record and make available episodes from the 1990 television season.

My thanks also to friends and colleagues at the following campuses for the opportunity to present various stages of this work: Center for African American Studies, UCLA; Department of Sociology, University of California, Santa Barbara; Ethnic Studies Department, University of California, San Diego; Ethnic Studies Department, University of California, Berkeley; Center for Cultural Studies, University of California, Santa Cruz; Humanities Research Institute, University of California, Irvine; Department of Communication, University of Michigan; Department of Communication, University of Texas; Annenberg School for Communication, University of Southern California.

1   Black Cultural Politics and Commercial Culture

In the contemporary politics of black popular culture, much critical attention has been given to identity and expressive culture. These critical discourses and the popular attention they have generated play a strategic role in the maintenance of and challenge to various systems of domination. My aim in this book is to extend these critical discourses and cultural strategies, particularly as they bear on commercial electronic mass-media forms, especially television. I examine critical debates about black expressive culture and black cultural productions within television as a means of exploring processes by which questions about the American racial order—and, within it, blackness—are constructed, reproduced, and challenged. Let me say early and directly that my focus on commercial network television and the struggles over the meanings and representations of blackness expressed and enacted there quite deliberately shifts attention to commercial media as a site of cultural politics.

The chapters that follow are guided by many of the theoretical advances and suggestions developed under the rubric of cultural studies, especially as these have been developed and applied by feminists and scholars of color. Most generally, I am concerned with trying to clarify just how we might talk about, theorize, and understand the representations of "blackness" presented in commercial culture, especially network television and the political projects in which these representations are deployed.

The decade of the 1980s constitutes the social and historical staging
ground for this examination. I have elected to situate the discussion in
the 1980s because it is a period rich with struggles, debates, and transformations in race relations, electronic media, cultural politics, and
economic life. As such, it constitutes a period in which it is possible to
chart the various ways in which the sign of blackness was constructed,
produced, claimed, performed, and struggled over in different social
arenas.

I want to take seriously commercial culture (especially commercial
television) and the kinds of representations that are produced and circulated there as the subject of critical reflection and analysis. I contend
that it is possible—indeed, very often necessary—to approach commercial culture as a place for theorizing about black cultural politics
and the struggles over meaning that are played out there. Hence, I
want to suggest that commercial culture serves as both a *resource* and
a *site* in which blackness as a cultural sign is produced, circulated, and
enacted.

I use the notions of *popular* and *culture* in terms of the wide-ranging but concrete and specific social practices, histories, desires, and
commonsense understandings of the world that are expressed, performed, and enacted within television texts, discourse, and material
life (Hall 1981a). I approach popular and commercial culture, then, in
terms of its power to organize, articulate, and disarticulate feelings
and understandings that move people, enlisting and positioning them
in different political and social configurations. To talk about popular
culture this way is to talk about the social, economic, and political
struggles operating in society as well as about cultural sites such as
commercial network television, film, and popular music in which
those struggles are made representable and take place.

This chapter details specifically how I use the model of cultural
studies to situate questions about the representation of and struggle
for the sign of blackness within the context of commercial television
entertainment, especially as they concern the issues of race, gender,
class, power, and inequality. This strategy of location, then, is necessarily about commercial television and the specific ways in which it
produces and represents the racial order, black Americans, and the
sign of blackness within that order through its complex strategies of
organization (both industrial and representational), narration, circulation, and exhibition. The issue remains just how American society,

through its dominant commercial institutions of representation, constructs, organizes, and represents blackness in the dominant popular imagination. In other words, how do our central institutions of representation (produced through rejection, appropriation, and marginalization) generally reconcile the presence of blackness with the American political, social, and cultural experience?

The field of cultural studies is a useful point of departure because its conceptual focus helps us think about the relationship between the representational practices produced "in" television and their relationship to the material experiences and locations of people who use, make meaning of, offer critiques on, and derive pleasure from their encounters with television.

Cultural Studies, Cultural Theory, and Black Cultural Politics

In thinking about cultural politics and commercial culture, I insist on keeping concerns with questions of power, inequality, domination, and difference at the forefront of analysis. I also aim to avoid the ahistorical and pessimistic tendencies of excessive structuralism as well as uncritical celebrations of the practices of collective and individual subjects (the working class, women, people of color) as resistance. These injunctions simply involve recognizing the central role of subjective discriminations, choices, and pleasures even while acknowledging the limits and constraints imposed on these experiences by the conditions, circumstances, and structures of cultural and material life in which we live and make meanings.

One of the most forceful critiques articulated by theorists and critics working within this framework has concerned the question of difference. The critiques and deconstructions of fixed and unified subject positions, identities, and historical forces have opened important new theoretical spaces. These conceptual openings have been especially important for studies of marginalized and subordinated peoples conducted by intellectuals and theorists of color. Such openings have been especially fruitful for studies of television and other popular media, because they have allowed for more complex understandings of televisual and cinematic practices, especially in terms of the relationships among race, class, and gender. No longer can our analyses be burdened unnecessarily by the weight of an eternal search for either "authentic" media representations of "blackness" or accurate reflections of African American social and cultural life. Nor are all of the representations operating at various sites of commercial culture simply and easily reduced to co-opted and weak approximations of African American life and culture. Our theoretical and critical readings are now open to the discoveries and identifications of a much broader and more complex range of representations. Moreover, these kinds of theoretical openings force us to take seriously the contradictory readings and interpretive strategies deployed by various segments of the audience, market, community, and so on. These openings have also forced a kind of deconstruction and critical interrogation of sites and conjunctions of domination and the exercise of power in liberal democracies such as the United States (Hall 1988).

These critiques have led to more complex and nuanced readings of television representations as well as the pleasures that various sectors of the audience derive from their encounters with television. Prompted by feminist as well as gay and lesbian scholars, these critical interventions have helped to destabilize and decenter simple and easy condemnations of media images and representations as evidence of secure and unified ideologies. Through such openings we have been forced to understand the complex, dynamic, and contradictory character of commercial forms such as television and the pleasures they produce. This has served to make scholars of popular culture and media, particularly those of us of color, take seriously the various locations and experiences of viewers and not reduce them to unified passive blocs on whom ideas are imposed.

Similarly, cultural critiques of essentialism and the recognition of the fluid and hybrid nature of identity and subjectivity in both the discursive and the nondiscursive have forced us to think in more complex ways about structures of power, sites of domination and contestation, and points of overlap and intersection, as well as to examine how and under what conditions we think about them (Collins 1990; Crenshaw 1989; Lorde 1990; Mercer 1992; Riggs 1991b; White 1990). These insights have placed at the center of theorizing the idea that practices, representations, and meanings, at the sites of the popular, are very much the subjects and objects of struggles across and within difference. Commercial culture is increasingly the central place where various memories, myths, histories, traditions, and practices circulate. At the site of commercial culture these practices and identifications are constantly assembled, torn apart, reassembled, and torn apart yet again by critics, viewers, and television makers such that they find discursive order resonance in everyday life (Fiske 1987).

Perhaps more important, on questions of identity, mass media, and popular culture these critical interventions have opened the way for critical intellectuals of color and students of popular and commercial culture to theorize how African Americans continually appropriate images and representations from commercial culture in order to reconstitute themselves and therefore transgress the cultural and social locations that constantly attempt to contain and police them. As I suggest in chapters 8, 9, and 10, advertising, rap music, sports, music videos, and television all provide materials (and cultural spaces) that people can appropriate, circulate, and recombine for their own meanings and uses beyond just those intended by the industrial commercial system. As I also show throughout this book, popular and commercial representations and cultural practices of blacks and blackness can also be used in racist, sexist, and homophobic ways; hence, they are not inherently resistant or automatically progressive.

To reiterate, then, the central thread of my argument is that commercial culture operates as both a site of and a resource for black cultural politics. Certainly the most difficult and challenging obstacle to the demonstration of such a claim is the construction of a theory incorporating the relationship between the representations and their productive practices in commercial culture (in this case, television) *and* the relationship of these representations to other discursive (and nondiscursive) sites and practices (e.g., legal, theoretical, and material). My hope is that, additionally, this book makes a convincing case that these cultural matters are also about politics and power, about struggle and transformation.

George Lipsitz (1990b) goes quite a way in helping to clarify the complexities of this relationship:

> Cultural forms create conditions of possibility, they expand the
> present by informing it with memories of the past and hopes for the
> future; but they also engender accommodation with prevailing power
> realities, separating art from life, and internalizing the dominant
> culture's norms and values as necessary and inevitable. *Politics and
> culture maintain a paradoxical relationship in which only effective
> political action can win breathing room for a new culture, but only a
> revolution in culture can make people capable of political action.
> Culture can seem like a substitute for politics, a way of posing only
> imaginary solutions to real problems,* but under other circumstances
> culture can become a rehearsal for politics, trying out values and
> beliefs permissible in art but forbidden in social life. Most often,
> however, *culture exists as a form of politics,* as a means of reshaping
> individual and collective practice for specified interests, and as long
> as individuals perceive their interests as unfilled, culture retains an
> oppositional potential. (p. 16; emphasis added)

It seems to me that too much of the uncritical celebration of commercial culture, or its easy condemnation by intellectuals and cultural critics, has missed the critical point directly addressed here by Lipsitz and elsewhere by Stuart Hall (1992a). Shortsighted and contemptuous dismissals of commercial culture often fail to appreciate the seminal

importance of the constant *articulations* or linkages at play in the relation between representational practices and social locations, dynam-
ics, and relationships (Grossberg 1992).

In order to establish the complexity and importance of the social
and discursive field in which social claims circulate, I devote chapters
2 and 3 to a mapping of various social, moral, and political claims on
blackness in the 1980s and the political projects, such as "Reaganism," to which these claims were put. More specifically, chapters 2 and
3 concentrate on the period of the 1980s. Chapters 2 and 3 appear in
the order that they do, not because I want to argue that black cultural
discourses are reactive, but because I aim to foreground Reaganism's
claims on blackness and at the same time to place these discourses on
blackness in dialogue with each other. I begin, then, with the discourse
of Reaganism because it constitutes the dominant discourse of the period. And although the subject of this book, television, may seem to
some largely secondary in these chapters, it is very present, for television constitutes part of the discursive field (and a major resource) in
which and over which these competing claims and struggles took
place.

As chapters 2 and 3 show, these multiple claims on blackness came
from white liberal democrats, white Reagan conservatives, black nationalists, critical black progressives, and black neoconservatives. I argue, too, that these claims and the discourses that structured them and
made their meanings readable and representable were staged primarily
through mass media, especially television. As Lipsitz (1990b) notes,
culture and the struggles over representation that take place there are
not just substitutes for some "real" politics that they inevitably replace
or at best delay; they simply represent a different, but no less important, site in the contemporary technological and postindustrial society
where political struggles take place. And it is the constant articulation
of representations to material circumstances, social formations, and
alliances of power that make a critical analysis and politics of culture
so very consequential. Chapters 2 and 3, then, function in this book as
a staging ground from which I will show just how competing productions and claims on blackness in the 1980s involved very real and very
consequential struggles that can be understood culturally.

Although cultural practices and traditions, including those on the
margins of the culture industry, remain important, their power to disrupt and destabilize, to generate alternative (even resistant) readings
and possibilities, is neither politically given nor text bound. Cultural
practices and the potential they hold are significant only in relation to
the political power, economic positions, social conditions, and lived
experiences of people. These practices, therefore, must be theorized

from inside the commodity form and inside market relations, where struggle is waged against the constant attempts to reconstitute and locate us as consumers in the cultural market (Willis 1991). To my mind, such struggles are significant because it is within the realm of commercial culture and representation that we are constantly being constituted and positioned, as well as reconstituting ourselves collectively and individually.

The logic of these dominating impulses and tendencies is always contingent and open to struggle, precisely because what things mean and how they register rest ultimately with their production in discourse as well as the moment of encounter and use (Fiske 1989; Hall 1989; Lipsitz 1990b). The meanings of things rest with what people do with them, how they use them, and under what circumstances pleasures and significance are produced (Fiske 1989). Thinking about culture as deeply contradictory and about culture's use by people sharpens our focus on its hegemonic as well as its counterhegemonic potentials. This strategy helps us to attend to the enormously complex and dynamic ways that people take from, identify with, reject, are duped by, and sometimes resist regimes of domination.

Black Cultural Politics and Commercial Television

The social, institutional, and historical contexts in which representations of blackness in television have been framed and located are the focus of chapters 4 and 5. Hence, this book is as much about "blackness" as it is about television. That is to say, it is not just about how television represents blackness or how blacks use television; rather, it is about the complex play between the sites of mass commercial media and black cultural politics.

I want to illustrate, in a somewhat preliminary way, these complex processes and relationships by examining the cultural politics operating in commercial television. At one level, these politics operate within the discursive confines of television as an industrial and aesthetic apparatus. At another level, they operate in relation to discourses, material circumstances, and social configurations within the broader society. The meaning, significance, and resonance of the representations of blackness on commercial network television cannot be understood at any one of these levels without taking account of their complex relationships to one another.

At one level, for instance, one might read television treatments of blacks in terms of how these treatments stand up against "reality" or the experiences of black folk as we know them empirically or from commonsense understandings. Although frames operating in such representations confirm some notions of how blacks are and how we live, they are also frames of containment that constitute and reproduce many of the class, gender, and racial discourses of American society. The debate over the construction and representation of black women and the black family is but one example.

At another level, we might read television treatments of blacks not just in terms of how they measure up to the empirical world beyond the small screen, but in terms of the aesthetic and formal strategies that challenge or reproduce historical treatments of blacks by the apparatus of television. Such readings, too, can be and often are evaluated according to the degree to which they correspond, as it were, to black experiences beyond the screen; their resonance and appeal may also be judged in terms of the degree to which they offer improvements and, even more, new possibilities for imagining blacks in America. The driving logic of television and black adjustment to historic stereotypes found in Marlon Riggs's (1991a) award-winning documentary *Color Adjustment* come to mind here.

Because television representations of blacks and people of color operate within structured material and discursive relations of power, at least in the realm of the popular imagination expressed by television (and other realms of popular culture, including film and popular music), subversive and alternative possibilities are constantly displaced, shut off, or occasionally appropriated and folded into the center. And yet, as deeply contradictory and conflicted a medium as television is, it must nevertheless appeal to utopian possibilities (Gray 1989; Jameson 1979). Thus, although my general focus is on the ways in which the hegemonic racial order is continually contested, renewed, and realigned in commercial popular culture, I also believe that television itself constitutes and expresses contradictions of and contestations to that order (Fiske 1987).

In chapter 4, I maintain that television has produced not just a textual or representational notion of blackness, but one defined and organized by the institutional and industrial character of television. In other words, I argue, though not exclusively, for an appreciation of the institutional and industrial production of blackness as a market category that emerged from the dramatic and far-reaching transformations of the television industry in the 1980s. I then lay out these institutional and aesthetic imperatives, particularly as they work to construct black viewers and to represent blackness. This discussion in turn leads to an analysis of the institutional character of television that accounts for the proliferation of television shows about blacks in the 1980s.

Just what are the organizing structures of contemporary television representations of blackness, and how do these structures constitute specific systems of representations and thereby engage a struggle and negotiation over the representation of blacks?[1] In chapter 5, I continue the angle of inquiry taken up in chapter 4, but shift the focus a bit from industrial organization and machinations to consider discursive strategies and operations. I identify three discourses that structure commercial network representations of blackness: assimilationist, pluralist, and multiculturalist discourses. How any one or a combination of these discourses is privileged or operates in dominance is determined not so much by the television text alone, but in terms of its relationship to a broader set of discourses and social configurations at work in the society.

Chapter 5 and the remainder of the book should be read in relation to the debates, discourses, and struggles over blackness detailed in chapters 2 and 3. The politics at work in all of these possibilities are indeterminate rather than fixed. The resonance and articulations that television may register depend not just on the careful reading of the texts of any one program, but on some understanding of the terms of discursive struggle and intertextuality operating in television and other cultural sites of the society, as well as the social locations and conditions in which people live and how they make meanings from television. The progressive, reactionary, and contradictory character of a program, representation, and image is historically and socially determined rather than politically guaranteed by the text.

The Social Production of Television Discourses of Blackness

Television is an extremely complex and contradictory medium, owing to its commercial imperatives, formal character, texts, organizational and industrial structure, technological apparatus, and relationship to everyday life. In order for television to achieve its work—that is, to make meaning and produce pleasure—it has to draw upon and operate on the basis of a kind of generalized societal common sense about the terms of the society and people's social location in it. The social ground and the cultural terms on which it works depend on assumptions about experience, knowledge, familiarity, and the accessibility of viewers to these assumptions.

It is my contention that television representations of blackness operate squarely within the boundaries of middle-class patriarchal discourses about "whiteness" as well as the historic racialization of the social order. These dominant social and cultural discourses maintain normative universes within which all other representations and marginalization of difference—race, class, ethnic, gender, sexual—are constructed and positioned. That is to say, black representations in commercial network television are situated within the existing material and institutional hierarchies of privilege and power based on class (middle class), race (whiteness), gender (patriarchal), and sexual (heterosexual) differences. On the matter of race and ethnicity this is especially important, because the very presence of African Americans in television discourses appeals to this normative "common sense," this working knowledge of the history, codes, struggles, and memories of race relations in the United States.

The reigning wisdom in critical television studies of race is still that television representations of blackness work largely to legitimate and secure the terms of the dominant cultural and social order by circulating within and remaining structured by them (Gray 1993b, 1993c). I largely agree with this assessment. Just as often, however, there are alternative (and occasional oppositional) moments in American commercial television representations of race, especially in its fragmented and contradictory character. In some cases, television representations of blackness explode and reveal the deeply rooted terms of this hierarchy. It is this struggle and politics of representation that I highlight in the chapters on *Frank's Place*, *A Different World*, and *In Living Color*.

Notes, Markers, and Warnings: A Reader Advisory

Discussions and analysis of certain kinds of programs, genres, and representations do not appear in the chapters that follow. I do not attend to those shows that feature one or two continuing black characters in otherwise all-white settings (e.g., *Designing Women*) or those shows with black casts that, for all practical purposes, are just like white shows (e.g., *Family Matters*). Nor do I deal in great detail with the genre of nighttime drama, especially such relevant and often powerful shows as *In the Heat of the Night*, *Equal Justice*, *L.A. Law*, *I'll Fly Away*, and *Laurel Street*. I have elected to focus on entertainment, variety, situation comedy, music television, and advertising because I regard these as the sites most completely saturated by representations of blackness. Shows in these genres are widely available in reruns and collectively they still generate wide attention from the press, scholars, and viewers. In short, I try to focus on the kinds of popular shows that African Americans, in particular, watch with the expectation of finding black images.

I have also framed this analysis largely within a timespan that begins with the election of Ronald Reagan as president (1980) and ends with the airing of the last episode of *The Cosby Show*, which took place during the Los Angeles riots on April 30, 1992. Hence, few shows beyond the 1992 season are included here. This decision makes theoretical and practical sense. Given television's voracious appetite and ability to replace new shows with still newer ones, a book like this has to end somewhere, lest it go on and on. The election of Bill Clinton, the end of *Cosby*'s reign, and the riots in Los Angeles together mark a significant shift in public discourses about race.

Framing a book about television and race within such a period may seem curious, but I do so in order that I may engage questions of text and context simultaneously. In this sense the book is located within the project of cultural studies; that is, it deliberately combines and appreciates the insights of social history, institutional analysis, textual readings, and the social locations of audiences. By using a concept such as discourse, rather than ideology, I also want to foreground questions of agency, agents, common sense, and the socially constructed nature of ideas and meanings. Hence, I am very much committed to acknowledging meanings organized in and produced by discourse. By the same token, the readings I offer are intended to engage the social positions, histories, shifts, and transformation within which people live and experience television representations of blackness.

The social positions that I bring into relief are multiple, shifting, and intersecting. I have tried to be especially alert to foregrounding possibilities, interpretations, and claims on blackness by multiply situated and complexly organized African American reading positions. The readings and analyses offered, therefore, are porous and especially attentive to the social conditions, patterns, and relationships that organize, structure, and enable them. My position should not be understood as relativist or pluralist, but as one that recognizes and appreciates the fact that different reading positions and readers continue to be structured and organized by racial, gender, and class relations of power (Gray 1993b). The political possibilities and transformative effects of such readings, although always present, are nevertheless contingent and open to the competing claims and enlistments of different political projects.

I also want to be clear on my view of culture and its specific application to African American experiences. What I intend is some specification of the ways in which the impulses, tones, and consciousness of contemporary black life in the United States—especially as these are lived, practiced, and understood by blacks—are expressed, framed, and organized in and by mass-mediated commercial culture in general and television in particular. I am especially interested in the ways in which the practices, traditions, and perspectives of people in marginalized and subordinated social positions, vis-à-vis dominant cultures, are expressed in the realm of mass-mediated popular culture. My aim, then, is to identify, specify, and make sense of the ways in which these specifically black "structures of feeling"—sensibilities, perspectives, and traditions—get claimed, expressed, articulated, mediated, and appropriated in contemporary mass-produced and -distributed commercial culture.

This analysis is also limited to programming found on the four major commercial television networks—ABC, CBS, NBC, and Fox. Cable, syndication, and pay-per-view and other services are no doubt increasingly important to television representations of race and blackness, but commercial network television is still the predominant form of service delivery for most black viewers. Hence, it is on the networks' construction and representation of blackness in the 1980s that I have elected to focus.

In this respect, readers will no doubt note the absence of any detailed and sustained analysis of the Black Entertainment Television (BET) cable network. The reasons for this absence are both practical and theoretical. Not all municipalities are wired for cable; hence, access to BET's programming schedule remains limited in some areas. Because BET's viewership is strongest in metropolitan areas in the East, South, Midwest, and parts of the West, the circulation and impact of the network's programming require carefully situated readings. Until quite recently, much of BET's programming, especially series and movies, was made up of reruns of syndicated programs. Network-produced entertainment and public affairs programming was confined primarily to music videos, news, talk and public affairs, and sports shows. To be sure, the organization of BET as a network, especially its specific and self-conscious structure, guiding philosophy, and identity, deserves careful analysis. For the moment I will offer, somewhat suggestively and tentatively, an observation developed in chapter 5, namely, that (in its formative period at least) BET fits within a separate-but-equal discourse. I offer this categorization not in some strict and narrow sense, but for purposes of qualification, as a way of seeing BET's representations and constructions, as well as the cultural politics they organize and perform.

Finally, an explanatory note on my use of the terms *blackness, black,* and *African American.* By using the word *blackness* I mean to focus attention on the operation of blackness as a cultural signifier that, although operating on the basis of specific histories, dynamics, and relations of power, nevertheless remains open to multiple and competing claims. More specifically, I use *blackness* to refer to the constellation of productions, histories, images, representations, and meanings associated with black presence in the United States. In chapters 1 and 2, I use contemporary examples to show how blackness is variously constructed, represented, and positioned by social formations to achieve different political objectives. Although I recognize that treating blackness this way places me in the choppy (and contested) seas of essentialist and antiessentialist debates, I nonetheless want to call attention to the constructed nature of blackness and the discursive work it does in mass media and popular culture as well as in the social, political, and cultural debates in which it is situated.

I purposely retain the term *black* to indicate specific communities, people, and agents who live and struggle in and against (historic and contemporary) racialized discourses and oppressive social conditions in the United States. Although I also use the term *African American* interchangeably with *black,* I specifically use it to signal broader and more inclusive dimensions of black social life and culture; in some specific instances I deliberately use *African American* to mark the recent shift from a discourse of race to one of ethnicity.

I do want to avoid any presumption that my varying use of *blackness, black,* and *African American* privileges some implicit claim to authenticity or essence about black life. Although I argue that African American claims on blackness suggest different social positions, histories, and distinct ways of seeing, I do not mean this to obscure or stand as a totalizing conception of black life in the United States. Rather, I mean to point to and accent diversity, especially in class, sexuality, gender, generation, and region, within blackness. Hence, I use the notion of *blackness* as a sign quite deliberately as a way to examine various positions and claims on it both from within the African American community and from outside of it. I begin, then, with an examination of claims on blackness by conservatives and the new right in the 1980s.

2 Reaganism and the Sign of Blackness

Americans, with Reagan leading them, were in no mood for
being bothered by problems. Reagan and television gave
them what they wanted most: a chance to feel good again.

Haynes Johnson, Sleepwalking through History, *1991*

Race and television were the twin pillars that anchored Ronald Reagan's decade of "feel-good politics." The 1980s were not the first
time that race and popular culture were enlisted in the service of mo-
bilizing the white American imagination to establish a different hegemonic bloc. Appeals to solidarity in the service of hegemonic orders
based in "whiteness" have historically used blackness (as well as different forms of othering based on ethnicity, sexuality, religion, and
gender) to counter alliances among and across class, race, and cultural
differences. As Clyde Taylor (1991), Toni Morrison (1992b), and
David Roediger (1991) show, race, popular culture, and the white
imagination were forged in nineteenth- and early-twentieth-century
popular forms of minstrelsy, film, and literature. Through the discursive production and organization of television news images and reports about black welfare "cheats" and moral panics about black
"family disintegration" and epidemic drug use and violence in the nation's cities, race and popular media, in particular television, were central to the consolidation of a conservative cultural and political hegemonic bloc. The very idea of America was in contention, especially the

terms in which it would be defined, who would be included, and cultural warrants for making claims on it.

Race and television were at the very core of the new right's largely successful efforts to establish a rightward shift in the political, cultural, and social discourse. This discourse established the foundation for matters ranging from the economy to morality (Edsall and Edsall 1991; Hacker 1992; Johnson 1991; Katz 1989). The "sign of blackness," its discursive production, contestation, and mobilization, was an essential element of the political and cultural realignments that helped to stage and install the neoconservative hegemony referred to as Reaganism (Edsall and Edsall 1991). The discourses of race in general and blackness in particular were neither limited to nor controlled by conservative Republicans. Traditional liberals and neoliberals were very much a part of the action, and, as I suggest in the next chapter, blackness (and race) was also a key sign over which African Americans struggled in order to contest and in some instances bid for a place in the newly emerging conservative order.

What the social and cultural representations of blackness on commercial television in the 1980s signified culturally and politically, how such constructions were used, and how people made sense of them hang within a complex web of shifting social positions, economic and political interests, and competing cultural discourses. Throughout the 1980s the production and mobilization of race as a political issue through the cultural sign of blackness produced an explosion of television images, photo opportunities, and campaign pledges that saturated the American popular imagination. And television was a central transit point and expressive vehicle through which popular debates and images about race circulated.[1] Whether explicit or implicit, constructions of blackness and by extension appeals to race, especially whiteness, found easy and ready access to media venues such as network news, popular films, television situation comedy, sports, and music television. Moreover, television was never just a neutral player, an invisible conduit, in these representations and constructions. Television itself also constituted a significant social site for shaping, defining, contesting, and representing claims about American society.

Although racialized claims and counterclaims about family, responsibility, character, and citizenship appeared in many televisual forms, their cultural and political importance rested on the fact that as a conceptual system, television's specific constructions of blackness and appeals to race were performed, as it were, under the glare of the hot lights of American commercial culture. Indeed, in this context Reagan (and the political discourse he articulated and embodied—Reaganism) functioned as a sort of grand and trusted anchor, reassuring whites that the menaces of the modern world—both foreign and domestic— were effectively held in check and that such sacred values as whiteness, individualism, private property, and family were protected (Reeves and Campbell 1994).[2] In other words, Reaganism is the major discursive formation within which conservative political, social, and cultural alliances, debates, policies, and claims were framed about the United States in the 1980s. Television, as Reeves and Campbell (1994) demonstrate in their analysis of the drug crusades of the 1980s, was central to constructing, packaging, and circulating popular understandings and common sense with respect to major social questions confronting the nation. I, too, regard the representations of and claims on blackness in television in terms of their discursive power to structure and circulate commonsense understandings about race in contemporary America.

American network television's representation of blacks as expressions of social menace and male irresponsibility (and its opposite—the *Cosby Show* ideal of responsibility and citizenship) cannot be understood apart from the aggressive (and largely effective) attempts on the part of the new right to reconfigure and establish a conservative hegemony hostile to progressive notions of racial entitlements. Although seldom framed explicitly in the language of "race" or "blackness," this offensive nevertheless set its popular sights on the popular and academic sectors, taking on such issues as affirmative action, multiculturalism, the welfare state, immigration, big government, and patriotism (Edsall and Edsall 1991; Johnson 1991; Omi and Winant 1986; Takagi 1993).

The New Right and the Discourse of Problems

The symbolic and political centerpiece of this reenergized conservative formation was Ronald Reagan, who, as the embodiment of Reaganism, functioned as the cultural and historical sign, for many whites, of the "real" America. Reaganism served as a key point of rearticulation for disparate political, social, historical, and cultural investments in an aggressive discourse of whiteness. Reagan functioned as the key signifier of the "authentic America" and the glory days of "American national preeminence" (Rogin 1987). He achieved this status of iconographic significance through his mobilization of and appeals to what Thomas and Mary Edsall (1991) call the discourse of race, rights, and taxes.

Symbolically, the centrality of the unnamed category of race— specifically, blackness—was evident from the very beginning of Reagan's first election campaign. Edsall and Edsall (1991) note, for instance, Reagan's strategic use of an often-repeated story that in effect linked and then demonized the welfare state and poor (black) women: "One of Reagan's favorite and most often repeated anecdotes was the story of a Chicago 'welfare queen' with 80 names, 300 addresses, 12 social security cards whose tax-free income alone is over $150,000. The food stamp program, in turn, was a vehicle to let some fellow ahead of you buy T-bone steak, while you were standing in a checkout line with your package of hamburger" (p. xx). Although unmarked, Reagan's references to this Chicago "welfare queen" and to "you" play against historic and racialized discourses about welfare at the same time they join law-abiding taxpayers to an unmarked but normative and idealized racial and class subject—hardworking whites.

Reagan's rhetorical celebration and symbolic embodiment of the good old days—articulated rhetorically and symbolically as a return to "traditional values"—turned on the complex post-civil rights discourse of race in general and blacks in particular (Omi and Winant 1993; Takagi 1993). This meant that regardless of historical and contemporary complexities of ethnicity, class, and racial composition, the new right effectively appealed to popular notions of whiteness in opposition to blackness, which was conflated with and came to stand for "other." In this and similar rhetoric we can detect the discursive labors of Reaganism as it constructs a notion of whiteness that found a good deal of resonance in the post-civil rights 1980s. Resurrecting the nativist language of reverse discrimination, traditional values, and anti-immigration, whiteness in the discourse of Reaganism no longer operated as a sign of victimizer, but was repositioned as a sign of victim. This rhetorical strategy did not rest solely on appeals to notions of white superiority, as was the case in the 1950s and 1960s; rather, it was mobilized by appeals to the putative unfairness of social policies such as quotas, affirmative action, and special treatment extended to women, blacks, and other communities of color.[3]

As a sign of this otherness, blackness was constructed along a continuum ranging from menace on one end to immorality on the other, with irresponsibility located somewhere in the middle. Only through such appeals to menace and irresponsibility, framed and presented in television news through figures of black male gang members, black male criminality, crumbling black families, black welfare cheats, black female crack users, and black teen pregnancy, could such claims on America (and its image of middle-class, heterosexual, masculine whiteness) find resonance within the discourse of traditional values. In short, Reaganism had to take away from blacks the moral authority and claims on political entitlements won in the civil rights movement of the 1960s.

This version of white populist claims on America could work only if white fears and resentments against what Katz (1989) calls the "undeserving poor" could be effectively figured and circulated in the contemporary white imaginary. This, of course, is the reason that the rearticulation of and appeals to whiteness mattered so much in the discourse of Reaganism. Such resentment and fear depended largely on the effectiveness of a shift in the political language from a focus on the poor and disadvantaged recipients of state-sponsored support to an emphasis on taxpayers, the white suburban middle class, and erosion in the quality of American life. Rhetorically, the blame had to be placed on someone, and the neoconservative formation that coalesced under Reaganism placed it on blacks, latinos, feminists, the poor, single mothers, gays and lesbians, and undocumented immigrants (Edsall and Edsall 1991; Katz 1989; Reeves and Campbell 1994). Whereas Reaganism gave discursive coherence to the growing backlash against the advances of communities of color and women, it also reworked and rewrote existing scripts on the politics of race. That is to say, Reaganism updated and reactivated the resentments of Dixiecrats who in the 1960s felt betrayed by Democratic support for initiatives that outlawed segregation in the South.

Given the climate and the post-civil rights "culture of civility" on matters of race, producing this discursive configuration was no simple or easy matter.[4] A cultural sign for race and difference was required to mobilize white resentment and fear, a sign that, by forcing a reckoning with the very definition of America, could encourage a rhetorical and imaginary return to tradition, family values, morality, individualism, authority, and prosperity. The increasing illegitimacy of the welfare state, the visibility of neoconservative black voices, and a post-civil rights culture of politeness meant that simpleminded and totalizing appeals to white fears (using the image of black menace) were not enough to consolidate the new hegemonic order. Reagan Republicans also appealed to a representation of blackness that was both familiar and acceptable to whites. Even when blackness functioned as the chief icon against which conservative Republicans ran for political office, it was important for them not to appear racist. Like their white middle-class counterparts, and yet distinct from the black poor, images of middle- and upper-class blacks with appropriate backgrounds, pedigrees, tastes, and networks were also part of the discourse of race articulated and mobilized by the new right.

People such as former head of the U.S. Commission on Civil Rights Clarence Pendleton or U.S. Supreme Court Justice Clarence Thomas (and commercial television's Cliff Huxtable) were seen by conservatives as possessing the requisite moral character, individual responsibility, and personal determination to succeed in spite of residual social impediments. These were the kinds of "model minorities" that neoconservatives celebrated and presented both to counter the dependence of the underclass and to affirm their commitment to racial equality. These African Americans were just like whites, loyal to the ethos of capitalism and bourgeois individualism, and that loyalty rewarded them with the same middle-class privileges as whites. In news media profiles of individuals such as Thomas and Pendleton, claims on blackness were not an excuse so much as a small accident of birth. Blackness was not a category requiring structural adjustments for the disadvantages of historic and systemic group disenfranchisement and social inequality. Rather, like other "differences," blackness was a minor facet of the larger American story of ethnic richness and incorporation (Lipsitz 1990a). This discursive rewriting and political realignment of the sign of blackness under Reaganism was carried to its full and logical conclusion in the spectacle surrounding the nomination (and subsequent confirmation) of Clarence Thomas to the U.S. Supreme Court by George Bush (Morrison 1992a).

Morality, Tradition, and Blackness

In their respective analyses of the rise and subsequent domination of the British government by Conservatives during the Thatcher years, Paul Gilroy (1990, 1991b), Stuart Hall (1988), and Kobena Mercer (1992) suggest that the Conservative party effectively used discourses of difference (in this case ethnicity and race) to reconfigure and realign British domestic politics and social policy. The Conservative party produced (and controlled) a conception of Britishness organized around a chain of images and associations that linked and equated Britain with tradition, conservatism, and whiteness. Gilroy, Hall, and Mercer show how this hegemonic discourse found resonances and identifications across various social locations, especially class, through appeals to a racially constructed threat of fear, loss, and erosion of British society. In this discourse, difference—signaled by the signs *immigrant, outsider, black*—was mobilized to appeal to such sentiments. Central to this discourse was a pivotal understanding of the centrality of images, symbols, and language (especially their production and circulation in media and popular culture) for the establishment of the discourse that Hall (1988) calls "Thatcherism."

The impact of this mobilization of Thatcherism in England rested with the Conservatives' ability to disrupt and reconfigure, at the level of national symbols and political discourse, colonialism, class, and race with appeals to popular fears and desires about Britishness (Mercer 1992). Though often contradictory, culturally these appeals enjoyed some measure of identification and legitimacy from various sectors of British society, especially labor, precisely because the Conservative party effectively established and controlled the dominant definitions and representations of Britishness in the popular imaginary.

Although the situations were distinctly different and characterized by vastly different histories, discourses, and material conditions, it seems to me that something quite similar occurred culturally in the United States under Reaganism (Grossberg 1992; Kellner 1990; Reeves and Campbell 1994). In the United States, race and, by extension, popular media images of blacks and latinos (especially undocumented immigrants from Latin America and Haiti) were effectively used by conservatives to disturb and reconfigure the symbolic chain of association through which "America" came to be represented and defined. Television news images of blacks and undocumented immigrants overrunning the borders and apparently competing for shrinking resources activated and in some cases reaffirmed deeply felt popular fears and resentments among middle- and working-class whites. Together with these racialized images of the "immigration problem," news footage of drug- and violence-ravaged urban communities made it seem as if (white) America were being attacked from within and without.

Such images activated deeply held feelings that cut to the very heart of the meaning of a United States enmeshed in social and economic transformation. The rhetorical claims, symbolic images, and social discourses that structured such feeling were expressed across a wide, but related, set of issues—citizenship, civic society, public and private responsibility, entitlements, rights and obligations, family, language, morality, and character (Edsall and Edsall 1991; Hacker 1992; Katz 1989). The specific racialization of these concerns and fears produced deep resentments that, as public policy issues, took the form of a taxpayer revolt against tax recipients as well as a defense of traditional values in matters ranging from the labeling of popular music with "offensive" content to the constitution of university curricula. This resentment was expressed most dramatically as a mostly white middle-class and working-class populist revolt against communities of color and the poor, who were constructed as "undeserving" (Katz 1989; see also Edsall and Edsall 1991). It was exacerbated by a conservative discourse that constructed the liberal welfare state (and its advocates) as protecting the interests of racial minorities, feminists, gays and lesbians, criminals, and undocumented immigrants, all of whom were constructed as the recipients of state-protected entitlements that came at the expense of hardworking, responsible (and white male) taxpayers.

Discursively, this resentment and the strategy on which it depended was underwritten and mobilized by the desire on the part of the conservative movement and the Reagan/Bush administrations to restore the United States to a position of dominance and strength economically and in foreign affairs. Rhetorically, Reagan attributed the loss of U.S. international economic competitiveness and the country's domestic stagnation to the cultural permissiveness and political liberalism of the 1960s, the erosion of the traditional work ethic, the lack of preparation of the U.S. labor force, excessive state regulation, and the cost of a large dependent and unproductive underclass (Edsall and Edsall 1991). This unproductive sector of U.S. society, together with the debilitating costs of a large and intrusive government, exerted a continual and long-term drag on the economy.

Composed of varying groups and factions, the new conservative formation rearticulated under Reaganism cut across geographic, occupational, age, ethnic, and class locations. At its core, this formation included religious fundamentalists, various single-issue groups (e.g., antiabortion, anticommunist), wealthy and influential political action committees, powerful members of the business and corporate sector, Ivy League moderates, the radical right, and those opposed to big government (Ehrenreich 1990; Johnson 1991; Katz 1989). At least two components of this rearticulated conservative formation—so-called Reagan Democrats and religious fundamentalists—were themselves made up of northern white ethnics, Catholics, and southern populists (Edsall and Edsall 1991). All, but especially the southern white populists (with their historic connection to an earlier generation of Dixiecrats), were distrustful and resentful of liberal Democrats. Southern populists never forgave or forgot those liberal Democrats who supported federal intervention in the form of court decisions and tax laws to halt the move of whites to privatize schools as a way to avoid participation in court-ordered busing to desegregate public schools (Edsall and Edsall 1991:123). Reaganism rearticulated and mobilized these resentments. Many whites joined and supported conservative Republicans, who promised to restore and protect their individual liberties, liberties that allowed them to avoid the financial support of such programs as public school desegregation, affirmative action, abortion, and the ban on school prayer.

As a formation, Reaganism was built on desires to dismantle the welfare state, to curb an intrusive government, to stimulate corporate growth through unrestrained market forces, and (through key judicial appointments) to ensure a long reign of conservative authority in key areas of public and private life (Johnson 1991). Rhetorically, on the one hand, Reaganism depended on intellectual and philosophical foundations based in deep conservative traditions and principles: an unfettered free market, emphasis on individual liberty, a strong military, and antigovernment and anticommunist sentiments (Ehrenreich 1990; Johnson 1991; Katz 1989). On the other hand, its symbolic and emotional appeal rested on the strategy of demonizing the (undeserving) poor and simultaneously attacking the discourse of entitlement.

Nothing more effectively captured, linked, and mobilized these feelings of fear and resentment among disenchanted whites than the representations and debates over race, individual rights, and taxes, especially the role of the state in extending and defining the direction and pace of their distribution (Edsall and Edsall 1991).[5] At the level of presidential politics, the conjuncture of race, rights, and taxes provided conservative Republicans with concrete issues and deeply felt sentiments with which to attack liberalism and redirect the role of the state. Of the three elements, race was by far the most salient:

> Race . . . crystallized and provided a focus for values conflict, for cultural conflicts, and for interest conflicts over subjects as diverse as social welfare spending, neighborhood schooling, the distribution of tax burdens, criminal violence, sexual conduct, family structure, political competition, and union membership. (Edsall and Edsall 1991:5)

In addition to a bloated and sluggish economy weighed down by federal spending and regulations, race operated at the center of conservative Republican political discourse as the often unnamed sign of erosion, menace, threat, and permissiveness—(black) welfare cheats, the (liberal) welfare state (and its largely minority dependents), (black and latino) teenage pregnancy, rising crime (committed largely by black and latino urban male youth). Perhaps the one media image that found the greatest resonance with whites as a sign of everything gone wrong with America was the racialized image of moral irresponsibility and criminal threat—the so-called urban underclass (Auletta 1983; Glasgow 1981; Hacker 1992; Johnson 1991; Katz 1989; Lemman 1984; Marable 1991; Reed 1991b; Wilson 1987). As a contemporary sign of social erosion in post-civil rights America, the racialized concept of the underclass was perfectly suited for cultural and moral labor in a conservative-controlled discourse on poverty, morality, and entitlements. Lacking any meaningful economic and cultural ties—hence their strangeness and otherness—to the reconfigured conservative (and neoliberal) mainstream, the black urban underclass provided the perfect symbol with which to launch a full offensive against the welfare state and those it serves (Katz 1989; Reed 1991b).

Although conservative Republican rhetoric and imagery often took the explicit form of white middle- and working-class revolts over taxes, rights, and individual responsibility, their rhetorical appeals were profoundly structured by the discourse of race. Thus, in the 1980s, popular media and policy debates over big government, the welfare state, traditional values, morality, civic responsibility, entitlements, and family were presented on television and in daily newspapers and weekly magazines through the emotionally charged figure of the black body (Reeves and Campbell 1994). Nightly television news reports of "rampaging" hordes of urban black youth robbing and raping helpless and law-abiding white (female) victims came to us in the Bernhard Goetz and Central Park jogger cases in New York City; television documentaries such as CBS's *The Vanishing Black Family* presented case studies of (mostly black and female) welfare parents who were usually uneducated, unemployed, and single; reality-based crime shows such as *Cops* showcased the apprehension and arrest of black inner-city crack cocaine users. The cultural work of political campaigns was also organized on the issue of race—think, for instance, of the Willie Horton ad from the 1988 presidential campaign, which showed a black convicted murderer whose rights and privileges were protected by a liberal criminal justice system to a far greater degree than were those of his victims; think also of music videos of (defiant) black male youth in the music videos of Ice-T and N.W.A., whose angry and often obscenity-laced language so offended the Parents' Music Resource Center's standards of decency and civility that they had to be policed by the state and the music industry.[6]

Discursively, then, the conservative Republican strategy to "get America moving" relied heavily on dramatic and racialized media images of an isolated and pathological underclass trapped in a culture of poverty. Adolph Reed (1991b) argues that, in the tightly sealed discursive system of the new right, it was the very construction of the underclass as socially isolated and culturally deprived that set the members of that class apart and marked them as sufficiently different that they required moral and cultural regulation.

Thus, according to conservative logic, welfare and the liberal permissiveness that created and nurtured it produced an underclass distinguished by sedation and satisfaction of bodily pleasures, dependency, immorality, hostility, erosion of standards, loss of civic responsibility, and lack of respect for traditional values. Led by conservative ideologues, policy analysts, and political pundits, conservative strategists used political speeches, popular-opinion journals, and television talk shows to construct a view that the behaviors of poor and disenfranchised African Americans were the best evidence that the price of large-scale state intervention and responsibility for caring for those in poverty was ineffective and produced massive public debt, intolerance, and antagonism (Murray 1984).

In the discourse of Reaganism, the only public remedy was to eliminate dependency, reduce regulation, and let the unfettered market regulate itself. To achieve these goals practically, Republican analysts and spin doctors foregrounded the rhetoric of traditional values, emphasizing patriarchal families, corporate competitiveness, capital punishment, charitable giving, and moral self-regulation in areas of sexuality, reproduction, and gender roles (Ehrenreich 1990; Hacker 1992; Johnson 1991; Katz 1989). As for the "rehabilitation" of members of the underclass, Reaganism resurrected what Jimmie Reeves and Richard Campbell (1994) call "cultural Moynihanism," or the idea that the inculcation of appropriate moral values, self-discipline, and a work ethic can effectively break the vicious cycle of dependency that cripples the poor and disadvantaged. Programmatically, they believed that together with a revitalized private sector, the return to the traditional family and the emphasis on individual moral rehabilitation would go quite far toward the elimination of black urban poverty.

In practice, this social vision and political philosophy was realized through "the Reagan philosophy of privatization of government and the protection of private citizens from the intrusions of big government. . . . such protection was essential to a healthy and functioning social order, autonomous, healthy and stable" (Edsall and Edsall 1991:137). Reagan, and later Bush, seemed to have little trouble reconciling the call to get government off the backs of the people with the practice of using government to dismantle the welfare state and redistribute wealth to the rich (Johnson 1991; Phillips 1991). Thus, although Reagan was vehemently opposed to most forms of state regulation and intervention into the private lives of U.S. citizens, he seemed to have little problem with government playing a strong role in the areas of sexuality, reproductive rights, school prayer, and related moral issues (Edsall and Edsall 1991:138). Through the interventions of an activist judiciary, Reaganism advocated stiffer jail sentences, more prisons, and less tolerance for prisoners' rights, believing that at the very least such measures would contain, if not reduce, the "abhorrent behavior" of the black underclass. With the conservative vision of America firmly entrenched in social policy and popular discourse, the new conservative coalition largely (but not without opposition) directed and controlled the central debates about poverty and race.

Conservative appeals to white fears and resentments also depended on a discursive construction of the Democratic party, which linked liberalism and Democrats with "welfare dependence and anti-egalitarian special preference" (Edsall and Edsall 1991:187). This Republican construction of the Democratic party and liberalism, especially the alignment with welfare and special preference, did double work. This construction played on white working-class fears and, more important, tried to make traditional liberal alliances among civil rights groups, labor, feminists, and the elderly largely responsible for the social ills the United States confronted throughout the 1980s. Indeed, this view so completely saturated public political discourse in the period that some traditional liberals either found points of agreement with the conservative arguments or responded with weak defenses of the welfare state. Put differently, this construction and the implicit racialization on which it depends provided safe havens of a sort for many (especially white middle-class) traditional and neoliberal Democrats who had grown uneasy about liberalism. These neoliberals were as committed as conservative Republicans to restructuring the public sector, bolstering the private sector, protecting traditional values, and curbing the entitlements claimed by women and communities of color. Although scattered and sometimes confined to the margins of the national debate, diverse voices and complex explanations that emphasized the combined and multiple impacts of racism, deindustrialization, historic and contemporary discrimination, and deep structural transformations in the economy were never completely silent.

Sign Wars: Cultural Standards, Political Entitlements, and the Welfare State

In the hands of conservative polemicists, academics, and critics, attacks on the erosion of "standards" in education, the arts, values, and morality paralleled the demonization of the black urban underclass and attacks on the liberal welfare state. For such guardians of "culture" and defenders of "standards," radical attacks on the very ideas of Western values, traditional family and sex roles, heterosexual privilege, and increasing racial and ethnic "tribalism" evidenced further American decline. Like their counterparts in policy and political debates, these conservative scholars, critics, and policy analysts repeatedly framed their defense of America's deep commitment to and formation in Western values; they too called for a return to standards, tradition, and a coherent American identity.

With books such as Bloom's *The Closing of the American Mind* (1987) and D'Souza's *Illiberal Education* (1992), conservative academics and intellectuals focused their attacks on policies such as affirmative action; on area studies, such as women's studies, African American and Chicano studies, and gay and lesbian studies; on theoretical interventions such as feminist theory, postmodernism, poststructuralism, and Marxism; and on cultural movements such as multiculturalism and diversity. Reverberations of these attacks were directly felt in areas that seemed, on the surface at least, immune to partisan-based policing and surveillance—tastes and aesthetics. At one point or another, public funding for the arts and humanities, programming on the nation's publicly funded and regulated Public Broadcasting System, gallery exhibitions, films, and popular music all became targets of conservative moral surveillance and attacks (Gates 1992b; Johnson 1991).

Conservatives' attempts to implement and codify their specific cultural and social vision were deployed in the form of multifocused, state-sanctioned assaults. The targets of campaigns to uphold "standards" and maintain "traditions" included public school and university curricula; affirmative action-based hiring and promotion in public sector employment; liberal and radical university professors; college, university, and professional school admissions policies; and government-based implementation, enforcement, and prosecution of state-mandated policies concerned with issues of diversity, equality, and fairness (Williams 1991). In a key move, the cultural wing of Reaganism marked and then repositioned the highly charged and culturally resonant 1960s as the signal moment in the decline of most sectors of public and civic life, especially the university.

For conservative ideologues, and enlightened neoliberals, post-civil rights America had finally reached a point in its history where we no longer needed a large and activist state that protected and distributed group-based entitlements. Furthermore, they argued, in a strong and stimulated free market, no longer encumbered by group-based privilege and entitlements, individual merit, character, and achievement should—indeed, must—regulate access to and distribution of the valued rewards of the society. Discursively, this emphasis represented a subtle but important shift from a traditional liberal focus on equality and justice to a focus on individual freedom and liberty, especially for (white) middle- and working-class taxpayers. Accordingly, the role of the state is to ensure the optimum functioning of the market rather than the protection and distribution of group-based claims to entitlements.

Political claims for access to social institutions and organizations based on merit *and* race, ethnicity, gender, or sexuality were met with counterclaims from white males, and their advocates, of reverse discrimination and lower standards (Institute for the Study of Social Change 1992; Wellman 1993). Different forms and transgressive expressions of family, sexual pleasure, and gender relationships were demonized as immoral threats to traditional standards of morality and decency. Like the 1960s, to which their origins were traced, these forms of social and cultural life were, by extension, responsible for defects and declines in American standards and moral character (Ehrenreich 1990).

Again, black bodies (especially adolescent males and single mothers) served as signs for the very worst and most unproductive impulses loose in the land (Crenshaw 1991; Katz 1989; Williams 1991). In the neoconservative discourse, rampant teenage pregnancy, premarital sex, and single (especially female) parents among black and latino youth suggested not only welfare dependency, but immorality and behaviors that placed them outside of the American mainstream (Edsall and Edsall 1991; Katz 1989; Lemman 1984; Reed 1991b; Wilson 1987). As black feminist scholars (e.g., Collins 1990; Crenshaw 1991; Williams 1991) have shown, black women were constructed and positioned by such discourses as oversexed and promiscuous, constructions that more than anything else labored to highlight the morality and propriety of white middle-class norms of decency.

Black Bodies and the Reagan Revolution

Along with its rhetorical and intellectual appeals to traditional values, morality, and the return to standards, the new right proposed and then implemented far-reaching and devastating fiscal and economic measures aimed at dismantling the welfare state. Led by David Stockman, George Gilder, Arthur Laffer, and other economists and policy analysts, conservative Republicans attempted to replace the welfare state with an unfettered free market, the increased productivity and prosperity of which would eventually "trickle down" to all members of the social order (Johnson 1991; Phillips 1991). Toward this end, the Reagan/Bush administrations enacted sweeping environmental, fiscal, monetary, and deregulatory policies that resulted in the largest redistribution of wealth to the top one-fifth of the stratification order since the Gilded Age (Nasar 1992; Phillips 1991).

Mergers, buyouts, hostile takeovers, relocations, and foreign investment eliminated old companies at the same time they created new companies, players, debts, and profits (Auletta 1991; Johnson 1991;

Kellner 1990). Those most able to play in the newly deregulated environment—international financiers, drug cartels, bankers, corporate deal makers, and yuppies—were the immediate beneficiaries of what seemed like unlimited prosperity. Those most vulnerable—the poor, women, people of color, children, and the homeless—and the least able to compete—unskilled and underskilled workers—were hurt directly or stood by and watched as the spectacle of what Kevin Phillips (1991) calls the "second Gilded Age" unfolded. Ronald Reagan, Donald Trump, Leona Helmsley, Michael Milken, and Ivan Boesky all personified this conspicuous display of new American prosperity and affluence.

Television and race were again central to the spectacular display and affirmation of this new mood of prosperity: race because poor blacks, among others, embodied the discursive and cultural sign against which the new affluence and how to achieve it were measured; television because it functioned as both witness to and participant in the new prosperity. Television's witness and complicity took the form of programs such as *Dynasty* and *Lifestyles of the Rich and Famous,* shows that could have been possible only in the 1980s.[7] As a participant in this new affluent environment, television itself underwent a dramatic transformation in its structure and organization as a network system and corporate enterprise (Auletta 1991; Kellner 1990).

In addition to facilitating the concentration of wealth in the top one-fifth of the population, the flood of economic activity in the 1980s was accompanied by the proliferation of homelessness (in part the result of wide-ranging deinstitutionalization of the mentally ill), housing shortages, soaring unemployment (especially in urban minority neighborhoods), and the rapid deterioration of central cities.

As amazing, and perhaps even more emblematic of the cultural and economic spirit of the times, was the proliferation of government and corporate scandal. From the most significant and costly—Iran-contra, HUD, Wedtech, EPA, the "Keating five," the failure of savings and loan institutions—to routine government largess, journalist Haynes Johnson (1991) reports that by the end of Reagan's two terms in office, "138 administration officials had been convicted, had been indicted or had been the subject of official investigations for official misconduct and/or criminal violations. In terms of the numbers of officials involved, the record of his [Reagan] administration was the worst ever" (p. 184).

As with the conservative-dominated discourse on welfare and morality, race too was at the center of at least two of the scandals—HUD and Wedtech. In both instances, despite public pronouncements about dependency and the failure of affirmative action, the principal financial beneficiaries of these scandals depended on and profited from the demonization of poor and minority communities (Rogin 1987, 1990). In fact, Johnson (1991) reports that several Reagan appointees and officials profited from the very "failed policies" of which they were publicly critical. What is more, in both instances, it was the climate of intolerance concerning big government and minority programs that provided both the cover and the opportunities for abuse. And in both cases it was the demonized members of minority and poor communities who were hurt most by the greed, abuse, and opportunism of high government officials (Johnson 1991:180; Rogin 1990). The rallying cry to get government off the back of the taxpayer proved to be, at best, a rationale for the continued privatization of the national government and, at worst, costly, inefficient, and beneficial for a few already powerful and wealthy individuals (Johnson 1991:180; Phillips 1991).

Conservative Republican Power/Liberal Democratic Orthodoxy: Electoral Politics and Blackness

In a flurry of recent books, most notably Kevin Phillips's *The Politics of Rich and Poor* (1991), conservative (and liberal) commentators and analysts have chronicled just how handsomely the Reagan Republicans rewarded their core business and corporate constituency (see also Johnson 1991; Katz 1989). First the Reagan and then the Bush administration enacted the dramatic transfer of wealth to the top of the stratification order principally through fiscal policies, corporate tax breaks, and deregulation that overwhelmingly favored corporate and wealthy interests. The flank of the neoconservative coalition made up of northern white ethnics, southern white middle- and working-class ethnics, and religious fundamentalists was also rewarded, if only symbolically. This symbolic gratification came in the form of actions on their behalf by an interventionist federal government that made good on its promise to protect entitlements from tax recipients and transfer them to taxpayers (Edsall and Edsall 1991). On issues such as school prayer, traditional values, abortion, individual responsibility, patriotism, abortion, and affirmative action, the Reagan pledge to defend and advocate for the rights and entitlements of this wing of the neoconservative coalition helped to blunt and forestall the reality and consequence of the growing and brutal material inequality that accompanied the Reagan revolution.

By playing to racist and homophobic fears, the state arranged it so that core elements of the new conservative coalition hurt most by the

dramatic shifts in economic wealth and social privilege remained tol-
erant, even patriotic, so long as they were assured that their sacred
rights and values were protected and that the "undeserving" others—
gays and lesbians, feminists, African Americans, latinos, and the
poor—were no longer the protected benefactors of tax-sponsored and
state-sanctioned entitlements (Edsall and Edsall 1991; Omi and
Winant, 1986). The discourse of race and rights, then, helped to frame
symbolically and consolidate politically the redistribution of wealth
and privilege from the middle class to the wealthy and the claims to
rights and entitlements from minorities, the poor, and the disenfranchised to the white conservative middle and working classes (Edsall
and Edsall 1991; Johnson 1991; Phillips 1991; Reed 1991b).

Already labeled and demonized as "undeserving" by conservative
policy-generating enterprises, black inner-city populations were the
moral and symbolic targets that legitimated this shift in the national
political discourse. Symbolically, the racialization of this discourse was
perhaps the key glue in the political mix that held together the precarious neoconservative coalition. For, given their social location in the
changing global economy, many of the class interests of working- and
middle-class members of the conservative coalition seemed more akin
to those articulated by traditional Democrats. After all, the economic
transfer of wealth to the rich enacted by Reagan and Bush came at
considerable expense to this core conservative constituency. Despite
their ideological responses to the fears and resentments of race, rights,
and taxes, as well as promises by Republicans to represent their interests, they were nevertheless affected directly by both the economic and
the social costs (and consequences) of implementing Reagan's vision of
"morning in America."

Nevertheless, politically, allegiance to and identification with the
neoconservative social, cultural, and political positions of working-
and middle-class whites were absolutely central to the discourse of
Reaganism. They provided Republicans with the rationale for policies
and actions in the name of those who, in the end, would benefit least.
The new right's strategy in constructing the representation of "blackness" as threat and menace and therefore undeserving of state-protected entitlements is brutally clear.

This racial imagery and the conservative-controlled rights discourse
in which it operated helped to reshape and rearticulate political con-
stituencies and to shift rightward the very terms of political debate at
the national and presidential level. Conservative Republicans, led by
Reagan, effectively used race and rights to challenge and neutralize the
old-line liberal vision of the Democratic party. The result of this effective challenge and neutralization was never more evident than in the

growing illegitimacy of traditional liberal claims on the efficacy of the welfare state and the attendant warrant, by traditional liberals, to a fair and equitable redistribution of the nation's public resources from the most to the least privileged members of the society. This neoconservative challenge to the efficacy of traditional liberalism and its endorsement of the welfare state forced traditionally Democratic liberals to adopt a neoliberal position on the domestic role of the state and in legislative procedures to generate such policies (Edsall 1984; Reed and Bond 1991). Forced to follow the lead of the corporate sector and neoconservatives, neoliberals joined in attacks on the welfare state, arguing for a redistribution of national government responsibilities to state and local levels and the private sector.

With this aggressive and effective shift to the right, the Democratic party acquiesced, signaling what John Brown Childs has called the demise of the concessionary wing of the ruling hegemonic formation in the United States.[8] The Democratic party's 1980 and 1984 national platforms rested on a weak and eroding alliance of New Deal-style liberalism, labor, civil rights, and bureaucratic sentiments. By 1988 the Democratic party, in response to the entrenched, but not uncontested, discourse of Reaganism, did little better by proposing neoliberal programs of limited government rooted in managerial and technocratic competence.

In each of the presidential elections since 1980, the Democratic party has at best generated empty responses and ineffective strategies to hold off the popular conservative racialization, resentment, and challenge to the welfare state, social permissiveness, and state-protected entitlements to the undeserving—all programs and policies attributed to traditional Democrats by conservatives. As I suggest in the next chapter, in the populist conservative discourse of the 1980s, it was clear for many people of color, women, gays and lesbians, and the poor that this rightward shift spoke in increasingly hostile and intolerant terms for a constituency whose members resented what they believed was a costly and unfair transfer of rights and privileges. Not only did conservative Republicans seize control over public debates about welfare, big government, and federal spending, they did so by conflating traditional liberalism with excess, radicalism, permissiveness, erosion, irresponsibility, and the "sign of blackness." This conflation provided the cornerstone of populist conservative resentment and fear. It effectively positioned "liberalism" and "permissiveness" to serve as yet further rhetorical proxies for race (Edsall and Edsall 1991; Ehrenreich 1990). In this less explicit, but no less devastating, language, liberalism (especially in the 1960s) and its advocates were deemed responsible for the continued erosion of American standards and values (Bloom 1987; Ehrenreich 1990).

As the key cultural and symbolic figure in American politics in the 1980s, the "sign of blackness" circulated in a conservative-dominated discursive field, where it continually served to galvanize, articulate, and mobilize the central issues facing frightened, angry, and resentful white Americans. From the Willie Horton political ads and nightly news representations of black criminality, which stirred and fed white fears, to *The Cosby Show*, which quieted them; from claims by Ronald Reagan that black single teen mothers openly abuse the civic goodwill and morality of white taxpayers to the string of black Miss Americas that reaffirmed responsibility and morality;[9] black male and female bodies served as the psychic and emotional surfaces onto which whites projected their fears and desires (hooks 1992; Rogin 1990). Black bodies and especially the constructions and representations on commercial television news provided the cultural symbols out of which whites fashioned their increasingly conservative, intolerant, and hostile positions (Reeves and Campbell 1994).

The strategy of using black bodies to mobilize white resentment was by no means new or simpleminded. What makes the 1980s version of this strategy interesting and notable, however, is the fact that it was effective largely because of at least two countercurrents in the black American cultural and social landscape. First, the 1980s were characterized by the emergence of a sizable black middle class, which found widespread visibility on American commercial television, in literature and academic debates, and in cinema. The very presence of this class faction of black America enabled Republicans to disguise their politics of resentment, based on racial fears, in personal rather than structural terms while appealing to the virtues of individual merit, strong moral character, and hard work. How could Republican policies under Reagan and Bush be racist, one might reasonably ask, when there were blacks in the administration and black neoconservatives and neoliberals raising many of the same questions, celebrating the same values, and offering the same critiques of traditional liberalism, big government, individual irresponsibility, and welfare dependency?

The Republican strategy of using race in general, and the sign of blackness in particular, to mobilize white resentment also benefited from the often deep skepticism and distrust by blacks of Reagan and Bush as well as the new-right coalition that sustained them. These suspicions, the presidential campaigns of Jesse Jackson, and general Democratic party ineffectiveness gave the Republicans a unique opportunity to use traditional liberalism, big government, rights, taxes, crime, and traditional values as a set of interchangeable proxies and in the process to mobilize white resentments. The Republicans made little effort to moderate their extreme positions in order to appeal to black voters. Because African American voters were not central to their voting base, the Republicans saw little need to make themselves accountable to African American concerns. In this political landscape, Republicans easily had the best of all possible worlds—an ineffective opposition, crumbling cities, rampant crime, and a Democratic Congress—all of which provided them with an always available set of easily mobilizable demons and villains. In their largely white constituency they also found deep fears and insecurities in whose service black, brown, gay and lesbian, poor, and female bodies could easily be exploited.

The New Right, the Politics of Race, and the Media

The new right's strategy to reconfigure and redefine notions of nation, individual, and state depended in large measure on cultural appeals to a popular common sense—sentiment, image, personality, spectacle—and the careful construction, management, and representation of the elements of that common sense in the media (Kellner 1990; Reeves and Campbell 1994; Rogin 1990). Overall, this strategy took many different forms and was played out in many different sites of contemporary American popular culture. Just as the successful reconfiguration of the electorate depended on the discourse of race and appeals to white resentment, the articulation and circulation of the new right's agenda depended heavily on the personality, background, and media image of Ronald Reagan. In Ronald Reagan, millions of whites found the perfect expression and resolution to their fears of loss and the desire to, as Reagan put it, "let America be America again." Ronald Reagan expressed these nativist impulses and at the same time resolved them through his media-tailored personality, demeanor, and familiarity with the camera (Rogin 1987).

Against conservative mobilization and demonization of "blackness" as the sign of cultural erosion and menace, Reagan functioned symbolically as the heroic (white) savior, the symbolic embodiment of the grand American patriarch. Within the discourse of Reaganism, Ronald Reagan could be represented as the forgetful but firm and lovable father figure who smoothed over the deep contradictions and ambivalences of a modern society in decline (Hoberman 1991; Rogin 1990). Where the discourse of Reaganism proposed a tightly sealed set of questions and then provided reassuring answers, the figure of Ronald Reagan comforted millions of Americans about their fears of loss, menace, and threat even as he expressed them. The "evil Soviet empire," "oversexed gays," or "irresponsible and drugged-out" blacks—according to Reagan's vision, American society was being overrun by one or some combination of these dreaded and dangerous "others."

In the final analysis, this appeal to the politics of race was mean-spirited and dangerous. However, in the spectacular environment of commercial media, especially television news, such racial politics were often expressed without confrontation or bitterness. In the landscape of commercial media, many whites could, through their symbolic identification with the figure of Reagan, safely express these racial fears without being labeled racist. They could express frustrations, concerns, and fears about their racial and economic self-interests without appearing intolerant or selfish. In this sense, Reagan, television, and the discourse of Reaganism perfectly complemented one another. Television is the medium that surrounds our everyday lives without appearing to do so, intrusive without being obnoxious, a part of our common sense. Like Reagan's rhetoric, television can confront, represent, and circulate immorality without appearing hostile, judgmental, or, most important, racist.[10]

We witnessed the formation and institutionalization of discourses, articulated by Reagan and engineered by his sophisticated spin doctors, that moved quietly but steadily from "blacks" to "welfare," from "equal opportunity" to "preferential treatment," from "racism/ discrimination" to "reverse discrimination," from "tax recipients and social entitlements" to "taxpayers and civic responsibility," from "morality" to "immorality," and from "shared public responsibility" to "private charitable giving." Through its immediacy and pervasiveness, television quietly framed these shifts, announcing the news daily in softer, shorter, more visually dramatic, and conceptually simpler bites. Throughout the Reagan/Bush 1980s, commercial network television news programs brought us more and more people, mostly blacks and latinos, who seemed beyond the reasonable comprehension of popular common sense of public and civic responsibility, except as deviants, dependents, and threats. If television news was to be believed, these mostly black and brown people seemed to commit more crime, have more babies, use more drugs, and be more incompetent with respect to individual and civic responsibility and indifferent with respect to their obligations. The discourses of Reaganism targeted and effectively marked poor and black clients of the welfare state as undeserving. Reaganism's discursive construction of blackness and the claims on race that underwrote them were locked into a struggle, a highly contested struggle, over the very meaning and use of the sign of blackness.

3 African American Discourses and the Sign of Blackness

The new right's use of race and blackness as a marker of internal threats to social stability, cultural morality, and economic prosperity did not go uncontested. Indeed, African Americans produced an explosion of cultural, political, and social debate that sought to establish black claims, control, and affirmation of blackness. Where academic and policy debates over the political salience of race were waged largely in social science and policy discourses, popular culture and mass media were the expressive sites and vehicles through which serious issues facing African Americans and the broader society were expressed. Media and popular culture are the cultural and social sites where theoretical abstraction and cultural representation came down to earth, percolating through the imagination of America. Television, film, popular music, and literature were the cultural battlegrounds where important struggles were waged in and over the sign of blackness. I therefore want to move away from the focus on the new right's use of race and blackness to consolidate a new hegemonic order to consider African American claims on blackness, claims that contested conservative claims, repositioned traditional ones, and imagined new ones.

In the 1980s, television, film, popular music, and literature (especially by black women) were, perhaps, the dominant media forms in
which salient representations, counterrepresentations, and debates
about blackness were constructed and contested. Although not always
present in the dominant regimes of media representation such as commercial television network news and entertainment, historically African Americans have always met white and conservative claims on the
sign of blackness with suspicion and counterclaims. In the 1980s,
black youth, already suspicious and critical of white attempts to control the meaning and use of blackness, generated constructions and
representations of blackness that were increasingly circulated and expressed at the very center of American commercial media and popular
culture (Rose 1994). Representations of blackness by African American filmmakers, writers, musicians, painters, hip-hop/rap artists, athletes, and intellectuals produced a powerful counterhegemonic force in
the cultural politics of American society (Diawara 1993; Guerrero
1993; Tate 1992; Wallace 1992a).

I want to locate television representations of blackness, then, at the
intersection of social and cultural discourses within African American
communities and the dominant culture. I shall suggest that what these
representations mean, and for whom, is contingent, often contradictory, and sometimes ambivalent. My argument, moreover, is that the
popular discourses and commercial media landscapes across which
these constructions of blackness circulate help shape their meanings
(and countermeanings) for differently situated publics. Hence, conservative claims and uses of the sign of blackness necessarily produce different effects and meanings for blacks and whites.

Led in large measure by the intellectual labors of critical black intellectuals, especially those operating in the terrain of cultural criticism, literary criticism, social policy, and cultural politics, the 1980s
were notable for heated and often productive debates among black intellectuals and critics about the meanings of the very sign of "blackness" that figured so prominently in the discourse of Reaganism. African Americans debated the shape, character, and terms of blackness,
particularly as the meanings of blackness became structured by the
growing struggles over such issues as nationalism, gender, sexuality,
masculinity, and social class.

Commercial media sites such as film, television, video, and music
were among the most fertile social arenas in which African Americans
engaged each other (and whites) over questions of African American
presence in the United States. Black representations in commercial culture were often immediate and urgent in staging the aspirations, frus-

trations, and critical visions of African Americans. These representations were distinctive because they were generated from many different sectors and quarters of African American life. Strident, critical, direct, and often innovative representations and critiques of a stable and homogeneous "blackness" came from gays and lesbians, the sons and daughters of the middle class, the urban poor, neoconservatives, feminists, and neonationalists. In opposition to the containment and policing by blacks and whites alike, the sign of blackness, and the debates surrounding it, was squarely at the center of a larger discourse about contemporary U.S. society.

As pervasive and compelling as some of these representations often were, the struggles over the sign of blackness that they enacted were not just about matters of discourse, image, and the new market in black intellectual stars, for at stake were shifting and competing cultural frames for making sense of the dramatic and often painful social and material circumstances facing African American communities in the United States. Most directly, these discursive struggles attempted to make sense of and find a means for expressing counterhegemonic visions to the social and material impact of Reaganism, which exacted a devastating material toll on vast sectors of the African American community. From disproportionately high rates of unemployment, school dropouts, drugs, crime, marital instability, and prison incarceration to epidemic violence, teen pregnancy, and community instability, the poorest and most disenfranchised sectors of black America felt the sting of the new Republican hegemonic order (Hacker 1992; Johnson and Oliver 1991; Wilson 1987). In the face of steadily worsening material circumstances for the black poor, traditionally liberal civil rights visions of political activism and social change faced increasing competition from black neoconservatives, black feminists, black neonationalists, the Nation of Islam, and Afrocentric academic and organic intellectuals for the hearts and minds of African Americans.

Daily, new and more troubling statistics and dramatic news reports appeared in the media, telling middle-class blacks and whites what poor black Americans already knew—that American society under Reaganism was not a particularly hospitable or welcoming place. In the hands of policy analysts, media pundits, and academics, these daily reminders were framed and debated in the public discourse so that conditions of social instability and erosion became synonymous with the sign of blackness. Within African American discourses these data and the interpretations in which they were framed provoked deep disagreements in the social sciences, in policy circles, and in the popular media over the status of race.

Social Science and the Discourse of the Underclass

Along with the empirical identification and discursive production of the urban underclass, social scientists noted the appearance of a small but highly visible and vocal black middle class, and within it a smaller and equally vocal neoconservative impulse (Landry 1987; Wilson 1980). This middle class is distinct from its African American predecessors of the segregated South in the sense that its class position more closely approximates that of its white counterpart in terms of occupation, education, and places of residence (Frazier 1957).

Middle-class blacks are more likely to live in integrated communities away from urban centers populated by their poor and working-class counterparts (Landry 1987; Wilson 1980). The occupational reach of this newly emergent black middle class includes a rather large proportion of public sector employees, faculty at prestigious public and private universities, and business and corporate managers and junior executives. (It should be noted as well that, for all of the ways this black middle class approximates its white counterpart, its middle-class character continues to depend on income rather than wealth, and its members continue to experience glass ceilings, discrimination, income disparities, and racism.) For many, black and white, liberal and conservative, the very visibility and stability of this black middle-class formation at worst confounded and at best evidenced the "decline" of race and, by extension, racism as a barrier to African American economic and social enfranchisement (Wilson 1980).

The most significant sociological statement of the period, William J. Wilson's *The Declining Significance of Race* (1980), suggests (by its title) that class rather than race was the major post-World War II determinant of life chances for African Americans—including the likelihood of incarceration, family and marital stability, educational attainment, and access to health care. Wilson argues that as a result of postwar changes in the structure of the U.S. economy and legal recognition resulting from the civil rights movement, race became a less salient factor in black political empowerment and social mobility. A second Wilson monograph, *The Truly Disadvantaged* (1987), extends the arguments advanced in the first book, but shifts the focus from the simultaneous emergence of this new middle class and the urban underclass as the basis of the argument for the increased salience of social class over race to a more sustained analysis of the black urban underclass. For most of the 1980s, Wilson's books remained at the center of academic and policy debates over the salience of race in the post-civil rights era. At the core of these debates was the intractable problem of just how to account for the persistent and increasing poverty and suffering of the black urban poor and at the same time explain the increased movement of middle-class blacks into the mainstream.

Meanwhile, on commercial network television, on any broadcast day in the 1980s, the different faces of blackness were readily apparent—here was the affable and successful Bryant Gumbel, anchor of NBC's network morning news show, followed in many markets by the comforting, provocative, and enormously popular Oprah Winfrey, hosting her own talk show. Later in the broadcast day were reruns of 1970s black situation comedies, such as *Good Times, The Jeffersons,* and *Sanford & Son.* On the evening network newscast there might be a black male correspondent covering the arrest of a black drug dealer, a black victim of a gang-style killing, a teenage welfare mother, or an urban inner-city neighborhood decimated by hardships of deteriorating urban inner cities (Reeves and Campbell 1994). Later in the evening, one could be entertained first by *The Cosby Show,* the most consistent and highest-rated prime-time television program of the 1980s, and later yet by Arsenio Hall, whose late-night talk show initially functioned as television's version of *Jet* magazine for black Americans, especially youth. This pastiche of "blackness" was, of course, punctuated with carefully selected and packaged images of famous black bodies and faces selling soap, breakfast cereals, popular music, sneakers, laundry detergent, hamburgers, and automobiles. Across the country, college and professional athletes became the chief sales reps of consumer commodities, corporate team logos, and affluent lifestyles. The representations of blackness played their part to confirm the notion that America was racially open—white fans were just as likely as black fans to own life-size posters of Michael and Magic. Commercial network television, it seems, offered one continuous parade of "blackness" across the media landscape and our cultural imaginary. But not all of these representations were equally commodified or equally resistant. My contention is that television both constructs a sign of blackness and is itself one of the floodlit stages on which struggles over the sign of blackness are waged.

Under Reagan/Bush conservative policies, both African Americans and whites seemed to gather steam in their insistence that in the post-civil rights period—where the state had effectively mediated and outlawed legal discrimination—the persistence of a black underclass could be explained only in terms of individual character, morality, motivation, and responsibility (Loury 1985). In spite of mounting evidence about the destructive effects of structural inequality, institutional racism, and economic restructuring, the discourse of Reaganism focused the debate on the role of the state: How much and to what extent does the persistence of black urban poverty require state intervention and mediation? At what cost to the principles of equality and justice for all citizens? And at what point will the social costs of such intervention begin to have a negative impact on the collective social good?

Black conservatives such as Glenn Loury, Thomas Sowell, Robert Woodson, Clarence Thomas, Shelby Steele, and Walter Williams vigorously challenged the continuing hegemony of liberal "Great Society" initiatives such as entitlements for the poor, affirmative action, and the effectiveness of federal civil rights policies predicated on enfranchising poor and disenfranchised communities of color. During the Reagan/Bush 1980s these black neoconservative voices found both a more receptive political climate and prestigious national platforms and forums from which to voice their positions on affirmative action, civil rights strategies, and the black poor (Marable 1991; Reed 1991b; West 1993).

From the offices and forums of conservative think tanks and policy centers such as the Heritage Foundation, the Hoover Institute, and the American Enterprise Institute, black conservatives began a steady challenge to the salience of liberal programs, the integrity of civil rights leadership, and the direction and efficacy of the Democratic party as the legitimate and sole protector of black political aspirations (Katz 1989; Marable 1991; Reed 1991b). Advocating a turn, or return, to the traditions of black community self-help and empowerment in the tradition of Booker T. Washington, black neoconservatives offered economic and social proscriptions that articulated quite nicely with the Reagan/Bush moral and economic vision. Black neoconservatives stressed a self-regulating market and, within that, individual character, responsibility, morality, and hard work (Loury 1985b; Sowell 1983). Although most neoliberals and even some conservatives continued to acknowledge the persistence of racism, for the most part others, such as black conservative supporters of Reagan/Bush, seemed to accept uncritically the idea that an unfettered free market, as opposed to an intrusive and morally debilitating welfare state, offered the greatest possibility for the social and economic uplift of the black urban poor.

Academics such as literature professor Shelby Steele (1990) and economist Glenn Loury (1985b) were especially vocal critics of what they took to be rampant individual and moral irresponsibility in poor urban African American communities. Various supporters of black nationalism, such as the Nation of Islam also took a similarly conservative view of the state of moral and individual irresponsibility among the black poor (Reed 1991a). In addition to nationalists, the more race-conscious wing of the new black conservatism took the black middle class to task for abandoning the black poor (Reed 1991b).

Out-of-wedlock births, female-headed households, violence, and drug addiction were not all merely the results of racism, changing economic structures, and attacks on the welfare state; rather, for many whites as well as blacks, especially conservatives, these conditions represented zones of individual moral and spiritual bankruptcy. Such behaviors, they argued, resulted from well-intentioned Great Society welfare programs and entitlements for the poor, which in the end produced and reproduced the very dependency they were designed to eliminate. In the hands of black conservatives, these and other criticisms provided legitimation and support for an already aggressive attack on the welfare state and its major clients—the poor, especially African American and latino urban poor (Katz 1989).

Whether discussion centered on moral character, work ethic, violent crime, family instability, or drug addiction, the urban underclass operated as the touchstone of various discourses about race and contemporary American society. Within and among these discourses, there was considerable disagreement about the levels of analysis, causes, and empirical distribution of misery and impoverishment within black communities by gender, age, education, social class, and region. Similarly, policy analysts and political spokespersons, especially within the black communities, disagreed about effective social and political strategies (including the role of the state, the market, and movements for social change) for addressing the conditions of blacks in the United States.

Cultural Politics and African American Struggles over the Sign of Blackness

Materially, the black poor continued to face worsening conditions. Culturally and socially, racism, though often coded in new signs and symbols, remained a dominant interpretive lens through which to rationalize the self-interests of whites, who felt alternately threatened by the black poor and comforted by the growing black middle class (Gray 1993b; Jhally and Lewis 1992). With the visibility and legitimacy added by black conservatives, political attacks on multiculturalism, affirmative action, and the welfare state under Reagan/Bush continued their steady and destructive effects. Despite—perhaps even because of—these frontal assaults on the signs of blackness, African American discourses in the 1980s were also sharply defined internally, by cultural debates and struggles over blackness, struggles whose aims, more often than not, were both critique and affirmation. As cultural practices, these debates and struggles were played out in many arenas—film, theater, television, the academy, literature—and took various expressive forms, including music, cultural criticism and commentary, dress, language, popular dance, and style.

The cultural meaning for the sign of blackness was no longer defined only in relationship to whiteness and some utopian desire for integration, nor was it only about black utopian desires for a unified and totalizing notion of blackness (Wallace 1992a). In the material and cultural climate of the 1980s, blackness emerged as a site of contested struggle over the very question of identity and difference within America in general and black America in particular. Questions of social class, gender, sexuality, masculinity, feminism, and their status within (and representation by) the sign(s) of blackness came to occupy a central place in discourses about black cultural politics in the 1980s. Not surprisingly, it was often in popular culture and commercial media—such as television (talk shows, situation comedy, variety, music video), popular music (especially avant-garde jazz and rap), film (commercial and black independents), literature, and the critical and journalistic discourses surrounding them—that the salience and resonance of social science data, everyday life experiences, and policy debates were most directly registered and challenged. Black cultural responses to racism and utopian visions of possibility boomed from the radios and tape and CD players of urban youth, the cinematic images of black filmmakers, the television situation comedies featuring African Americans, and the language and dress that, taken together, expressed a dynamic and lived relationship to blackness (Rose 1994; Zook 1994). Politically, then, many of the most salient and most hotly contested African American counterhegemonic responses to the rightward shift in American society (and in African American communities) were organized and articulated culturally—not as social science "facts" or even political "realities" in organized mass social movements, but as expressive cultural practices and the lived experiences in which they were embedded (Lipsitz 1994).

Through popular music, videos, film, television, literature, and personal style, different publics, audiences, and communities came to see, encounter, and stake claims on the central issues facing various African American communities.[1] Struggles to define and control the "image" and "representation" of blackness in popular culture were important ways in which black urban youth, lesbians, Afrocentric nationalists, neoconservatives, liberal democrats, middle-class professionals, and gay men came to press claims, name themselves, and give voice to the hurts, pains, injustices, and brutalities of their experiences (Lorde 1990). It was also through rap music, cable television, novels, and cultural criticism that different sectors of the African American community forcefully and directly expressed alternative visions and social desires that critiqued as well as affirmed African American notions of blackness. Broadly speaking, these claims on blackness found resonance in the cultural imagination and social common sense of Americans in television programs such as *The Cosby Show*, nightly news broadcasts, the videotape of the Rodney King beating, broadcast footage of the Los Angeles riots, films such as *Boyz N the Hood* and *Do the Right Thing*, and, of course, rap music and music videos.

Because cultural and identity politics, especially its effectiveness in the project of social transformation, remains at the center of much debate, I want to be clear on this point. I do not mean to suggest or imply, as some postmodernists might, that cultural and identity politics has, in some dramatic way, come to displace materially based social protest and mass movements for social change. Recent evidence and events clearly suggest otherwise—the Los Angeles riots in the spring of 1992, mass support for the 1984 and 1988 candidacies of Jesse Jackson, mobilization against drugs, violence, crime, and job losses in urban black communities across the country. Nor am I suggesting that commercial and popular culture has emerged as "the only" site of the political. Rather, it seems to me that popular culture, and more specifically commercially mediated forms and representations, has become one of the chief means through which all Americans engage, understand, negotiate, and make sense of the material circumstances of their everyday lives (Grossberg 1992; Hall 1981a; Kelley 1992; Lipsitz 1990a; Rose 1994; Zook 1994). Young African American rappers as well as Reagan Republicans and their coalition of neoconservative supporters clearly understand this.

Although images of blackness saturated the televisual, cinematic, and advertising landscape in the 1980s to a far greater extent perhaps than ever before, it is the interpretive and discursive lens through which these images and representations of blackness are framed and understood that remains the object of cultural and political struggle in the realm of cultural politics. In an era of neoconservative domination, what does one, especially if one is black and female, make of this televisual and cinematic presence (or absence)? How are we to read these representations? How are we to relate to them? And by what standards and referents are they judged? And what of our own pleasures, desires, experiences, suspicions, criticisms that derive from the experience of living black lives in America? How do we confront the social science data, the journalistic accounts, the everyday lives, and the media representations in this cultural struggle over the meaning and use of the sign of blackness?

Ultimately, then, my concern is with the meaning of blackness and its circulation in a medium such as television. But, as I have been suggesting, cultural and social meanings are precarious matters; they too are subject to the constant shifts, contradictions, and struggles for power that punctuate all aspects of contemporary social life. It is this "politics" of representation, culture, and blackness that moved to the foreground of the struggle for blackness within African America. It is this cultural struggle for the politics of blackness as a sign that challenged the discursive productions and claims of Reaganism as well as totalizing constructions from inside black communities.

To be sure, academic and policy debates (and facts) did finally circulate beyond the specialized conference proceedings and journals read and critiqued by a small group of specialists; they made it to television network news broadcasts, to daily television talk shows and nighttime talk radio, to issues-oriented television specials and documentaries, and to television situation comedies, dramatic nighttime series, and miniseries. As a forum for the circulation of representations and discourses about blackness, commercial and cable television, popular films, and novels did not displace social scientific and policy discourses on the "facts" of African American life. Instead, these commercial and popular forms served to infuse passion and urgency into such questions, making the issues and images through which they were represented living realities and not just empty abstractions.[2] Of course, there is always the danger that in the postmodern condition media representations will and often do displace and subsequently stand in for the very material and social conditions in which they are situated. Accordingly, representations themselves can and often do become "the" crisis. Absent any social and cultural context, the crisis of representation (yes, even in the hands of African American filmmakers, novelists, and television producers) on the issue of race and blackness can become hyperreal.

Nonetheless, socially and culturally, popular culture and mass media operated as significant arenas within which and through which African American counterhegemonic responses to neoconservative hegemony were mobilized and articulated. But, of course, such counterhegemonic responses and their cultural meanings were more than mere televisual and cinematic representations or reflections of the real material conditions of black life in America. And they were not just limited by responses to the dominant conservative attacks on black communities and blackness. If the explosion of black popular and expressive culture was, in some respects, about a crisis of representation, it was also about something more. It was the place and means by which new, different, and alternative ways of imagining blackness (and African American life) were created and expressed. For example, in the music videos of Arrested Development, Queen Lati-fah, Salt-N-Pepa, and even Michael Jackson, one could readily find representations and constructions of an African homeland, the pasto-ral life of the black American South, and women defining the terms of their bodies and sexuality (Rose 1990; Zook 1992, 1994).

Before taking up the specific question of the cultural meanings and responses activated by televisual representations of blackness that oc-cupies the remainder of this book, I want to map, in rather broad strokes, some of the salient issues and discourses within African American cultural politics that constitute the cultural field within which televisual representations of blackness circulated in the 1980s. These African American cultural discourses, together with neoconser-vative assaults and claims on blackness, help to establish the symbolic landmarks with which to begin to make sense of television's construc-tions and representations of African Americans. These landmarks, their tensions, alliances, and positions, help to situate the terms of what I regard as a set of shifting meanings (and positionalities). Along with the social science and policy data debates about the social con-figuration of African American communities in the 1980s, I offer this preliminary siting of cultural landmarks to bring into sharper focus the contours and range of positions through which and by which cer-tain kinds of readings are enabled and disenabled.

In the final analysis, my argument is that one cannot begin the task of understanding the complex cultural meanings of black television representations and television's representations of blacks without situ-ating them in terms of the cultural discourses in which these represen-tations are produced and the social locations across which these im-ages and representations circulate. Following this analytic strategy, for example, one could, as Robin Kelley (1994) has so brilliantly shown, make sense of the complex and doggedly masculine and heterosexual constructions of nationalism and Afrocentricity that pervade so much of the cultural construction of rap music and its visual representation. By locating "gangsta" rap within the complex web of cultural mean-ings and social locations of black youth in Los Angeles, Kelley sees this music as, among other things, an expressive response to and engage-ment with the new right's surveillance, policing, and demonization of black male youth.

In a similar fashion, I locate some of the cultural scenes and con-versations enacted on television shows such as *Frank's Place, A Dif-ferent World,* and *In Living Color* within the context of the new right's construction of blackness as well as that of black imaginative produc-tions, expressions, conflicts, and visions in film, theater, popular music, cultural criticism, and literature. Within these discursive arenas, questions of black sexuality, social class, gender, and difference more broadly defined are explored and debated. Not surprisingly, these debates found their way into various television episodes, where they percolated up occasionally to challenge and subvert dominant neoconservative racial discourses. At the same time, they were articulated with (and by) and repositioned in (and against) some of the most totalizing (e.g., Afrocentric nationalism) and intolerant (heterosexual dominance and sexism) impulses in the African American social formation.

Black Popular Culture and the Cultural Politics of Difference

In the 1980s, African American cultural struggles over the sign of blackness centered on tensions between unity and difference. Could African Americans, especially critical intellectuals and cultural workers, represent the complex and wide-ranging differences of class, color coding, sexuality, gender, region, and political ideology without compromising the necessity for a public stance of unity? Does the desire—indeed, necessity—for a unified antiracist position based solely on racial identity and identification with "blackness" come at the cost of repression and containment of deep and growing internal differences? Would representing these complex differences amount to airing dirty laundry, in effect fueling stereotypes and eroding black political power, social legitimacy, and cultural visibility? And could—indeed, should—the already burdened sign of "blackness" continue to perform the discursive labors necessary to balance these implicit tensions?

By the 1980s these complex social and cultural questions were debated and enacted in such public cultural arenas as commercial network television, films, novels, popular music, and cultural criticism. For African Americans, questions of difference within the sign of blackness clustered around a host of core issues—gender (especially feminism and masculinity), social class, and sexuality. These issues were also connected to a related set of highly charged concerns, such as nationalism and Afrocentricity, multiculturalism, and the relationship of African Americans to latinos, Asians, whites, gays and lesbians, and members of the Atlantic Diaspora—blacks from Europe and the Caribbean.

In addition to the very public and often provocative representations and enactments of these tensions in black popular culture (especially film and rap music), a parallel set of key theoretical interventions provided the frameworks through which debates about difference could be examined. By critically interrogating rather than assuming the cultural and political labors of "blackness," these theoretical and cultural interventions forced a reckoning with the assumed hegemonic (masculinist and heterosexual) power of blackness. Stuart Hall, Cornel West, Greg Tate, Paul Gilroy, Angela Davis, Michelle Wallace, Ntozake Shange, Kobena Mercer, Marlon Riggs, Audre Lorde, Alice Walker, Bill T. Jones, Julius Hemphill, Essex Hemphill, and bell hooks were among a group of artists, performers, critical black intellectuals, and cultural critics who questioned, in a critical and sustained way, the tensions between unity and difference within the sign of blackness.

Quickening the demise of the essential black subject, scholars in the humanities, especially African American literature, began to expose and critique the masculinist and heterosexual control of the discourse of blackness. These and other writers critiqued the silence and marginalization of black heterosexual and lesbian women, black gay men, and people of mixed-race origin. Ever alert to the masculinist character of the representation of blackness in black popular culture, black feminists encouraged, celebrated, and wrote from the vantage point of black, often gay, women. At the center of many of these early and often pointed exchanges were the works of black women writers such as Ntozake Shange (*for colored girls who have considered suicide / when the rainbow is enuf*), Michelle Wallace (*Black Macho and the Myth of the Superwoman*), and Alice Walker (*The Color Purple*).

In the critical spaces created by the works of these and other black women writers came heated debates concerning African American unity, black masculinity, nationalism, moral responsibility, the urban underclass, the middle class, questions of violence in urban communities, the objectification of women, and homophobia. Underlying these debates were urgent and difficult questions about the political efficacy—indeed, luxury—of essentialist and totalizing constructions of blackness for African Americans in the United States (White 1990). From the heat and smoke of these debates came an increasing number of African American claims on blackness that ranged from the uncompromising authority of cultural nationalism and certain forms of gangsta rap to the flat-out rejection of blackness as a viable sign capable of handling the complex issue of difference among African Americans (and blacks within the Atlantic Diaspora) (Gilroy 1993). Though by no means the first, the national campaign led by Jesse Jackson to adopt *African American* in preference to *black* as a group and individual descriptor is part of this moment, as are contemporary debates about the political and cultural legitimacy of the status of mixed-race people within the African American community who make claims on all elements of their cultural and racial makeup (Gates 1987).

In the call for a new cultural politics of difference, Cornel West (1990) forcefully articulated and sharply focused the complex issues at stake in the cultural debates over the sign of blackness. West and others, such as E. Francis White (1990) and Kimberle Crenshaw (1989, 1991), recognized and exposed the theoretical fallacy and political seduction of constructing a totalizing definition built on false unities that are themselves structured by tensions, contradictions, and the repression of significant differences within blackness. Hence, many critical black intellectuals argued against a totalizing and authoritarian conception of blackness built on a romantic African past, an imagined nation, racial purity, or a cultural authenticity that denies differences of gender, sexuality, class, and history. By acknowledging the salience of difference among African Americans, critics articulated productive ways of thinking about black differences and the contemporary conditions of blacks in the United States, conditions that of necessity demanded recognition of the different modalities of black experiences and the historical, material, and cultural circumstances that structured those experiences.

Critical black intellectuals such as West enacted theoretically and culturally a new cultural politics of difference within the sign of blackness that was, itself, enabled and linked to theorizations and critiques of contemporary Western society stimulated by ethnic studies, African American studies, postmodernism, poststructuralism, feminism, deconstruction, and cultural studies. In their own ways, all of these intellectual developments presented important challenges to the stability and power of grand theory, unified subjects, disinterested knowledge, and the authority of positivist epistemologies (Collins 1990). Explored in the critical areas of legal studies, cultural criticism, film theory, and literary theory, these interventions challenged existing regimes of knowledge, especially ways of representing the world (Taylor forthcoming).

To their credit, critical black intellectuals in the United States in the 1980s gave a particularly African American character to questions about difference within the sign of blackness. However, similar questions were being debated among feminists, communities of color, gays and lesbians, and postcolonial scholars throughout the world, especially in the black Atlantic formations in England, Canada, and Caribbean. Outside of the United States one of the most productive and influential discussions of blackness for blacks in the United States was taking place in England.[3] African American cultural critics and scholars entered into important and productive dialogues with the work of black intellectuals in England. Scholars, filmmakers, and cultural critics—Stuart Hall, Kobena Mercer, Isaac Julian, Paul Gilroy, Angela McRobbie, Linton Kwesi Johnson, members of the Sankofa Collective, Courtney Pine, Jim Pines, and Dick Hebdige, among others—

performed, described, and analyzed the rather precarious and shifting status and labors of blackness in England. Theorizations about difference necessarily began to reckon with just how blackness in Britain functioned—where, for whom, and under what conditions. Stuart Hall's (1988, 1989, 1992b) seminal insights and the works that extend them took up the task of making sense of the trope of blackness as an oppositional strategy, a source of affirmation, an object of demonization, and a place from which to speak with power. For critical black intellectuals in the United States who were interested in popular culture and media representations of blackness, these theorizations proved important. If nothing else, such theorizations and the interventions they produced forced critical thinkers west of the Atlantic to reckon seriously with the specificity, hegemony, and travels of our claims on blackness both abroad and at home.[4]

In the United States, distinctions and tensions within African American formations certainly are not new; I call attention to the discursive force of the interventions of West (1990), Hall (1989), and others loosely working in the tradition of cultural studies and cultural politics because they are pivotal to the establishment of the theoretical and cultural terms in which contemporary media representations and self-representations of blacks came to be analyzed. Although written well into the decade of the 1980s, the theorizations of cultural studies and black studies scholars focused and opened debates about important issues throughout the decade in African American popular and intellectual discourses about blackness. Debates over the analytic status and location of class, gender, and sexuality within the sign of blackness centered on the power and cultural labors of blackness as a complex trope of affirmation, opposition, menace, and authority. In distinct ways, West (1990), Hall (1989), and others emphasized the continuing necessity to describe, theorize, and evaluate our assumptions about the cultural labors and social effects of blackness as force of political solidarity, social change, and cultural identity.

By interrogating the epistemological status of blackness rather than assuming its political, cultural, and social essence, the contributions of West, Hall, and others created the possibility for a more explicit social and cultural analysis of African American representations. Gender, sexuality, class, and other critical distinctions within blackness could no longer be taken for granted or go untheorized in the service of opposition, unity, and affirmation. As a result, political claims on blackness as a social and cultural place from which to speak require, at the very least, recognition of and grappling with the complex interplay, intersection, and tension among class, gender, and sexuality (Crenshaw 1989; Hall 1992b).

In popular and intellectual discourses alike, the representations of blackness—its status, authenticity, oppositional force, pleasures, appropriations, commodification—all seemed to weigh heavily on the productions, meditations, and reflections of cultural workers, from musicians to writers, academics, and playwrights. Blackness seemed to bear, as James Baldwin put it, a rather considerable burden of representation.[5]

As with the mobilization of blackness by neoconservatives under Reagan/Bush, blackness loomed large in discussions and debates about affirmative action, multiculturalism, political correctness, and related cultural skirmishes. In this climate one of the major questions facing black intellectuals and cultural workers was how to mobilize blackness effectively as the leading edge of an oppositional and affirmative place from which to stand without feeding the project of demonization and marginalization of Reaganism. Debate proceeded at a rapid pace and often rose to a fever pitch in popular films, popular music, monographs, academic and popular journals, and media talk shows.

I turn, then, to a brief focus on media discourses on blackness in the 1980s as a way of seeing various enactments of African American struggles for the sign of blackness. By focusing on the internal struggles for and over the meaning of blackness as an expression of opposition and affirmation, I want to underscore the provisional and contingent nature of cultural struggles and note the multiple and contradictory ways in which the trope of blackness operates in media—as opposition, as affirmation, as difference. That is to say, blackness was (and continues to be) mobilized by African Americans in opposition to conservative claims about race and blacks, as a place of cultural affirmation, and as a contested space of difference. Blackness labors on all of these fronts. I map media and popular culture this way because it offers a productive way of situating commercial network television as a site of cultural struggle and, within television, blackness as one of the key points of struggle and contention.

In addition to political and social science discourses, claims and counterclaims over the meanings and uses of blackness that found their way to television were shaped by and deeply embedded in the rich representations that emerged from black popular culture. Like the political and social science debates, popular media representations were formed and pressured by the contradictions of difference and unity within blackness.

In theater, for instance, Charles Fuller's *A Soldier's Play* (which was later adapted for the screen as *A Soldier's Story*), Ntozake Shange's *for colored girls who have considered suicide / when the rainbow is enuf,* and George C. Wolfe's *The Colored Museum* all offered irreverent, satirical, and sometimes painful confrontations with stable and time-honored visions of monolithic and homogenized black selves. These plays explore the underbelly of this stability, unearthing questions of difference and the burdens of black representations in political movements and social institutions, in gender and sexual relations, and in theater itself. August Wilson offered his plays *Ma Rainey's Black Bottom, Fences,* and *Two Trains Running,* which in a different way forced a long and lingering look inside twentieth-century African American cultural memory and the power of African American vernacular culture. Whether these critical and irreverent impulses reappeared in contemporary black films such as *School Daze, I'm Gonna Git You Sucka,* and *Hollywood Shuffle* or such television shows as *In Living Color* and *A Different World,* the critical power of irreverence and satire as expressions of difference and critiques of monolithic blackness by black playwrights, directors, and producers is unmistakable.[6]

Black cinema is perhaps second only to black music as a fertile and vibrant sector of black popular culture where African Americans, especially youth, debated, imagined, claimed, and represented black life, culture, and experience.[7] As I argue in chapter 4, the visibility and commercial success of black (mostly male) filmmakers in the late 1980s and early 1990s—Spike Lee, Keenen Ivory Wayans, Robert Townsend, John Singleton—led directly to the quickness of television to capitalize on the visibility and popularity of blackness as a cultural sign. For the moment, however, I call attention to these forms of black commercial and popular culture for another reason: film and music are the dominant cultural spaces where black self-representation is explored in mass commercial culture. In black films and popular music throughout the 1980s, utopian visions of blackness as the glue of political solidarity and cultural authenticity were constantly interrupted by persistent questions of economic mobility and middle-class responsibility; questions of gender, masculinity, and sexuality; questions of family and neighborhood disintegration; questions of racial and cultural authenticity. Where these and related questions were not explicitly explored musically and cinematically, representations of blacks in film and music certainly provoked commentary and debate (Crenshaw 1991; Diawara 1993; Early 1992; Guerrero 1993; Jones 1991; Tate 1992; Wallace 1992a; West 1993).

Two significant films from the 1980s that illustrate the range, depth, and passion of debates over questions of gender and sexuality are Steven Spielberg's movie based on Alice Walker's novel *The Color Purple* (1985) and Spike Lee's *She's Gotta Have It* (1986). Released only a year apart, both films staked out polemical positions (Bobo

1988; Guerrero 1993). Together with the growing visibility and influence of black feminist criticism and fiction, these films in different ways served to quicken the debate about a monolithic and unified blackness underwritten by masculinity, sexism, and homophobia.

Not surprisingly, both films were hotly contested and criticized for their treatment of sexuality and gender: *The Color Purple* for its representation of and critique of black men and its bashful presentation of a lesbian relationship (much more forthrightly depicted in the novel), and *She's Gotta Have It* for its representation of black women and its homophobic hostility toward lesbianism. Nevertheless, and this is the central point of these examples, both films served as important touchstones for internal debates about blackness among African Americans. These films and the debate they generated helped to illuminate, within the terrain of commercial popular culture, the terms, stakes, passions, and histories of different African American claims on blackness. Each film and the polemic it produced revealed the discursive strategies, interests, and power relations at work in different claims on blackness. These films contributed to, if not the end of what Stuart Hall calls the essential black subject, a reconsideration of blackness and black subjects in terms of difference. Perhaps more than the films themselves, the debates over *The Color Purple* and *She's Gotta Have It* meant once and for all that black difference and black diverse subjects could not be discursively packed away to labor exclusively in the service of masculinist, homophobic, and sexist representations of blackness.

One other point about the success of these films and the debate they stimulated is worth considering. As commercially successful and provocative films, they anticipated—indeed, helped to establish—the critical commercial power of black cinema in contemporary American popular culture. These films demonstrated to advertisers and television networks that issues, images, and debates among African Americans could find successful crossover appeal in the media and cultural environment of the 1980s. The issues of gender and sexuality raised and debated among African Americans easily articulated with broader questions of gender, black feminism, and violence toward women in general.

As the critical discourse over the cultural representation of difference within blackness continued to heat up, black commercial culture, especially music, upped the cultural and political ante—African Americans were aesthetically and politically preoccupied with questions of authenticity (especially the search for its locations and affirmations in a mythical African past), the urban streets, unity, masculinity, and class. Within the realm of these specific concerns, young black (mostly male) filmmakers and rappers imagined and enacted these concerns in representations that privileged and glamorized drugs, violence, gangs, power, and misogynist images of women. In rap and film, the particular representations of and identifications with "authentic blackness," although urgent and immediate, were often narrow and inflexible. This blackness was necessarily masculine, its nationalist cultural vision of unity at all cost seemed to suggest, because it had to negotiate divisive internal differences and racist external threats.

Black popular forms such as rap and cinema mobilized and then helped to consolidate visions and representations of blackness that articulated the pains, fears, joys, and aspirations of black youth. Because they catalyzed and drew together so many issues, these forms of black expressive commercial culture hovered at the center of contemporary black cultural politics. Beginning (in 1989) with *Do the Right Thing* and continuing through *Boyz N the Hood, Juice,* and *Menace II Society,* black commercial film and popular music constructed powerful images of African American youth from within the cultural space of blackness (Jones 1991).

Perhaps the richest and most consistently provocative claims on blackness as opposition and affirmation came from rap music. Where film works the imaginative space by representing blackness as spectacle writ large, rap works the terrain of representation through the experience of everyday life, the body, and language. As music, it operates as perhaps the quintessential cultural sensibility through which blackness is constructed and represented. Rap emerged out of the fiscal and social crisis of New York in the 1970s and in response to the demonization and marginalization of black youth. Its complex combination and use of black oral and vernacular tradition, technology, and music combined (at least in its earliest stages) with its ingenious neighborhood-based production and distribution network to make it the most exciting and compelling cultural innovation in twenty-five years (Baker 1991; Garofalo 1992; George 1992; Keyes 1984; Rose 1994; Tate 1992; Zook 1992).

So far, rap has developed a wide range of genres, styles, and innovations that have been felt throughout American popular culture. Indeed, by the 1990s, film, advertising, fashion, and television all felt the cultural force of blackness through rap. Rap, like film, articulates claims on blackness that, in the end, are powerful wagers for control over its representation, meaning, and use. These claims are constructed at social (schools, neighborhoods) and cultural sites (film, television) and in terms, assumptions, and representations filled with tension and contradiction. At the center of rap's claim on blackness is a vision of cultural politics in which blackness serves symbolically as the cultural resource with which to contest white racism, social invisibility, and cultural disrespect—whether from the state (and its representatives, such as the police), racists, other blacks, browns or yellows, women, or gays and lesbians. Gender, sexuality, class, power, and respect are the central tropes around which struggles for control are waged. Like *The Color Purple, She's Gotta Have It, Do the Right Thing,* and *Boyz N the Hood,* rap stimulated heated debates in all sectors of U.S. society, including intellectual circles, law enforcement, parents, schools, electoral politics, the recording industry, and the criminal justice system. These debates focused on questions of homophobia, misogyny, reverse racism, traditional values, the glorification of violence, and the celebration of certain forms of black nationalism (Crenshaw 1991; Gray 1989; Grossberg 1992; Kennedy 1990; Rose 1994; Zook 1992).

With great authority, young rap musicians aggressively claimed and celebrated their right to speak and represent blackness. Articulated from multiple locations and voices, rap not only voices the frustrations, aspirations, and realities of urban life for black youth, but does so through its ability to express and represent its vision through the body and pleasures (Rose 1994). Rap's cultural power is precisely its ability to structure and mobilize multiple fields of alliance and interest, often across racial, gender, class, and cultural difference, both within and across blackness (Grossberg 1992; Lipsitz 1994).[8] These "always ready" interests and alliances that are mobilized in the realm of popular culture operate at shifting points of articulation and disarticulation, where they can be put into the service of various ends, interests, and desires, including those that do not always serve the interests of African Americans.

Like cinema, then, rap occupies a central place in debates and discourses about blackness, particularly in the mobilization and organization of counterclaims to neoconservative demonization of blackness. As representations of blacks and blackness moved into commercial network television in the 1980s and beyond, the meanings, identifications, and resonances they activate and produce cannot be read in isolation. Rather, they must be understood dialogically in relationship to shifting and multiple discourses—neoconservative, social science, and difference within blackness (Lipsitz 1990b).

Conclusion

Black cultural representations and the debates they stimulate are in dialogue with, borrow from, organize, and structure television representations of blacks. Along with film and popular music, black expressive culture offers television a black cultural vocabulary of style that can be seen politically (Hebdige 1979, 1989; Lipsitz 1994; Rose 1994; Tate 1992; Zook 1994). They constitute a bricolage of dress, attitudes, language, postures, gestures, habits, and tastes, all of which are constantly replenished and travel with increasing frequency and velocity across the landscape of commercial media—in advertising, situation comedy, sports, talk shows, fashion runways, magazine layouts, comedy, music television, and the news.

Some of the most familiar and provocative representations of blacks in commercial television—Clarence Thomas/Anita Hill, the urban basketball court, Michael Jordan, Colin Powell, Homey the Clown, Willie Horton, black welfare mothers, Bill Cosby, Mars Blackman and Spike Lee, KFC, Arrested Development, Eddie Murphy, Mike Tyson, the Los Angeles riots, Michael Jackson, Oprah Winfrey, Fresh Prince, *It's Showtime at the Apollo,* Sister Souljah, Carole Simpson and Charlayne Hunter-Gault, Ice-T—are necessarily related to the wide range and circuits of images and discourses that television organizes, packages, and circulates. These images are socially and culturally meaningful in relationship to their continuing dialogue with neoconservative attacks on African Americans, intraracial struggle and competition, and claims on blackness by African Americans.

For all of their limits and contradictions, commercial network television representations of blackness are socially and culturally rooted someplace and are in dialogue with very real issues. How commercial popular culture and mass media construct and represent these dialogues, organize and appeal to the desires that underwrite them, and articulate them with and against various political positions is part of their power (Grossberg 1992; Hall 1981b; Kelley 1994).

When approached relationally, the varied and rich representations and claims on blackness waged by African Americans in commercial media defy simplistic and reductionist analyses. And here I mean to point to those analyses that shun or dismiss black commercial representations because of their commodity character and those that uncritically celebrate representations that circulate outside of commercial media as inherently resistant and authentic. Representations of blackness that are produced and circulate within commercial media and popular culture constitute strategic cultural resources and social spaces where the traces, memories, textures, definitions, and, above all, struggles for and over social and cultural life are lived and waged (Lipsitz 1990b). Whether the middle-class privileges of the Huxtables on *The Cosby Show* or the irreverent, often disturbing, b-boy sensibilities of *In Living Color,* in their own ways they each labor to identify and organize claims on blackness that must be theorized and situated in relation to the formations, communities, affinities, structures, and histories that threaten and support their interests. Judgments about the positive or negative effects of black television and media representations are not productive for a project that of necessity begins with the recognition that the meaning and power of black representations in popular commercial media do not rest with images or texts alone. For different and multiply situated audiences, the significance of these images rests in the ways these images situate, activate, and structure alliances of identification and pleasure.

My point here is neither to privilege certain black representations as more desirable nor to dismiss others as worthless, though certainly both kinds of representations have been abundant since the 1980s. Nor is it my aim simply to beg the question with overtheorized qualifications and directives about what is to be done culturally and politically. Rather, in the remainder of this book I treat commercial network television and popular culture as active sites where representations of and issues about African Americans circulate. I argue, therefore, that television constitutes an important site of cultural politics. As I have suggested in these preliminary examinations of claims on the sign of blackness, television and the signifying practices that operate there, then, are crucial resources and sites over which and within which alliances, experiences, pleasures, and desires are organized and mobilized. Struggles for and over the representation of blackness are important and meaningful, not just for the choosing of moral and political sides that such struggles constantly force, but also for the very way in which they organize and structure choices, construct oppositions, and shape our commonsense understandings. Struggles over (and within) blackness are not just about the representation and control over the sign or the meaning of blackness—they are tactical resources to which people, all of us, turn in the struggle to make a life, to make sense, to affirm our humanity, and to counter the assaults and attacks that we all face in our daily lives (Lipsitz 1990b). As resources, these images and the site in which they circulate serve as enabling conditions—conditions of possibility and imagination that are registered and struggled over and for in the cultural arena.

4 The Transformation of the Television Industry and the Social Production of Blackness

Why the sudden proliferation of black-oriented situation comedies in the mid- to late 1980s? Although it can carry us quite a way toward an explanation, the focus on discursive struggles, cultural politics, and textual analysis alone does not provide completely satisfactory answers. Hence, in this chapter I center the apparatus of television a bit more by shifting the focus of my argument slightly toward a more detailed consideration of the complex institutional and industrial machinations of American commercial network television.

This chapter explores how structural transformations in the television industry, as a cultural institution, constructed and produced black audiences as a key element in the operation of the industry in the middle and late 1980s. I approach television by way of its political economy, industrial organization, and technologies, because these structures are central to television's construction, organization, and circulation of blackness. I give the institutional character of television this central status because it, and the signifying practices through which its representations are presented, is situated at the center of the production, organization, and circulation of the sign of blackness in commercial media. Along with popular music and cinema, commercial television is the site where meaning maps are registered and affective alliances are articulated (Grossberg 1992). For now, I consider commercial network television's own institutional practices, economic imperatives, market constraints, and organizational structures as they relate to the construction, representation, and circulation of blackness.

Registering Shifts and Packaging Cultural Moods

In order for television to produce cultural effects and meet its economic imperatives (that is, to produce identifications and pleasures necessary to maintain profitability), it has to operate on the basis of a popular awareness and general common sense about the currents adrift in the society (Campbell and Reeves 1989b; Fiske 1987, 1989; Gitlin 1983; Hall 1981a; Press 1991; Reeves and Campbell 1994). To do this, commercial television must constantly negotiate and renegotiate, package and repackage, circulate and recirculate this common sense; it must, of necessity, frame its representations in appropriate and accessible social terms that express the shared assumptions, knowledge, and experiences of viewers who are situated along different alliances of race, class, and gender (and, increasingly, sexuality).

American television representations of blackness in the 1980s were structured by a number of complex historical, economic, technological, and cultural factors.[1] In the mid-1980s, television representations of black Americans proliferated when the big three television networks, ABC, CBS, and NBC, experienced a decline in total viewers as a result of competition from cable programming, increased use of videocassette recorders and video games, the rise of a fourth television network, and an increase in original programming on independent stations (Butsch 1990). Commercial television network executives, program makers, and advertisers were forced to define their audiences ever more precisely in terms of demographic characteristics such as income, class, race, gender, and age (Block 1990a; Gitlin 1983; Taylor 1989; Williams 1989). This crisis was further exacerbated by the introduction of new ratings devices and reporting services (e.g., the People Meter) that methodologically challenged the dominance of such ratings systems as Arbitron and Nielson (Atkins and Litman 1986; Bierbaum 1990; Butsch 1990; Gitlin 1983; Koch 1990; Meechan 1990). In this climate of new technologies, new delivery systems, and new corporate players, network executives and programming bosses quickly found that "quality" shows that appealed to very specific markets of upper-income viewers could both find their audiences and remain profitable (Auletta 1991; Tartikoff 1992). Moreover, NBC's financial and popular success with *The Cosby Show* was pivotal to the proliferation of network programs about blacks and the network's use of a more focused marketing strategy to reach black audiences (Bierbaum 1990; Block 1990a, 1990b; Fuller 1992; Jhally and Lewis 1992).[2]

From the 1980s on, this strategy of "narrowcasting" helped to establish NBC as the leading television network. Programs such as *Hill Street Blues, St. Elsewhere, L.A. Law, The Cosby Show, Cheers, Miami Vice,* and *A Different World* evidenced this shift to more precisely targeted demographics as well as a new approach to scheduling (Tartikoff 1992). Reporting in the *Wall Street Journal* on the influence of television producer Stephen Bochco, Kevin Goldman (1991) characterized the marketing and aesthetic impact of *Hill Street Blues:* "The gritty realism of his [Bochco] 1981 hit *Hill Street Blues* made it one of the first prime-time dramas to woo large numbers of baby boomers back to their television sets, while *L.A. Law,* which makes tens of millions of dollars a year for NBC, practically defined the decade's yuppie careerism" (p. A1). This conscious strategy of going after affluent baby boomers produced noticeable changes in the form, content, and look of programming on NBC in the 1980s (Auletta 1991; Bierbaum 1990; Tartikoff 1992).

Such changes were not only the result of concerns about scheduling, programming, or the ratings war, however; something more significant was at work in the social and cultural landscape. Todd Gitlin (1983) and Ella Taylor (1989) characterize this "something more" sociologically, noting, in particular, the shifts in the social and cultural mood of the nation. In their analyses, both are alert to the crucial role of television in registering, packaging, and circulating significant social and cultural shifts. In the 1970s, for instance, with such shows as *All in the Family, M*A*S*H, The Mary Tyler Moore Show,* and *The Bob Newhart Show,* CBS's programming executives engineered that network's response to a social and demographic sea change by shifting programming away from shows aimed at older rural adults to those with younger, more explicitly urban sensibilities and lifestyles (Du Brow 1990; Gitlin 1983; Taylor 1989). Following CBS's success with these programs, the networks began to schedule shows that more directly addressed contemporary issues, such as race relations, gender, and family and generational conflicts (Press 1991; Taylor 1989).

Following the logic of Taylor and Gitlin, my contention is that by the mid- to late 1980s yet another shift was under way. This time the networks moved away from issues-oriented comedies to light comedies and sophisticated nighttime dramas about the lives, trials, and excesses of upper-middle-class professionals and the wealthy. Shows such as *L.A. Law, Miami Vice, Moonlighting, China Beach, Tour of*

Duty, Designing Women, Murphy Brown, and *thirtysomething* appeared in the network schedules. These and similar shows articulated the angst, frustrations, and dilemmas of a generation of affluent (predominantly white) and aging baby boomers who were reconciling their 1960s political and cultural ideals with the realities of social responsibility and generational accountability. At the same time, black-oriented situation comedies such as *227, Homeroom, Family Matters, True Colors, The Cosby Show, Amen, Frank's Place,* and *A Different World* found their way to network television's prime-time schedule.

As I suggested in chapter 3, these representations appeared during the dominance and growing legitimacy of neoconservatives' assaults on what they saw as a pervasive culture of permissiveness and immorality (Ehrenreich 1990; Johnson 1991; Kellner 1990; West 1993). Amid conservative attacks on gays and lesbians, feminists, and women of color, black popular culture was squarely at the forefront of national political debate about morality, permissiveness, teenage sexuality, affirmative action, single parenthood, and multiculturalism.

The force of neoconservative cultural assaults on liberal permissiveness (including attacks on black popular forms such as film and rap music) taking place at the same time as the proliferation of network television representations of blackness seems paradoxical. One possible key to this paradox might be found in the textual character and cultural meanings of network shows about blacks, which registered a range of social and cultural concerns. For example, programs about blacks were largely confined to proven genres: situation comedy, variety, music television, talk, and sports. Shows such as *In the Heat of the Night* and, later, *I'll Fly Away* were notable exceptions, because these hour-long dramas not only featured blacks in primary roles but explicitly addressed race relations. More to the point, most of these shows were set in domestic spaces—the home, and within that the family, where they reinforced values of individualism, responsibility, and morality (Spigel 1992; Taylor 1989). Of necessity, most focused on "universal" issues, such as social relations within the family, child rearing, teenage maturation, and conflicts within the domestic sphere (and sometimes at work) (Taylor 1989). These issues were neither different nor far removed from concerns that dominated the agendas of the moral entrepreneurs of the new right; hence, some black-oriented shows found a degree of resonance within the dominant cultural mood of the 1980s. *The Cosby Show, Family Matters, 227, True Colors,* and *Amen* all fit neatly with public preoccupations with the domestic sphere and, within it, concerns about individuals, family, and relationships (Christon 1989; Dyson 1989; Greenly 1987).

In rare (and all-too-brief) instances, black-focused shows such as *Frank's Place, A Man Called Hawk, A Different World,* and *In Living Color* stretched thematic boundaries and occasionally challenged the reigning conservative social and cultural sensibilities that anchored them. These shows occasionally ventured into tougher issues: racism, rape, community cohesion, color coding, gang violence, and apartheid in South Africa.

Given the social and cultural mood of the 1980s, what is remarkable is not so much the network's use of such strategies as narrowcasting, but (and this point is central to my argument) the increasing centrality of black popular culture to the networks' offerings. By making race, for example, one of the central and continuing themes in shows such as *Hill Street Blues* and later anchoring its Thursday-evening lineup with *The Cosby Show* and *A Different World,* NBC made shows about black life central to its definition of "quality" programming; in so doing, the network helped to establish the financial and aesthetic terms within which blackness was represented and circulated in commercial television (Bierbaum 1990). Of course, by the 1990s this strategy was pushed to its logical limit by other networks with such shows as *Fresh Prince of Bel Air, Martin, Hangin' with Mr. Cooper, Sinbad, Thea, Living Single,* and *Where I Live.*[3] These programs draw directly on black popular forms of music, dress, language, and style for their representations.

In the 1980s, then, a discursive space was opened in commercial network television where black programs, stars, and audiences figured more centrally than ever before in the economic viability and aesthetic vitality of commercial television (Block 1990b). No longer choked by the long-standing, and limited, principle of least objectionable programming, the networks were forced to reckon more seriously with black audiences and black programming (Braxton 1992c; Gunther 1990; O'Connor 1990; Siegel 1989a; Waters and Huck 1988). In spite of neoconservative discourses hostile to affirmative action, feminism, and multiculturalism, television programs that refused, at the very least, to acknowledge the complex and changing realities of race, gender (though not sexuality), and class in U.S. society were no longer profitable or popular (Steenland 1987, 1989). By the late 1980s, most commercial television programming acknowledged, if only minimally, the economic viablility and cultural force of women and African Americans.[4]

Structural Transformations of Television in the 1980s

If the networks recognized and responded to shifts in the public moods on questions of gender and race, actually hitching themselves up to and exploiting these changes by creating and scheduling programs that packaged and expressed these moods remained risky (Tartikoff 1992). In the increasingly unstable crisis environment of commercial television in the mid-1980s, there was little guarantee that audiences would view programs about blacks in the kinds of numbers that would be profitable for the networks.

Hence, any account of the enabling conditions that produced the proliferation and cultural significance of black shows (and their audiences) cannot rest simply on textual explanations alone. The enabling conditions that produced the proliferation of programming about blacks involved the conjunction of cultural, social, and economic circumstances; these conditions were prompted by the large-scale transformations—in ownership, profits, service delivery, technology, and regulation—that occurred in network television throughout the 1980s. I want to move away from the emphasis on social and cultural moods and, within them, the thematic and cultural significance of television representations of blacks to consider the various ways that television representations of blacks are tied to and enabled by the political economic transformations and institutional conditions in the television industry.

Todd Gitlin (1990) and Mark Crispin Miller (1990a) maintain that the look of commercial media, especially film and television, in the 1980s was transformed by increasingly symbiotic relationships among film, television, popular music (music television), and advertising.[5] The economic imperatives, institutional logic, and signifying practices of television have become almost indistinguishable from those of related mass media. Because of changes in the structure and ownership of media industries, from those making movies to those producing computers, as well as the training and circulation of directors, producers, and agents among major film studios, networks, management agencies, and advertisers, all have become more dependent on one another for talent, management, financing, distribution, and exhibition (Butsch 1990; Gitlin 1990; Koch 1990; Mathews 1990; Miller 1990; Vianello 1984; Zook 1994). In the end, of course, this symbiosis is driven by powerful economic opportunities and the desire for greater organizational control and power in a changing media environment. These pressures and desires have resulted in the creation of larger, more powerful, and more diverse multinational media conglomerates.

Nothing illustrates these pressures and the transformations they have produced in media better than the dramatic changes in ownership that took place at all three commercial television networks in the mid-1980s. In addition to these changes in ownership, I would certainly include the following as further important influences: the formation in 1986 of the Fox Broadcasting Company, the fourth television network; the rise and impact of cable and pay-per-view services; the 1988 writers' strike and the subsequent creation of relatively inexpensive reality-based programming; the increasing power of independent stations (especially the superstation concept, pioneered by Ted Turner); satellite transmission capabilities; the emergence of home shopping networks; the popularity of videocassette recorders and video games as major home entertainment alternatives to commercial network programming; a more permissive and relaxed regulatory environment under Reagan/Bush, which resulted in changes in rules governing prime-time access and syndication/finance, and in regulations governing independent stations as well as network-owned and -operated stations (Block 1990a, 1990b; Butsch, 1990; Koch 1990).

As new network owners, Capital Cities Broadcasting (ABC), General Electric (NBC), and Laurence Tisch (CBS) took over network operations that were bloated, inefficient, and often redundant (Auletta 1991).[6] Of the three, perhaps Capital Cities Broadcasting/ABC was in the best position to weather the short-term changes required to scale down operations and at the same time maintain profitability. As experienced broadcast managers, the executives at Capital Cities instituted cost-saving measures and cutbacks at ABC without producing a debilitating climate of fear and intimidation (Auletta 1991; Williams 1989).

At NBC, the leading and most profitable network throughout the 1980s, General Electric, the network's new owner, faced a different challenge—to maintain NBC's profitability and cut waste while increasing productivity. This proved to be a formidable task, especially because of G.E.'s seeming disregard for the particular managerial skills required to run a network and, by extension, its lack of understanding and disinterest in television's distinctive culture (Auletta 1991; Fabrikant 1992).[7] Although the network maintained its dominance in programming and revenue throughout most of the 1980s, it did so at the expense of some three thousand members of its workforce (Fabrikant 1990:C1). By the beginning of the 1989 season, the press began to report trouble at NBC. With a stable of successful but aging shows, the network filled out its prime-time schedule with a mixture of tabloid journalism, T&A comedies, and bad movies (Cox 1989). By the early 1990s, NBC's dominance had clearly eroded; by 1993 the erosion was sealed with the loss of its two signature (and most profitable) programs—*The Cosby Show* and *Cheers*.

For most of the 1980s CBS was in the worst shape of the three networks in terms of ratings, programming, revenues, and morale. Writing in *Newsweek*, Powell and Alter (1986) described life at the network in the months prior to its takeover:

> Once the most prestigious corporation in the most glamorous of industries, CBS today is a financially ailing, deeply demoralized organization churning with dissension. After two years of seemingly ceaseless turmoil, the broadcaster is in the midst of a civil war that has brought it to the brink of a complete management overhaul—and maybe even new ownership. Its chairman and chief executive, Thomas Wyman . . . is fighting a nerve-racking tactical battle for control of the company. . . . His opponent . . . is a man he once considered an ally: New York investor Laurence Tisch . . . chairman of the Loews Corp. conglomerate and one of the richest men in the United States. (p. 46)

In what Powell and Alter called a "twisted plot worthy of a TV series" (p. 46), Laurence Tisch engineered a takeover of CBS.[8] In the short run, this climate, and the subsequent takeover, had its most far-reaching impact on the morale of CBS staff and the reputation of the network (Auletta 1991). Its greatest asset—its tradition as a great broadcast news organization—seemed in greatest turmoil and was emblematic of larger troubles at the network (Auletta 1991; Du Brow 1990). A number of related factors contributed to the low morale at CBS, especially in the news division: uncertainty about the ownership, direction, and management of the company; the encroachment of entertainment values on the news division; the increased use of new technologies (e.g., satellite) that privilege immediacy over substance; and threats of massive layoffs (Moyers 1986; Powell and Alter 1986).

After acquiring the network, Tisch and his advisers set about streamlining, downsizing, and reorganizing all the major divisions at CBS.[9] The frenzy and uncertainty of this activity produced greater fear, suspicion, and public fights, especially in the news division (Auletta 1991; Du Brow 1990; Powell and Alter 1986).[10] (This was the volatile and unstable climate in which the innovative *Frank's Place* appeared in the CBS schedule. In this climate, the show proceeded to get lost in the shifting network schedule, where it found little stability or support, and was ultimately canceled because of poor ratings; see Reeves and Campbell 1989; White 1991.)

Through internal reorganization, staff reductions, and programming changes, the new network owners tried to make their operations more efficient, more productive, and ultimately more profitable. At all three networks one of the first targets of this strategy was a network culture deeply rooted in traditions, relationships, and appearances— generous expense accounts, opulent offices, and extravagant parties were all reduced or eliminated. Traditional assumptions, arrangements, and expectations that structured the culture of network television and drove the deals on which so much depended were rethought in light of the new condition of austerity. In short, the post-takeover environment "brought an end to the high-living, free-spending days in network television" (Powell and Alter 1986:48). Network owners and managers sought ways to reduce operating costs, to run their companies more efficiently, and to halt the loss of viewers and profits.

As important, the climate at the three major networks was also affected by the emergence of a new network, Fox Broadcasting (Block 1990a). The formation of Fox changed the terms of the television game. Initially, Fox's programming was confined to two prime-time evenings per week. By the end of the decade, however, Fox offered a weekly prime-time schedule with programming every evening, including the innovative animated program *The Simpsons,* which it placed head-to-head with *The Cosby Show* on NBC, and *In Living Color,* an irreverent comedy/variety show featuring African Americans. The lineup also included *Married . . . with Children, 21 Jump Street, America's Most Wanted,* and *The Joan Rivers Show.* For the big three networks, the mere presence (and potential growth) of Fox meant that the traditional cut of the audience (and, hence, advertising revenues) could no longer be split three ways. The presence of Fox meant that potential revenues remained, but they had to be shared differently (Block 1990a; Koch 1990).

In the traditional three-network structure, audience shares were split relatively evenly, with no one network dominating far out of proportion to the other two. The mere presence of Fox and especially other alternative programming outlets changed the structure of the game, and with it the bargaining position of the three major networks. In the post-1986 merger environment, ratings points now had to be split four ways. As a fourth network, Fox stood to pick up potential revenues from the other networks and, more important, changed the pricing structure of advertising (Block 1990a; Koch 1990). In addition to Fox Television, advertisers could also go elsewhere to promote their products. The presence of superstations, independents, and cable outlets eroded the kinds of audiences the commercial networks could deliver to advertisers and, in return, the kinds of advertising rates they could demand. By 1986 the commercial networks were no longer seen by advertisers as the only game in town:

> After consistent double-digit ad revenue gains annually during the early 1980s, the rate is now almost flat. Advertisers, moreover, are rebelling against the increasing amount of clutter on network TV:

since 1975 the average number of commercials per week on the
networks has gone from 3,500 to 5,100. Worried that their products
get lost in the shuffle, advertisers are looking to place their
commercials elsewhere. (Powell and Alter 1986:48)

In the high-stakes ratings game, where hundreds of thousands of dollars are at stake per ratings point, these subtle shifts translated to millions of dollars in potential advertising revenues.

The emergence of Fox also introduced a new form—the hybrid independent affiliate (Koch 1990; Mathews 1990). As the number of players
in the television game increased, and as the stakes became higher, niche
marketing and narrowcasting became more important strategies for negotiating an increasingly complex and competitive environment. Fox,
plus other forms of service delivery and programming options, made each
of the three once-powerful and dominant networks only one among
many in a rapidly changing broadcast media field.

Along with organizational changes they developed to maintain and,
where possible, extend their dominance, the networks found some
comfort in the Reagan and Bush administrations. Both administrations initiated, supported, and relaxed regulation and enforcement of
federal policies governing prime-time access, antitrust regulations, fi-
nance and syndication rules, ceilings on network-owned and -operated
stations, and cable franchise monopolies, all of which are central to
network survival in the always changing media environment (Auletta
1991; Johnson 1991; Kellner 1990). Because of a more permissive
regulatory environment, the networks were able to remain financially
competitive by diversifying their operations and, in some instances,
consolidating and expanding their holdings in the areas of programming and copyrights, the production of programming for cable, and
the acquisition of cable operations (Auletta 1991; Butsch 1990;
Haithman 1990; Johnson 1991).

The political, organizational, and economic conditions at the networks in the 1980s resulted in such network responses as narrowcasting, niche marketing, and the development of inexpensive, cost-efficient programming (reality-based shows, made-for-television movies
based on dramatic news stories). It was within this shifting set of political, economic, and institutional conditions that programming
aimed at black audiences emerged as a low-risk, potentially profitable
object of television.[11]

The Institutional Production of Blackness—Audiences

This media environment and the responses it generated from the networks goes some way toward explaining the proliferation of black television programs and representations of blackness in the middle and late 1980s. Consider, for example, the issue of viewership. Throughout the decade, the networks experienced a steady decline in their share of viewers—from a high of 76 percent in 1983 to 62 percent in 1989 to 60.1 percent by 1990 (Baker 1988; Bierbaum 1990; Carter 1990; O'Connor, 1992). Commercial television viewing, however, for minorities, women, children, the working class, and the elderly during this period either remained constant or increased. In fact, as early as 1988, *Newsweek* reported that "in an average week, black viewers watch nearly 40 percent more television than the rest of the population" (Waters and Huck 1988:52). By 1989 this demographic was so important to the networks that *Boston Globe* television critic Ed Siegel noted that "network programmers have become convinced that they've lost upper income viewers to home video and cable television, particularly pay cable." "After years of wooing those viewers," Siegel (1989b) continued, "it may be that the networks now think it's advisable to go for the less affluent" (p. 74). Hence, though the networks experienced steady losses in the rate of television viewing among affluent and middle-class whites, an underserved and reliable pool of viewers was there waiting to be served (or, at the very least, acknowledged).

With their programming decisions the networks finally began to pay attention to the fact that blacks watched television at rates far higher than the rest of the population. They also became alert to the fact that black audiences were concentrated in the country's largest urban markets, where network-owned and -operated stations were located and where the networks could be competitive with cable outlets. Because of prohibitive costs and the monopoly nature of cable franchising, many black urban households were "slower to purchase VCRs and be wired for cable, the two technologies that most threaten the networks' franchise. No wonder the TV industry is finally wooing black audiences" (Waters and Huck 1988:52). What independent stations, cable operators, syndicators, film studios, and Fox already knew, the three remaining commercial networks soon discovered— African American audiences as a ready-made, already organized, and exploitable market niche (Block 1990a).

With the successful marketing of black personalities and stars such as Spike Lee, Arsenio Hall, Oprah Winfrey, Michael Jordan, Charles Barkley, and Bill Cosby, by the end of the decade the networks and their advertisers increasingly looked to black programming and talent as a cost-efficient product investment with potential for crossover appeal. Within the structure of the post-1986 television environment, the growing commodification and appeal of blackness are evident in all aspects of the television landscape. In addition to the proliferation of black-oriented television programs, one only need note the proliferation of fast food, sneakers, personal grooming and household products, and cars that are marketed to blacks. Alone, black-oriented programming and the audiences it delivers to advertisers could not get the networks through the fiscal and structural crisis they faced, especially given a saturated environment full of new players, delivery systems, and program suppliers. As they must do, the networks keep trying to refine and control the most irrational part of their environment—audience mood, taste, and desire. By targeting and rationalizing their work process and their products, the networks attempt to identify as precisely as possible which schedules, audiences, advertisers, and programs will yield the greatest return on investment. In the shifting television and media environment of the 1980s, the sensibilities, choices, and habits of black audiences were becoming far more central to the look, rhythm, and feel of commercial television, especially in the genre of situation comedy (Zook 1994).

The recognition and engagement with blackness were not for a moment driven by sudden cultural interest in black matters or some noble aesthetic goals on the part of executives in all phases of the industry.[12] In large part they were driven, as most things are in network television, by economics. To the extent that black-oriented programs were cost-efficient and advertisers could be attracted, such programs were well worth the risk. This risk was limited to proven and cost-efficient genres such as situation comedy, entertainment/variety, and talk programs, because, as part of their broader strategy the networks had to complement rather than jeopardize their investments in more expensive and proven program staples such as nighttime dramas and movies of the week (Gitlin 1983). In the end, black programs and the audiences they could deliver were worth the risk because black audiences often have fewer options and therefore depend on commercial television for their primary programming choices.

This logic has been taken to its conclusion in the areas of advertising, entertainment, and sports. Such highly visible media personalities as Spike Lee, Michael Jordan, Arsenio Hall, Oprah Winfrey, and Bill Cosby helped to focus, organize, and translate blackness into commodifiable representations and desires that could be packaged and marketed across the landscape of American popular culture. So central were representations of racial, ethnic, and class difference to network programming that in 1989 television critic Ed Siegel (1989a) of the *Boston Globe* was prompted to ask, "Why are the networks suddenly stirring the melting pot?" Not at all bashful about the response, he noted, "It is probably, at least in part, an extension of the networks' recent success with programs like *The Cosby Show* and *Roseanne,* where audiences showed that they would accept people and families who looked and talked differently from the white middle-class norm. ... If class differences are a salable commodity for the networks, maybe they figure ethnic differences will be as well" (p. 7). Television representations of blackness organize and articulate different audiences, desires, identifications, and meanings within the media space of commercial culture. Like film and popular music, television programmers at the networks pursued these images and representations more aggressively and consistently, incorporating them into a strategy that would do what television does best: generate profits by identifying and packaging our dominant social and cultural moods.

5 The Politics of Representation in Network Television

A long with the structural shifts, cultural discourses, and institutional transformations of the television industry, contemporary television representations of blackness are linked to the presence and admittedly limited influence of a small number of highly visible black producers, writers, directors, and on-screen talent in the entertainment industry. Within the institutional constraints and cultural traditions of a collaborative and producer-driven medium such as television, the successes of Bill Cosby, Oprah Winfrey, Stan Lathan, Arsenio Hall, Marla Gibbs, Keenen Ivory Wayans, Stanley Robertson, Kellie Goode, Dolores Morris, Suzanne de Passe, Topper Carew, Frank Dawson, Sherman Hemsley, Quincy Jones, Thomas Carter, Carl Franklin, Michael Warren, Debbie Allen, and Tim Reid increased their individual abilities at studios and the networks to shape the creation, direction, and tone of television representations of African Americans (Gunther 1990; Horowitz 1989; O'Connor 1990; Zook 1994).[1]

Of course, there is nothing particularly remarkable about the presence of black producers, writers, and directors in network television. Indeed, directors and producers Michael Moye, Thomas Carter, Suzanne de Passe, and others have been central to the production of such critically acclaimed programming as *Equal Justice* and *Lonesome Dove* (Gunther 1990).[2] What is remarkable, however, is that these critically and commercially successful shows have not necessarily been organized around black themes and black cultural sensibilities. Television clearly needs more of this kind of black presence.

At the other extreme are television shows that traffic heavily in themes and representations about blacks, but that, by and large, operate under the creative control and direction of white studio and network executives. Successful comedies such as *Sanford & Son*, Norman Lear/Bud Yorkin staples *The Jeffersons* and *Good Times*, and more recent shows such as *Amen* and *227* come immediately to mind. To be sure, these shows employed black writers and actors, and they drew their creative direction, look, and sensibility from African American culture. But ultimately, the overall creative responsibility for these shows rested with white executive producers—Bud Yorkin, Norman Lear, the Carsey-Werner Company, Irma Kalish, Ed Weinberger, and Miller-Boyett Productions (Newcomb and Alley 1983).

In the final analysis, the creative vision of the white producers predominated even if situations and themes they explored were drawn from African American culture (Newcomb and Alley 1983; interviews with black writers from *227*, 1990). Although the programs were shows about blacks (rather than black shows), there were clearly boundaries concerning cultural representations, social themes, and professional conventions that they dared not transgress. As some of the black television writers from *227* explained to me, the nuances and sensibilities of African American culture that many of them found funny and attempted to bring to particular scripts or scenes became points of professional contention or were eliminated because white head writers and producers thought otherwise.[3] Black writers seldom had the same veto power over white characters, situations, and themes (interview with writers from *227*, 1990).

For many of the shows based on the situations and experiences of blacks, the conventions of television production (especially collaborative writing) serve to discipline, contain, and ultimately construct a point of view. Not surprisingly, this point of view constructs and privileges white middle-class audiences as the ideal viewers and subjects of television stories. In the producer-driven medium of television, a paucity of producers of color continues to be the rule. In a 1989 report issued by the National Commission on Working Women, researcher Sally Steenland (1989) notes that "minority producers constitute only 7% of all producers working on shows with minority characters. Minority female producers comprise only 2% of the total. Of 162 producers working on 30 shows containing minority characters, only 12 are people of color, while 150 (93%) are white. Of the 12 minority producers, 8 are male and 4 are female" (p. 11).

African American writers, directors, and producers in the television industry must still negotiate the rough seas of an institutional and cultural system tightly but subtly structured by race and gender (Dates 1990).[4] It is all the more remarkable, then, that a small number of visible and influential black executive producers, directors, and writers forced open creative spaces within the productive apparatus of television. And within this discursive and industrial space—between black invisibility and white-authorized representations of blackness—black producers such as Cosby, Wayans, Hall, and Jones have had some impact. Rather than simply placing blackness and black themes in the service of the creative visions of white producers or inserting blackness within existing aesthetic visions, these producers have helped to challenge and transform conventional television treatments of blackness by introducing black viewpoints and perspectives (Hampton 1989). In short, they have introduced different approaches and placed existing aesthetic and production conventions in the service of blackness and African American cultural perspectives (Gunther 1990; O'Connor 1990; Ressner 1990). By trying to construct and represent the experiences, nuances, and explicit concerns of African Americans, these producers offer not only different stories, but alternative ways of negotiating and realizing them. Indeed, Kristal Brent Zook (1994) argues quite convincingly that in the 1980s and 1990s television has been an especially important discursive and institutional space because it serves as a vehicle for intertextual and autobiographical dialogue for blacks.

In a business long criticized for the absence of people of color in decision-making positions and authority, efforts on the part of black executives to hire and train African Americans are, to say the least, hard to sustain.[5] In terms of hiring, training, and placement of black talent in all phases of the industry, Bill Cosby, Quincy Jones, and Keenen Ivory Wayans have been singled out. For example, Susan Fales, former executive producer of the The Cosby Show spinoff, A Different World, began her television career in television as an intern with The Cosby Show (interview with Susan Fales, 1990).

The impact of this small cohort of influential black producers occasionally, but all too rarely, reaches beyond the generic and thematic boundaries of situation comedy and the thematic dominance of streetwise masculinity that pervades so much of contemporary television representations of blacks. The Women of Brewster Place, Lonesome Dove, and Motown 25: Yesterday, Today, Forever, Polly, and The Mary Thomas Story were all projects created, engineered, or produced by black women: Oprah Winfrey (Harpo Productions), Suzanne de Passe (Motown), and Dolores Morris (Disney Television). As core members of *A Different World*'s production team, black women such as executive producer Susan Fales, director and writer Debbie Allen, and writers Neema Barnette and Yvette Lee were all responsible for the creative look, feel, and direction of the program. As Jacqueline Bobo (1991) points out, these and other black women tell stories about black women that are different from those told by others, and they tell those stories differently. Thus, these black women contribute to the more general project of "fleshing out their female characters to become more multi-dimensional and like actual women and . . . experimenting with important issues and themes" (Steenland 1987:24).

Like their counterparts in cinema and literature, this recent cohort of black television producers has experienced growing visibility and success that has heightened the expectations of black audiences and critics. These heightened expectations have, in turn, produced conflict among and criticism from African Americans. For instance, heated public criticism has been directed toward Keenen Ivory Wayans, creator and former producer of *In Living Color*, for staging his irreverent humor at the expense of blacks; toward Arsenio Hall for his failure to place more blacks on the staff and technical crew of his late-night talk show; and toward Bill Cosby because his series often failed to address social issues facing black Americans (Braxton 1991; Christon 1989; Collins 1990; Dyson 1989; Fuller 1992; Gray 1989; Jhally and Lewis 1992).

The mere presence of a critical group of successful black producers, directors, and writers has, nevertheless, helped to bring different, often more complex, stories, themes, characters, and representations of blackness to commercial network television. Questions about the continuing presence of racism and sexism in the television industry as well as the social impact and cultural meaning of these stories are ongoing subjects of heated debate and study. The fact remains, however, that the variety and sheer number of stories about blacks proliferated in the 1980s to a degree perhaps unparalleled in the history of television (Siegel 1989a; Waters and Huck 1988).

The Historical and Discursive Formation of Television Treatments of Blackness

Alone, the argument that television representation of blackness is primarily shaped by changing industrial and market conditions that enabled a small number of black producers, directors, and writers to tell stories about black life from the perspective of blacks is reductionist. To avoid such reductionism, I want to argue also for a reading of the social meaning and cultural significance of television's representations of blackness in terms of their political, historical, and aesthetic relationship to earlier generations of shows about blacks. I contend that contemporary television representations of blacks depend heavily on shows about families, the genre of (black) situation comedy, entertainment/variety programming, and the social issue traditions of Norman Lear (Allen 1987; Dates 1990; MacDonald 1983; Spigel 1992; Taylor 1989).

Ultimately, then, I argue that our contemporary moment continues to be shaped discursively by representations of race and ethnicity that began in the formative years of television (Lipsitz 1990b; Riggs 1991a; Spigel 1992; Winston 1982). The formative period of television and its representation of race and ethnicity in general and blacks in particular is central to my argument in two crucial ways: first, together with dominant representations of blacks in film, radio, the press, and vaudeville, this inaugural moment helped to shape the cultural and social terms in which representations of blacks appeared in mass media and popular culture (Dates 1990); second, as illustrated by Marlon Riggs's (1991a) documentary film, *Color Adjustment,* this formative period is a defining discursive and aesthetic moment that enabled and shaped the adjustments that black representations continue to make. It remains the moment against which all other television representations of blackness have reacted. And it is the defining moment with which subsequent representations, including those in the 1980s and beyond, remain in dialogue (Dates 1990; Riggs 1991b; Taylor 1991; Winston 1982).

In the early 1950s, programs such as *Amos 'n' Andy, Beulah, The Jack Benny Show,* and *Life with Father* presented blacks in stereotypical and subservient roles whose origins lay in eighteenth- and nineteenth-century popular forms (Cripps 1983; Dates 1990; Ely 1991; Winston 1982). Blacks appeared primarily as maids, cooks, "mammies," and other servants, or as con artists and deadbeats. These stereotypes were necessary for the representation and legitimation of a racial order built on racism and white supremacy. Media scholars and historians have clearly established the formative role of radio in the institutional and aesthetic organization of early television (Czitrom 1982). As Winston (1982), Barlow and Dates (1990), and Ely (1991) suggest, the networks, first with radio and later with television shows such as *Beulah, Amos 'n' Andy,* and *The Jack Benny Show,* played an active and crucial role in the construction and representation of blacks in American mass media.[6] In the televisual world of the early 1950s, the social and cultural rules of race relations between blacks and whites were explicit: black otherness was required for white subjectivity; blacks and whites occupied separate and unequal worlds; black labor was always in the service of white domesticity (*The Jack Benny Show, Life with Father, Beulah*); black humor was necessary for the amusement of whites.[7]

Culturally, because blackness served whiteness in this way, the reigning perspective of this world was always staged from a white subject position; when television did venture inside the separate and unfamiliar world of blacks—in, say, *Amos 'n' Andy*—viewers found comforting reminders of whiteness and the ideology of white supremacy that it served: here was the responsible, even sympathetic, black domestic in *Beulah;* there were the responsible but naive members of the world of *Amos 'n' Andy.* But seldom were there representations of the social competence and civic responsibilities that would place any of the black characters from these shows on equal footing with whites (Dates 1990:204). Black characters who populated the television world of the early 1950s were happy-go-lucky social incompetents who knew their place and whose antics served to amuse and comfort culturally sanctioned notions of whiteness, especially white superiority and paternalism. These black folk could be trusted to manage white households, nurture white children, and "restore balance and normalcy to the [white] household" (Dates 1990:262), but they could not be trusted with the social and civic responsibilities of full citizenship as equals with whites.

In the racially stratified and segregated social order of the 1950s United States, there was enough about these representations to both comfort and offend. So pervasive and secure was the discourse of whiteness that in their amusement whites were incapable of seeing these shows and the representations they presented as offensive. At the same time, of course, many middle-class blacks were so outraged by these shows, particularly *Amos 'n' Andy,* that the NAACP successfully organized and engineered a campaign in 1953 to remove the show from the air (Cripps 1983; Dates 1990; Ely 1991; Montgomery 1989). As racist and stereotypical as these representations were, the cultural and racial politics they activated were far from simple; many poor, working-class, and even middle-class blacks still managed to read against the dominant discourse of whiteness and find humor in the show. However, because of the charged racial politics between blacks and whites, as well as the class and cultural politics within black America, the tastes, pleasures, and voices in support of the show were drowned out by the moral outrage of middle-class blacks.[8] To be sure, although blacks and whites alike may have found the show entertaining and funny, these pleasures meant different things. They were situated in very different material and discursive worlds. The social issues, political positions, and cultural alliances that shows such as *Amos 'n' Andy* organized and crystallized, then, were powerful and far-reaching in their impact, so much so that I believe that contemporary representations remain in dialogue with and only now have begun to transcend this formative period.[9]

By the late 1950s and throughout the 1960s, the few representations of blacks that did appear on network television offered more benign and less explicitly stereotypical images of African Americans. Shows such as *The Nat "King" Cole Show* (1956–57), *I Spy* (1965–68), and *Julia* (1968–71) attempted to make blacks acceptable to whites by containing them or rendering them, if not culturally white, invisible.[10] In these shows the social and cultural "fact of blackness" was treated as a minor if not coincidental theme—present but contained. In the racially tense and stratified United States of the middle 1960s, Diahann Carroll and Bill Cosby lived and worked in mostly white worlds where whites dare not notice and blacks dare not acknowledge their blackness. Where the cultural and social "fact of blackness" was irrepressible, indeed, central to the aesthetics of a show, it had to be contained. (Whiteness also operated as the dominant and normative place of subjectivity both on and off the screen. In this racialized world of television common sense neither whites nor blacks had any need to acknowledge whiteness explicitly.)

This strategy of containment was used with Nat Cole, the elegant and sophisticated star of *The Nat "King" Cole Show*.[11] An accomplished jazz—read black—pianist, Cole was packaged and presented by NBC to foreground his qualities as a universally appealing entertainer. Cole was the host of a television variety show that emphasized his easy manner and polished vocal style, and the containment of his blackness was clearly aimed to quell white fears and appeal to liberal white middle-class notions of responsibility and good taste. In the social and cultural climate of the times, NBC thought it necessary to separate Cole from any association with the black jazz life (an association made larger than life with the sensational press coverage of Billie Holiday, Charlie Parker, Charles Mingus, and Miles Davis), equating black jazz artists with drugs, sex, rebellion, and social deviance. Despite this cautious strategy, the network's failure to secure national sponsors for the show, especially in the South, resulted in cancellation of *The Nat "King" Cole Show* after only one season. Sanitized and contained representations of blacks in the late 1950s and the 1960s developed in response to the stereotypical images that appeared in the early days of television. They constitute signal moments in discursive adjustment and readjustment of black representations in commercial television (MacDonald 1983; Montgomery 1989; Winston 1982).

Against this discursive backdrop as well as the social rebellions of the 1960s, the representations of black Americans that appeared throughout the 1970s were a direct response to social protest and petitions by blacks against American society in general and the media in particular for the general absence of black representations (MacDonald 1983; Montgomery 1989; Winston 1982). Beginning in 1972, television program makers and the networks produced shows that reached for "authentic" representations of black life within poor urban communities.[12] These programs were created as responses to angry calls by different sectors of the black community for "relevant" and "authentic" images of black people.

It is easy to see now that both the demand for relevant shows and the networks' responses were themselves profoundly influenced by the racial and cultural politics of the period. The new shows offered were designed to contain the anger and impatience of communities on the move politically; program makers, the networks, and "the community" never paused to examine critically the notions of relevance or authenticity. As a visible and polemical site of cultural debate, television moved away from its treatment of blacks in the previous decade. The television programs involving blacks in the 1970s were largely representations of what white liberal middle-class television program makers assumed (or projected) were "authentic" accounts of poor black urban ghetto experiences. *Good Times* (1974–79), *Sanford & Son* (1972–77), and *What's Happening!!* (1976–79), for example, were all set in poor urban communities and populated by blacks who were often unemployed or underemployed. But more important, for the times, these black folk were good-humored and united in racial solidarity regardless (or perhaps because) of their condition. Ironically, despite the humor and social circumstances of the characters, these shows continued to idealize and quietly reinforce a normative white middle-class construction of family, love, and happiness. These shows implicitly reaffirmed the commonsense belief that such ideals and the values they promote are the rewards of individual sacrifice and hard work.

These themes appeared in yet another signal moment in commercial television representations of African Americans—in the hugely successful miniseries *Roots*. Inhabiting the televisual space explored three years earlier in the miniseries *The Autobiography of Miss Jane Pittman*, *Roots* distinguished itself commercially and thematically as one of the most-watched television shows in history. Based on Alex Haley's book of the same name, *Roots* presented the epic story of the black

American odyssey from Africa through slavery to the twentieth century. It brought to millions of Americans, for the first time, the story of the horrors of slavery and the noble struggles of black Americans. This television representation of blacks remained anchored by familiar commitments to economic mobility, family cohesion, private property, and the notion of America as a land of immigrants held together by shared struggles of hardships and ultimate triumph.

There is little doubt that the success of *Roots* helped to recover and reposition television constructions and representations of African Americans and blackness from their historic labors in behalf of white racism and myths of white superiority. But the miniseries also contributed quite significantly to the transformation, in the popular imaginary, of the discourse of slavery and American race relations between blacks and whites. That is to say, with *Roots* the popular media discourse about slavery moved from one of almost complete invisibility (never mind structured racial subordination, human degradation, and economic exploitation) to one of ethnicity, immigration, and human triumph. This powerful television epic effectively constructed the story of American slavery from the stage of emotional identifications and attachments to individual characters, family struggles, and the realization of the American dream. Consequently, the social organization of racial subordination, the cultural reliance on human degradation, and the economic exploitation of black labor receded almost completely from the story. And, of course, this quality is precisely what made the television series such a huge success.

From the distance of some seventeen years, I also want to suggest another less obvious but powerful effect of *Roots*, especially for African American cultural struggles over the sign of blackness. My criticisms of the dominant labors of the series notwithstanding, I want to propose that for an entire generation of young blacks, *Roots* also opened—enabled, really—a discursive space in mass media and popular culture within which contemporary discourses of blackness developed and circulated. I think that it is possible to locate within the media discourse of blackness articulated by *Roots* some of the enabling conditions necessary for the rearticulation of the discourse of Afrocentric nationalism. In other words, I would place *Roots* in dialogue with the reactivation and renewed interest in black studies and the development of African-centered rap and black urban style, especially their contemporary articulation and expression in popular culture and mass media. It seems to me that *Roots* enabled and facilitated the circulation and saturation of the popular imaginary with television representation of Africa and blackness. Finally, relative to the televisual construction of African Americans and blackness in the 1950s and 1960s,

Roots helped to alter slightly, even momentarily interrupt, the gaze of television's idealized white middle-class viewers and subjects. However minimal, with its cultural acknowledgment of black viewers and subjects, the miniseries enabled a temporary but no less powerful transitional space within which to refigure and reconstruct black television representations.[13]

In black-oriented situation comedies of the late 1970s and early 1980s, especially the long-running *The Jeffersons,* as well as *Benson, Webster, Diff'rent Strokes,* and *Gimme a Break,* black upward social mobility and middle-class affluence replaced black urban poverty as both setting and theme (Gray 1986).[14] Predictably, however, the humor remained. Even though these situation comedies were set in different kinds of "families"—single-parent households, homes with cross-racial adoptions—that were supposed to represent an enlightened approach to racial difference, in the end they too were anchored by and in dialogue with familiar themes and emblems of familial stability, individualism, and middle-class affluence (Gray 1986). Although blackness was explicitly marked in these shows, it was whiteness and its privileged status that remained unmarked and therefore hegemonic within television's discursive field of racial construction and representation (Kelley 1992). As with their predecessors from the 1950s and 1960s, blacks in the shows from the 1970s and early 1980s continued to serve as surrogate managers, nurturers, and objects of white middle-class fascination (Dates 1990; Steenland 1989). Furthermore, as conventional staples of the genre, they required unusual and unfamiliar situations (e.g., black children in white middle-class homes) for thematic structure and comedic payoff. In appearance, this generation of shows seems more explicit, if not about the subject of race, at least about cultural difference. However, because they continued to construct and privilege white middle-class viewers and subject positions, in the end they were often as benign and contained as shows about blacks from earlier decades.

The Cosby Moment

Discursively, in terms of television constructions of blackness, *The Cosby Show* is culturally significant because of the productive space it cleared and the aesthetic constructions of black cultural style it enabled. Pivotal to understanding the social position and cultural significance of contemporary television representations of blackness is what I shall call the Cosby moment. Like the miniseries *Roots, The Cosby Show* reconfigured the aesthetic and industrial spaces within which modern television representations of blacks are constructed.

Indeed, under Bill Cosby's careful guidance the show quite intentionally presented itself as a corrective to previous generations of television representations of black life. In countless press interviews, Cosby voiced his frustrations with television's representation of blacks. Here is just one:

> Run down what you saw of black people on TV before the
> Huxtables. You had "Amos 'n' Andy," one of the funniest shows
> ever, people say. But who ever went to college? Who tried for better
> things? In "Good Times," J. J. Walker played a definite
> underachiever. In "Sanford & Son," you have a junk dealer living a
> few thousand dollars above the welfare level. "The Jeffersons" move
> uptown. He owns a dry-cleaning store, lives in an integrated
> neighborhood. Where are the sociological writings about this?
> (quoted in Christon 1989:45)

Positioning *The Cosby Show* in relation to the previous history of programs about blacks helps explain its upper-middle-class focus. More significantly, the show's discursive relationship to television's historical treatment of African Americans and contemporary social and cultural debates (about the black underclass, the black family, and black moral character) helps to explain its insistent recuperation of African American social equality (and competence), especially through the trope of the stable and unified black middle-class family (Dates 1990; Downing 1988; Dyson 1989; Fuller 1992; Jhally and Lewis 1992).

In *The Cosby Show*, blackness, although an element of the show's theme, character, and sensibility, was mediated and explicitly figured through home life, family, and middle-classness. Cosby explained the show's treatment of race: "It may seem I'm an authority because my skin color gives me a mark of a victim. But that's not a true label. I won't deal with the *foolishness* of racial overtones on the show. I base an awful lot of what I've done simply on what people will enjoy. I want to show a family that has a *good* life, not people to be jealous of" (quoted in Christon 1989:7; emphasis added).[15] The Huxtable family is universally appealing, then, largely because it is a middle-class family that happens to be black (Dates 1990; Dyson 1989; Fuller 1992; Gray 1989; Greenly 1987; Jhally and Lewis 1992).

In an enactment of what Stuart Hall (1981b) calls the "politics of reversals" in black-oriented shows from the 1970s, the merger of race (blackness) and class (poverty) often provided little discursive and textual space for whites and many middle-class blacks to construct meaning for the shows that was not troubling and derisive. *The Cosby Show* strategically used the Huxtables' upper-middle-class status to invite audience identifications across race, gender, and class lines. For poor, working-, and middle-class African Americans, Asian Americans, latinos, and whites it was impossible simply to laugh at these characters and make their blackness an object of derision and fascination. Rather, blackness coexisted in the show on the same discursive plane as their upper-middle-class success (Dyson 1989; Jhally and Lewis 1992).

In this respect, *The Cosby Show* is critical to the development of contemporary television representations of blacks. The show opened to some whites and affirmed for many (though by no means all) blacks a vast and previously unexplored territory of diversity within blackness—that is, upper-middle-class life.[16] On the question of *The Cosby Show*'s importance to the representation of differences within blackness, Michael Dyson (1989) perceptively notes:

> *The Cosby Show* reflects the increasing diversity of African American life, including continuous upward social mobility by blacks, which provides access to new employment opportunities and expands the black middle class. Such mobility and expansion insures the development of new styles for blacks that radically alter and impact African American culture. *The Cosby Show* is a legitimate expression of one aspect of that diversity. Another aspect is the intra-racial class divisions and differentiation introduced as a result of this diversification of African American life. (p. 29)

Discursively, the show appropriated the genre of situation comedy and used it to offer a more complex representation of African American life than had been seen previously.

This ability to organize and articulate different audiences together successfully through televisual representations of upper-middle-class African Americans accounts for *The Cosby Show*'s popularity as well as the criticisms and suspicions it generated (Dyson 1989; Gray 1989; Jhally and Lewis 1992). If, to its credit, the program did not construct a monolithic and one-dimensional view of blackness, then, as Dyson points out, its major drawback was its unwillingness to build on the very diversity and complexity of black life that it brought to television. That is to say, the show seemed unwilling to critique and engage various aspects of black diversity that it visually represented. In particular, *The Cosby Show* often failed even to comment on the economic and social disparities and constraints facing millions of African Americans outside of the middle class.

The show seemed unable, or unwilling, to negotiate its universal appeals to family, the middle class, mobility, and individualism on the one hand and the particularities of black social, cultural, political, and economic realities on the other. While effectively representing middle-class blackness as one expression of black diversity, the show in turn submerged other sites, tensions, and points of difference by consistently celebrating mobility, unlimited consumerism, and the patriarchal nuclear family (Dyson 1989; Gray 1989). Notwithstanding its political and cultural desires, *The Cosby Show* seemed nevertheless underwritten by the racial politics of "unity," which comes at the cost of subordinating key differences within that unity. In the social climate of the Reagan and Bush years and amid debates about affirmative action and the urban underclass, the show as Dyson (1989) puts it,

> presented a black universe as the norm, feeling no need to announce the imposition of African American perspectives since they are assumed. Cosby has shown us that we need not construct the whole house of our life experience from the raw material of our racial identity. And that black folk are interested in issues which transcend race. *However, such coming of age progress should not lead to zero-sum social concerns so that to be aware of race-transcending issues replaces or cancels out concerns about the black poor or issues which generate interracial conflict.* (p. 30; emphasis added)

As Dyson suggests, *The Cosby Show*'s strategic stance on the "foolishness of racial overtones" has its limits. This was made painfully obvious in April 1992 with the entirely coincidental, but no less poignant, juxtaposition of the show's final episode with news coverage of the Los Angeles riots. The televisual landscape that evening dramatically illustrated that no matter how much television tries to manage and smooth them over, conflict, rage, and suspicion based on race and class are central elements of contemporary America. Next to the rage that produced pictures of Los Angeles burning, the representations and expressions of African American life and experience on *The Cosby Show* (and so much of contemporary television) seemed little more than soothing symbolic props required to affirm America's latest illusion of feel-good multiculturalism and racial cooperation.

Many of the same contradictions and labors of blackness found in the representations of African Americans on *The Cosby Show* were also present in other black-oriented shows that appeared in the aftermath of the show's success. *Amen, Homeroom, 227, Snoops, Family Matters,* and *True Colors* all provided familiar (and comfortable) renderings of black middle-class family life in the United States. The cultural traditions and social experiences and concerns of many African Americans, although much more explicit, nevertheless functioned in these programs as comedic devices, to stage the action or signal minor differences. Although often staged from a black normative universe, these shows seldom presented black subjectivities and cultural traditions as alternative perspectives on everyday life.[17] That is to say, as a cultural and experiential referent, blackness was seldom privileged or framed as a vantage point for critical insights, guides to action, or explanations for what happens to African American people in modern American society.

By contrast, *Frank's Place*, some of the programming on the Black Entertainment Television cable network, *A Man Called Hawk*, early programs on *The Arsenio Hall Show*, *Yo! MTV Raps*, *Pump It Up*, *Rap Street*, *A Different World*, and *In Living Color* often deployed race and class in different ways.[18] As I argue in the remaining chapters, these shows present visions and perspectives in which African American social locations and experiences are more central to the programs' structure and viewpoint. Of course, all of these shows operate squarely within the conventional and aesthetic boundaries of their particular genres—situation comedy, variety, talk, or whatever. But, as I suggest below—in significant respects these shows are different from the others, including *The Cosby Show*. At the same time, however, they are dependent on *Cosby* and the shows that preceded it for representations of black experiences in America. That is, how they construct black subjects can be read only against previous shows. In this respect, I regard *The Cosby Show* as a critically important moment, a transitional point, if you will, in the development of television representations of blacks. *The Cosby Show* and some of the innovative shows that followed it (e.g., *Frank's Place*, *Roc*, *A Man Called Hawk*) form part of a continuing discourse of adjustment and dialogue with the history of television representations of blacks.

The Cosby Show's most significant contribution to television's representations of blacks and the ongoing discursive adjustments that are central to such a project has been the way that it repositioned and recoded blackness and black (middle-class) subjectivity within television's own discursive and institutional practices. To be sure, the limitations and criticisms of the show, especially the cultural labors it performed in the rearticulation of a new, more "enlightened" racism, as well as the consolidation of Reaganism on the question of race and morality, must be registered (Gray 1993a; Jhally and Lewis 1992; Miller 1988). However, coming as it did in the midst of neoconservative assaults, African American cultural debates, and the transformation of the television industry, the show has also had an enabling effect within television. Indeed, *The Cosby Show* itself became the subject of parody and imitation. In its last few seasons the show turned its thematic gaze away from its narrow preoccupation with familial domesticity to pressing social issues, including education and employment, affecting urban black youth.[19]

For most of its run I remained ambivalent about *The Cosby Show.* As a regular viewer, on many occasions I found pleasures in the predictable humor and identified with the idealizations of family, mobility, and material security represented on the show. I took particular delight in the program's constant attempt to showcase black music and such musicians as John Birks (Dizzy) Gillespie, B. B. King, Mongo Santamaria, and Betty Carter. On the other hand, in my classes, at conferences, and in print I have criticized the show for its idealization of the middle class and its failure to address issues that confront a large number of African Americans. I have often regarded this ambivalence as my unwillingness to stake out a position on the show, to make up my mind. But this unwillingness, I am increasingly convinced, is part of the show's appeal, its complexity in an age of racial and cultural politics where the sign of blackness labors in the service of many different interests at once. As I have been arguing, *The Cosby Show* constructed and enabled new ways of representing African Americans' lives. But within black cultural politics of difference the strategy of staging black diversity within the limited sphere of domesticity and upper-middle-class affluence has its costs.

Discursive Practices and Contemporary Television Representations of Blackness

Having mapped the institutional and discursive history of commercial network television representations of blackness, I now want to suggest that contemporary images of African Americans are anchored by three kinds of discursive practices. I shall refer to these as assimilationist (invisibility), pluralist (separate but equal), and multiculturalist (diversity). In each of these discursive practices, I am interested in how the strategies of signification employed in representative television programs construct, frame, stage, and narrate general issues of race and, more specifically, black subjectivity and presence in contemporary U.S. society.

These practices are historically and discursively related to one another and to contemporary social discourses about race. Thus, the dominance and primacy of a particular set of images and representations from each of these television constructions and representations of blackness are contingent on the social, technological, and institutional conditions in which they are situated. Through reruns, cable networks, syndication, and independent stations, viewers have virtually unlimited access to the complete body of television representations of blacks. Thus, these programs constitute a vital part of the contemporary television landscape and should be examined by media and television scholars in terms of the shifting meanings and pleasures they offer in our present moment (see Butch 1990).

Assimilation and the Discourse of Invisibility

Assimilationist television discourses treat the social and political issues of black presence in particular and racism in general as individual problems. As complex social and political issues, questions of race, gender, class, and power are addressed through the treatment of racism and racial inequality as the results of prejudice (attitudes), and through the foregrounding of the individual ego as the site of social change and transformation. I consider shows assimilationist to the extent that the worlds they construct are distinguished by the complete elimination or, at best, marginalization of social and cultural difference in the interest of shared and universal similarity. These are noble aspirations, to be sure, but such programs consistently erase the histories of conquest, slavery, isolation, and power inequalities, conflicts, and struggles for justice and equality that are central features of U.S. society (see Lipsitz 1990b). Programs organized by such assumptions are framed almost entirely through codes and signifying practices that celebrate racial invisibility and color blindness (see Gray 1986). Beginning with I Spy and continuing with Julia, Mission: Impossible, and Room 222, these early shows integrated individual black characters into hegemonic white worlds void of any hint of African American traditions, social struggle, racial conflicts, and cultural difference.

Contemporary variations on this theme remain with us today. In the 1980s, assimilationist television representations of African Americans could be found in daytime soaps, advertising, and local and network new programs as well as in such prime-time shows as Family Ties, The Golden Girls, Designing Women, L.A. Law, and Night Court. Without a doubt, some of these shows, including L.A. Law, The Golden Girls, and Designing Women, featured episodes that explicitly addressed issues of contemporary racial politics, but I nonetheless maintain that where such themes were explicitly addressed they were underwritten and framed by assumptions that privilege individual cooperation and color blindness. In other words, at their best these shows acknowledged but nevertheless framed cultural distinctions and conflicts based on race in ways that ultimately appealed to visions of color blindness, similarity, and universal harmony. In terms of black participation (and inclusion), black characters' acceptance seemed to be inversely related to the degree of separation from black social life and culture. Unique individual black characters (such as Anthony in *Designing Women*) seemed to demonstrate the principle of racial exceptionalism. That is, they seemed to be appealing because of their uniqueness and their neatness of fit into a normative television universe.

Assimilationist programs construct a United States where the historic and contemporary consequences of structured social inequality and a culture deeply inflected and defined by racism are invisible and inconsequential to the lives of its citizens. Seldom on these shows is there ever any sustained engagement with the messiness, confusion, and tension caused by racism and inequality that punctuate the daily experience of so many members of our society. In these televisual worlds American racial progress is measured by the extent to which individual citizens, regardless of color, class, or gender, are the same and are treated equally within the existing social, economic, and cultural (and televisual) order. When they exist, race, class, and gender inequalities seem quite extraordinary, and they always seem to operate at the level of individual experience. Put differently, to the extent that these tensions and conflicts are addressed at all, they figure primarily through individual characters (white and black) with prejudiced attitudes, who then become the focus of the symbolic transformation required to restore narrative balance.

In keeping with television's conventional emphasis on character and dramatic action, assimilationist television discourses locate the origins and operation of prejudiced attitudes at the level of the individual, where they stem from deeply held fears, insecurities, and misunderstandings by individual whites who lack sufficient contact with blacks and other peoples of color. For blacks, on the other hand, they are expressed as the hurts and pains of exclusion that have inevitably hardened into victimization, anger, and irrationality. Typical examples from episodes of *Family Ties* and *The Golden Girls* used the presence of black neighbors and a potential romantic interest, respectively, to identify and draw out white prejudices and suspicions about blacks. In the end, misunderstandings and mistrust were revealed as the source of fear and suspicion. With television's conventional reliance on narrative resolution, once identified, such troubling issues as racial prejudice are easily resolved (or contained) in the space of thirty minutes.

One other characteristic defines shows embedded in an assimilationist discourse: the privileged subject position is necessarily that of the white middle class. That is to say, whiteness is the privileged yet unnamed place from which to see and make sense of the world. This very transparency contributes to the hegemonic status of this televisual construction of whiteness, placing it beyond critical interrogation. Indeed, relative to the hegemonic status that whiteness occupies in this discourse, blackness simply works to reaffirm, shore up, and police the cultural and moral boundaries of the existing racial order. From the privileged angle of their normative race and class positions, whites are portrayed as sympathetic advocates for the elimination of prejudice.

Pluralist or Separate-but-Equal Discourses

Separate-but-equal discourses situate black characters in domestically centered black worlds and circumstances that essentially parallel those of whites. Like their white counterparts, these shows are anchored by the normative ideals of individual equality and social inclusion. In other words, they maintain a commitment to universal acceptance into the transparent "normative" middle class. However, it is a separate-but-equal inclusion. In this television world, blacks and whites are just alike save for minor differences of habit and perspective developed from African American experiences in a homogeneous and monolithic black world. In this televisual black world, African Americans face the same experiences, situations, and conflicts as whites except for the fact that they remain separate but equal.

I have in mind such programs as *Family Matters, 227, Amen,* and *Fresh Prince of Bel Air;* earlier shows with predominantly black casts that currently run in syndication from previous seasons, such as *The Jeffersons, What's Happening!!, Sanford & Son,* and *That's My Mama;* as well as some of the programming featured on Black Entertainment Television.[20] What makes these shows pluralist and therefore different from the assimilationist shows is their explicit recognition of race (blackness) as the basis of cultural difference (expressed as separation) as a feature of U.S. society.[21] As in so much of television, the social and historical contexts in which these acknowledged differences are expressed, sustained, and meaningful are absent. The particularity of black cultural difference is therefore articulated with(in) the dominant historical, cultural, and social discourses about American society. It is possible, then, to recognize, indeed celebrate, the presence of African Americans, latinos, Asians, Native Americans, and women and the particularly distinct tradition, experiences, and positions they represent without disrupting and challenging the dominant narratives about American society. In other words, race as the basis of inequality, conquest, slavery, subordination, exploitation, even social location is eliminated, as are the oppositions, struggles, survival strategies, and distinctive lifeways that result from these experiences. In this manner cultural difference and diversity can be represented, even celebrated, but in ways that confirm and authorize dominant social, political, cultural, and economic positions and relationships. From the separate-but-equal televisual world inaugurated by *Amos 'n' Andy*, a large number of black representations remain separate, even if they have gained, symbolically at least, a measure of equality.

Contemporary black-oriented shows and the representations they offer occupy a discursive space still marked by their relationship to an unnamed but nevertheless hegemonic order. Like assimilationist representations, pluralist representations are constructed from an angle of vision defined by that normative order. The assumptions organizing pluralist representations of black life offer variations and modifications of the representations in the assimilationist paradigm. These shows are also tethered to this hegemonic white middle-class universe in yet another way—through the conventional formulas, genres, codes, and practices that structure their representations. Hence, on the face of it, shows from *227* to *Family Matters* present themes, experiences, and concerns that seem, and in some instances are, "uniquely African American"—for example, the black church (*Amen*) and black women's friendships (*227* and, more recently, *Living Single*). Of course, the images of black life in these shows do represent one mode of black participation in American society. However, representations of blackness in these separate-but-equal worlds depend on an essential and universal black subject for their distinction from and similarity to the normative center. On programs such as *Amen, 227,* and *Family Matters,* black people live out simple and largely one-dimensional lives in segregated universes where they encounter the usual televisual challenges in the domestic sphere—social relations, child rearing, awkward situations, personal embarrassment, and romance.

Culturally, these shows construct a view of American race relations in which conflict, tension, and struggles over power, especially claims on blackness, depend on the logic of a cultural pluralism that requires a homogeneous, totalizing blackness, a blackness incapable of addressing the differences, tensions, and diversities among African Americans (and other communities of color).[22] Shows organized by such pluralist logic seldom, if ever, critique or engage the hegemonic character of (middle-class constructions of) whiteness or, for that matter, totalizing constructions of blackness.

Discursively, the problem of racial inequality is displaced by the incorporation of blacks into that great American stew where such cultural distinctions are minor issues that enrich the American cultural universe without noticeably disturbing the delicate balance of power, which remains unnamed, hidden, and invisible. Obscured are representations of diversity within and among African Americans, as well as the intraracial/ethnic alliances and tensions that also characterize post-civil rights race relations in the United States. Together with assimilationist discourses, these television programs effectively work for some viewers to produce pleasures and identifications precisely because their presence on commercial network television symbolically confirms the legitimacy and effectiveness of the very cultural pluralism on which America's official construction and representation of itself depend. Obscured in the process is the impact (and responses to it) of structured social inequality and the social hierarchies that are structured by it.

Multiculturalism/Diversity

I argued earlier in this chapter that *The Cosby Show* reconfigured representations of African Americans in commercial network television. Although this program marked an aesthetic and discursive turn away from assimilationist and pluralist practices, key elements of both continued to structure and organize aspects of *The Cosby Show,* which remained rooted in both sets of discourses. In style and form, the show operated from the normative space of a largely black, often multicultural world that paralleled that of whites. It appealed to the universal themes of mobility and individualism, and it privileged the upper-middle-class black family as the site of social life.

At the same time, the show moved some distance away from these elements through its attempt to explore the interiors of black lives and subjectivities from the angle of African Americans. *The Cosby Show* constructed black Americans as the authors of and participants in their own notion of America and what it means to be American. This transitional moment was most evident in the show's use of blackness and African American culture as a kind of emblematic code of difference.

More central to the transition from assimilationist and pluralist discourses to an engagement with the cultural politics of difference, however, are *Frank's Place* and, more recently, *Roc* and *South Central.* The short-lived *Frank's Place* was coproduced by Tim Reid and Hugh Wilson and aired on the CBS television network during the 1987–88 season. The show was distinguished by its explicit construction and positioning of African American culture at the very center of its social and cultural universe. From this position the show examined everyday life from the perspective of working-class as well as middle-class blacks. It seldom, if ever, adjusted its perspective and its representation of African American cultural experiences to the gaze of an idealized white middle-class audience. The discursive practices that structured

Frank's Place (and *Roc*) are also distinguished by an innovative approach to television as a form—the program's explicit attention to African American themes, the use of original popular music from the African American musical tradition (i.e., blues), the blurring of genres (comedy/drama), the lack of closure and resolution, the setting and location, and the use of different visual and narrative strategies (e.g., a cinematic look and feel, lighting, and production style). (In the case of *Roc*, I would add to these the use of live/real-time production.)

In addition to *Frank's Place* I would count some of the very early seasons of *The Arsenio Hall Show*, *A Different World*, and *In Living Color* as representative programs that have explicitly engaged the cultural politics of diversity and multiculturalism within the sign of blackness. Television programs operating within this discursive space position viewers, regardless of race, class, or gender locations, to participate in black experiences from multiple subject positions. In these shows viewers encounter complex, even contradictory, perspectives and representations of black life in America. The guiding sensibility is neither integrationist nor pluralist, though elements of both may turn up. Unlike in assimilationist discourses, there are Black Subjects (as opposed to black Subjects), and unlike in pluralist discourses, these Black Subjects are not so total and monolithic that they become THE BLACK SUBJECT.

The issue of cultural difference and the problem of African American diversity and inclusion form the social ground from which these shows operate. As illustrated by *The Cosby Show*, the discourse of multiculturalism/diversity offers a view of what it means to be American from the vantage point of African Americans. But, unlike *The Cosby Show*, this is not a zero-sum game. The social and cultural terms in which it is possible to be black and American and to participate in the American experience are more open. Although these terms often continue to support a "normative" conception of the American universe (especially in its class and mobility aspirations), in other respects shows such as *Frank's Place* and *Roc* stretch this conception by interrogating and engaging African American cultural traditions, perspectives, and experiences.[23]

In shows that engage cultural politics of difference within the sign of blackness, black life and culture are constantly made, remade, modified, and extended. They are made rather than discovered, and they are dynamic rather than frozen (Hall 1989). Such programs create a discursive space in which subject positions are transgressive and contradictory, troubling, and pleasurable, as are the representations used to construct identity (see Lipsitz 1990b), a space that is neither integrationist nor pluralist—indeed, it is often both at the same time.

Not surprisingly, black middle-class cultural perspectives and view-points continue to shape and define these shows; however, they are driven less by the hegemonic gaze of whiteness. (This gaze is detectable in the assimilationist attempt to silence cultural difference and in the pluralist attempt to claim that African American cultural experiences are parallel to white immigrant experiences.)

It is not that the representations that appear within this set of discursive practices and strategies simply offer a more culturally satisfying and politically progressive alternative to assimilationist and pluralist discourses. Indeed, they often do not. They do, however, represent questions of diversity within blackness more directly, explicitly, and frequently, and as central features of the programs. As I show in the chapters that follow, *A Different World, Frank's Place, Roc,* and *In Living Color* have consistently and explicitly examined issues of racism, apartheid, discrimination, nationalism, masculinity, color coding, desegregation, and poverty from multiple and complex perspectives within blackness.

In these shows, differences that originate from within African American social and cultural experiences have been not just acknowledged, but interrogated, even parodied as subjects of television. *In Living Color* and *A Different World,* for instance, have used drama, humor, parody, and satire to examine subjects as diverse as Caribbean immigrants, black fraternities, beauty contests, black gay men, the Nation of Islam, Louis Farrakhan, Jesse Jackson, Marion Barry, racial attitudes, hip-hop culture, and white guilt. The richness of African American cultural and social life as well as the experience of otherness that derives from subordinate status and social inequality are recognized, critiqued, and commented on. The racial politics that helps to structure and define U.S. society is never far from the surface.

Watching Television, Seeing Black

In many of the programs located in both pluralist and multiculturalist discourses, African American culture is central to the construction of black subjects as well as program content, aesthetic organization, setting, and narrative. These discourses, especially those that I regard as multiculturalist, operate at multiple levels of class, gender, region, color, and culture, and though fractured and selective, their dominant angle of vision, social location, and cultural context are African American (Fiske 1987; Hall 1980, 1989; Newcomb 1984). In all of the television representations of cultural difference there remains a contradictory character, one where the leaks, fractures, tensions, and contradictions in a stratified multicultural society continue to find expression.

Although contained within the larger hegemonic terms of the dominant American discourse on race and race relations driven by the narrative of inclusion, many of the shows circulating within these various discursive practices provide different representations of African Americans on commercial network television (Hall 1981b). Within commercial television representations of African American culture, the most compelling and powerful representations mark, displace, and disarticulate hegemonic and normative cultural assumptions and representations about America's racial order. At their best, such representations fully engage all aspects of African American life and, in the process, move cultural struggles within television and media beyond limited and narrow questions of positive/negative images, role models, and simple reversals to the politics of representation (Fregoso 1990a; Hall 1989).

As I demonstrate in the remaining chapters, contemporary television representations of blackness require a sharper, more engaged analytic focus on the multilayered, dialogic, intertextual, and contradictory character of racial representations in commercial network television. I do not claim, of course, that these representations are inherently resistant or oppositional. The hegemonic terms and effects of racial representation are no longer hidden, silenced, and beyond analytic and political interrogation. To make sense of television representations of blackness politically, we must theorize and understand them in relation to other television representations and to discourses beyond the television screen. The readings, affirmations, and interrogations that follow attempt just such a critical practice.

6 It's a Different World Where You Come From

On the evening that I visited the set of *A Different World,* the taping ran late into the night. Until the actual taping began, those of us in the studio audience were entertained by and placed under the general care of Louis Dix, a black stand-up comic. Dix's hip African American-based humor assumed a certain familiarity with black youth culture, personalities, and events specific to contemporary black life in America. This kind of comedic priming, as it were, is standard practice for live studio tapings in television. What was especially notable to me, however, was the fact that this immersion in this decidedly black cultural and comedic world seemed just the thing, just the right setting to prepare us for our venture into the sitcom world of black college life at Hillman. Once taping began, the cast and crew seemed spirited, and willingly cooperated when scenes had to be redone or when lines were blown or when there were long pauses in the taping. There was even a surprise visit to the set (arranged by the director, Debbie Allen) by black heartthrob Denzel Washington. The studio audience went wild, and even members of the cast and crew seemed surprised. And, of course, there was the pride and confidence that comes with producing a show that has consistently been at the top of its game and in the top ten in ratings since the second season of its run.

The Carsey-Werner Company, producer of *The Cosby Show* and *Roseanne*, also produced *A Different World*. The presence and authority of black women permeated every aspect of this television production—in the production offices, on the set, in the credits, in the theme song accompanying the opening montage, and especially in the teleplays that found their way to the small screen. Under the guidance of executive producers Marge Peters, Thad Mumford, and Susan Fales, the television representation of life at Hillman College came close enough to the world that I knew as an undergraduate at historically black Florida A&M University to draw me back week after week. This was no small feat, for mainstream media such as television are often mashed and shaped by considerable pressures to show the familiar, to rely on the tried and true.

For me, *A Different World* merits careful consideration for the way it commandeered mainstream television conventions to present black life and issues in new, entertaining, and sometimes poignant ways. As I learned from visiting the set of the show and interviewing its then executive producer, Susan Fales, representing the interiors of black life through television's dominant conventions without completely falling prey to its structuring and authorizing codes was not easy. *A Different World* faced a far greater challenge than simply bringing black characters to the small screen or staging action in all-black settings. After all, beginning with *Amos 'n' Andy*, television had by 1990 become quite adept at constructing separate televisual worlds for African Americans. To make good on its weekly promise to present a "different world," the show had to inhabit and then use the existing television conventions to construct different perspectives, experiences, and visions.

Formally, and perhaps not surprisingly, *A Different World* was really quite conventional. Narratively, the show seldom deviated from the standard plot structure of stasis, conflict, resolution, stasis. As in most weekly situation comedies, the camera shots, framing, and perspective were established through the conventional use of close-ups, medium shots, and long setup shots; the action took place primarily on a sound stage (though this conventional set was punctuated with one important location setting—in the streets of Los Angeles—in the aftermath of the 1992 riots). The brightly lit sets guaranteed the familiarity and comfort of idealized middle-class interiors that dominate so much of television. The characters were attractive, pleasant, articulate, and smart. They moved with ease in their worlds, usually overcoming whatever uncertainties, crises, and obstacles they faced.

A Different World was also conventional in its presentation and resolution of conflict. Individually and collectively, the characters, quite predictably, negotiated the challenges, ambivalences, discoveries, disappointments, and triumphs of college life and young adulthood. The stories were usually told from several perspectives, the sign of a commitment to liberal television notions of balance conveyed as much through narratives themselves as through the characters, who symbolically represented different sides of various issues. (For instance, Whitley usually represented self-interest, Freddie was the embodiment of political correctness, and Ron was entrepreneurealism incarnate.)

With such obvious commitments to conventional strategies of telling stories, why should the show be characterized as exemplary, even distinctive, for its representation of diversity and engagement with black cultural politics? And on the question of blackness, why not frame this show in the same terms as those I call assimilationist and pluralist? The answers lie in the specific ways that the producers, directors, writers, and cast used existing television conventions to construct the world of black life at Hillman College. The producers and writers explored a remarkable range of themes, situations, stories, sensibilities, and characters from various locations within African American social and cultural experiences.

From the opening visual montage, which rode over the catchy but powerful thematic hook sung by Aretha Franklin, the show explicitly commented on cultural difference and celebrated the social and cultural traditions of black college life. The opening montage, and the stories it framed, announced these differences (and similarities) without the primary requirement or expectation of identification on the part of white audiences. These representations invited identification, but not the kind of familiarity that necessarily assumes and privileges whiteness as the ideal subject position. They challenged analytic and interpretive positions that assume that for these television representations of blackness to work, they must be organized, structured, and deployed through whiteness. To its credit, *A Different World* seemed explicitly to refuse this powerful aesthetic temptation and structural pressure. Time and time again, the show refused to retreat into the politically safe, culturally familiar televisual world of whiteness. How, then, did *A Different World* manage to tell stories about blackness through the conventional practices of television? And what kinds of stories were these, anyway?

Managing Conventions and Representing Blackness

When I interviewed her in spring of 1990, Susan Fales had just taken over, from Thad Mumford, the post of executive producer of *A Different World*.[1] Fales is a Harvard graduate and one of the few black female executive producers of major television series. She broke into television first as an intern and later as a writer for *The Cosby Show*. She subsequently moved to *A Different World* when it was created by Bill Cosby as a spin-off from *The Cosby Show*.

A Different World was originally conceived as a feature vehicle for Lisa Bonet, then a cast member on *The Cosby Show*. The second-oldest Huxtable daughter, Denise, Bonet's character, decided to attend historically black Hillman College. One of the initial problems facing the new show, according the Fales, was how to build it around Bonet's character. This problem was especially challenging because it was not at all clear that Bonet could carry the show or that the potentially rich possibilities of a fictional black college setting would generate the kind of ratings necessary to sustain it.

As might be expected, during the first season Denise faced the usual anxiety of leaving home, the uncertainty of a different environment, and adjustment to a new life of freedom and responsibility. Upon her arrival at Hillman, Denise found a white roommate named Maggie, a skirt-chasing smart-mouthed fellow freshman named Dwayne Wayne, and a cohort of students not unlike herself. By the end of the first season the show's promise was still, at best, questionable. With more than its share of jokes, antics, and wisecracks, *A Different World,* according to Fales, degenerated into a youth-focused comedy that veered dangerously close to a black television version of *Animal House*. Needless to say, the program failed to develop a distinct identity. Indeed, as Fales recalled, the show was so bad and embarrassing that Bill Cosby threatened to have it taken off the air.

Instead of cancellation, *A Different World* underwent an overhaul to eliminate the high jinks, give it more serious academic credibility, and bring some degree of dignity and integrity to its representation of black college life. Toward that end, the show's core production team toured historically black colleges such as Howard, Morehouse, Spelman, and Huston-Tillotson to get a closer look at and better feel for black college life.

Actress/choreographer/director Debbie Allen was brought onto the production team as director, writer, and consultant. This was an important move; the energetic Allen brought professionalism, fun, a sense of teamwork, and firsthand knowledge of black college life to the show (Allen attended Howard University).[2] Denise and her white roommate were eliminated. Jasmine Guy's Whitley Gilbert, who had been a supporting character in the first season, eventually replaced Bonet as the primary female lead in the ensemble. Kadeem Hardison's

Dwayne Wayne became more complex and studious, and less of a smart-aleck skirt chaser. (In one episode, Dwayne was inducted into the Phi Beta Kappa honor society.) Other primary cast members included Charnele Brown as Kim Reese, Darryl Bell as Ron Johnson, Cree Summer as Freddie Brooks, Dawnn Lewis as Jaleesa Vinson, Glyn Turman as Colonel Taylor, Sinbad as Coach Walter Oakes, and Lou Myers as Mr. Gaines. A new arrangement of the show's opening theme song, originally performed by Phoebe Snow, was sung by Aretha Franklin. Needless to say, these explicit turns toward blackness quickly established a clear identity for the show, one firmly rooted in African American social experiences and cultural sensibilities.

With a clearer sense of direction and identity, the series settled into a regular time slot—Thursday at 8:30 p.m., following *The Cosby Show*—where it consistently enjoyed solid ratings. There is little doubt but that some part of the show's commercial success and longevity can be attributed to solid scheduling, especially the lead-in it enjoyed from *The Cosby Show*. But *A Different World* also distinguished itself from *The Cosby Show*, as well as other existing television shows about blacks, by explicitly situating itself within a broader set of African American social and cultural discourses, especially cinema, hip-hop, sports, popular music, and African American studies. *A Different World*, in a sense, formed part of the cultural bloc that contributed, at least on the television front, to a process Cornel West (1993) describes as the "African Americanization" of American popular culture.

Structurally and from within the center of the form, the show's producers mobilized and staged representations of blackness by adjusting and adapting the conventions of casting, writing, characters, setting, and narrative to fit their own vision. I want to consider the show's adaptation of each of these conventions in order to explore just how they were managed and used in the service of making claims on and representing blackness.

Characters/Casting

In the 1980s a growing tension between the demands of unity and the reality of difference within representations of blackness became critical points of debate among African Americans. Often at the heart of these debates were various claims on blackness. These claims included visions of nation, community, authenticity, masculinity, and heterosexuality. Points of contention in such debates often centered on sexuality, interracial relationships, mixed-race heritage, and social class. The cultural force of these debates and the claims on blackness that they underwrite are evident in the images and discourses surrounding such films as *Jungle Fever, School Daze,* and *Boyz N the Hood* and events such as the selection of Vanessa Williams as Miss America and the subsequent stripping from her of that title, Mike Tyson's trial and subsequent conviction for rape, and Professor Anita Hill's testimony at the Clarence Thomas confirmation hearings.

In television representations of African Americans, *Frank's Place, Roc,* and *A Different World* were the few shows that engaged cultural tensions and debates stemming from such issues as sexuality, violence against women, and color coding within blackness. Although *A Different World* alone by no means subverted the deeply rooted psychic and ideological scars of racism, the show was not at all shy about addressing them. Indeed, by deliberately casting the principal ensemble to emphasize differences in backgrounds, classes, histories, complexions, and politics, the show's producers broke with television's conventional construction of African Americans as monolithic.

When asked about the deliberateness of this casting strategy, Fales emphatically stated that the choice was quite intentional, and that the aim was to highlight diversity among African Americans; attention to the issue of difference did not stop with exterior matters of complexion, but extended to gender, age, and class. For example, Mr. Gaines, manager of the Pit, was a fixture on the campus who gave the writers the opportunity to explore issues of generation and class. Similarly, Jaleesa was an older returning student when the series began, 26 and divorced, in a world of 18- and 19-year-olds.

The show raised questions of black diversity not just through the composition and range of its cast; issues of difference were also the explicit subjects of various episodes. In one episode, for example, the character of Kim, an attractive premed student, confronts some painful memories from elementary school, where she had been the object of jokes and ridicule because of her dark complexion. Recalling the pain of her past when confronted with stereotypical images in memorabilia from the old South, Kim initially refuses to participate in a campus event for Black History Month. (In the same episode, the fair-skinned Whitley discovers that her great grandparents were slave owners.) Here is an example of the show's attempt to tackle an important topic, and not just through plot or a single character. For many African Americans, the figure of Kim, a young black woman, is vitally important to the meaning of this episode. Through her, the show, symbolically at least, acknowledges the injuries, ambivalence, and strength of African American responses to life in an oppressive racialized social order. But more significantly, the figure of Kim makes explicit the specific and complex ways in which black women's bodies are often at the intersection of race, class, and gender, both within blackness and in the relations between blacks and whites.

In this episode, and in the representation of the characters in general, one could sense the show's conscious attempt, as Fales put it, to subvert expectations about class and race. All of the show's primary characters functioned within the ensemble to embody a variety and range of positions and experiences within blackness—Whitley, the pampered and fair southern belle; Freddie, the politically correct neo-urban hippie; Dwayne Wayne, the b-boy computer engineer; Ron, the self-absorbed budding entrepreneur; Kim, the serious and gifted pre-med student; Jaleesa, the returning student and sometimes adult voice of experience. By imbuing the characters with such qualities and then having them play against type, the show's writers and producers seemed quite self-conscious in their intention to make their characters neither blacks in whiteface nor one-dimensional.

Writers and Writing

As with the deliberate decisions to cast the show to convey the diversity within blackness, the show's production team represented diversity through the composition of the writing staff. The writers for *A Different World* were themselves from different racial and ethnic backgrounds. The production staff included Thad Mumford, Susan Fales, and Marge Peters, each of whom at one time or another served as producer, executive producer, co-executive producer, and writer. The seven members of the writing team included more women than men, all of whom Fales described as politically liberal.

As is true for many television shows, especially sitcoms, the writing was done in combinations of individual and group writing. And, of course, script ideas were developed on the basis of personal encounters, memories, and experience. Fales recalled, for example, that the story dealing with Whitley and Freddie's encounter with prejudice and racism in an upscale shopping mall came from the experiences of two of the black women members of the production staff.

The deliberate emphasis on gender and racial diversity in all aspects of production, Fales seems convinced, contributed to the distinctive character and identity of the show. According to Fales, this distinctive character turned up on the show in several ways: the show's producers and writers were much less apprehensive than they may otherwise have been about drawing on the cultural, social, and imaginary resources available to them, especially those based on their own distinctive backgrounds; members of the production team were willing to take the risks necessary to put out stories about the interiors of black life because they, as Fales put it, constitute a segment of the industry where they (and the stories they want to tell) have not been listened to or taken seriously. Fales is the first to admit that as executive producer she was interested in having people on the show who understood or at the very least were open to stories and ideas that explored what it means to be black in America. Within the generic boundaries of the form and its structuring conventions, then, Fales, Mumford, and Peters employed people sensitive to issues of diversity, especially in terms of ethnicity, gender, class, and age.

Along with the cultural themes and social concerns that informed the show's stories, the distinctive identity of the show and its treatment of issues involving race and African American culture were related to how the program used the conventions of television writing to tell stories. That is, the writers cleverly used themes, plot devices (i.e., multiple and overlapping plot lines), and settings to examine issues facing African Americans and to express, highlight, and celebrate black cultural sensibilities.

Instead of being labeled "message" shows or "issue" shows by members of the industry, both *A Different World* and *The Cosby Show* developed reputations as shows built on good writing (interviews with the writers of *227, 1990*). In other words, writers on these shows were seen by others in the industry as competent and imaginative, capable of telling stories beyond the balkanized orbit of so-called black shows. Certainly this characterization indicates some of the subtle and persistent ways in which racism is expressed in the culture of television.[3] It is not so much that *A Different World*, for instance, was "less black" or aesthetically "better" than shows that I have called pluralist; rather, my argument is that blackness in *A Different World* labored toward different ends by using existing television conventions in a different way.

Like many successful shows in the genre of situation comedy, *A Different World* effectively utilized multiple plot structures (A and B stories) in its teleplays. Conventionally, the dominant story (A) is the site of the major message and moral of the play; in *A Different World* the A stories usually involved the major characters in situations where they were faced with difficult circumstances, the resolution of which usually ended in lessons or insights about social relations, romantic tensions, or individual character. Minor plots, or B stories, are more likely to focus attention on minor characters involved in minor action, often away from (sometimes even parallel to) the dominant plot. As often, however, separate stories are closely related to the major plot. Minor plots are often used to break up the action, shift scenes and time frames, add humor and variety, or showcase guest talent.

As deployed in *A Different World*, however, minor plots were not used only in these conventional ways; rather, they often served as the structural devices or hooks on which the writers hung explorations of social issues and cultural practices central to African American life and culture. The show routinely used classroom scenes, for instance, to narrate stories about key historical figures and significant events in African American culture. With references to sports figures, musicians, and events that might require an insider's knowledge, seemingly minor dialogue was used to highlight and comment on contemporary issues, controversies, and events within African American social and cultural discourses.

By using minor themes, characters, and settings in this way, the show's production team was able to saturate the show with cultural knowledge central to African American life without necessarily being didactic, exclusive, or derisive. This use of minor plots, characters, and settings enabled the writers to construct and represent the sensibilities of an African American youth culture full of intertextural references to black popular culture, current events, and contemporary debates about blackness. As in the images found in music video and black cinema, black bodies were routinely adorned with hairstyles and draped in clothing that clearly signaled the rich repertoire and vernacular of black youth culture. In this way the show integrated the looks, styles, and feels of black youth culture without seeming artificial or forced.[4]

Again, there is nothing especially remarkable about the presence of these emblems of blackness in commercial television. Today, in fact, they are easily found in varying degrees of imitation and replication in music videos, sports events, advertising, and other situation comedies. What I do find remarkable, however, is the specific way that African American television makers have drawn on these elements and integrated them into their televisual constructions and claims on black life and culture. Here the presence of director Debbie Allen and other African Americans on the show was unmistakable. These African Americans and their colleagues were collectively responsible for the subtle nuances that heightened the look and feel of the show.

Setting

By most television standards, *A Different World*'s construction and representation of black life would certainly be fairly routine were it not for the show's imaginative use of setting. Because it was set in the exterior world of college life, rather than just the interior spaces of the domestic family, the show by and large sidestepped many pressures to construct and package African American life primarily within the conventional requirements of the universal television family (Dyson 1989). In fact, Fales told me that early on the producers and writers saw an opportunity to use the university setting to break free of the aesthetic confinements and thematic isolation of the domestic family. It is the setting of home-place domesticity, indeed, that accounts for so much of television's preoccupation with domestic relations, romantic troubles, and life-cycle issues.

Now, I do not simply mean that a shift to the public arena of college life is any guarantee that such issues cannot be addressed, or that, when they are, they will be handled differently. As Ella Taylor (1989) reminds us, in the 1970s and 1980s the domestic family simply moved its key characters, troubles, and jokes to the workplace. I do want to argue, instead, that *A Different World*'s move away from the confines of the domestic family into the fictional world of Hillman College freed the writers and directors to explore a broader range of issues, to construct more complex and diverse representations, and to engage a wider range of historical and contemporary issues of concern to African Americans. Setting the show at historically black Hillman College enabled the writers to confront, far more directly and consistently, issues of difference without succumbing to the seductions of the zero-sum game of universal appeal at the expense of the specificity of African American diversity.

A Different World effectively used the milieu of Hillman College not just to stage blackness but to construct and engage in debates on such topics as gender, sexual harassment, color coding, and violence against women. The campus hangout (the Pit), the classroom, the dorm room (and, later, the off-campus student apartment), the workplace, parties, the basketball court were all places where characters experienced themselves and each other fully. These interior and exterior spaces were actually central to the expression of personality, imagined community, tradition, and aspirations of people who lived and developed in them. Because these interior and exterior spaces exist in the same time and space, *A Different World*, far more than domestic situation comedies that remain isolated in the home, helped to break down the genre's idealization and reproduction of the split between the public and the private. On the show, such issues as rape, sexism, and racism were debated and struggled over in the privacy of the dorm, at home, and on dates, and the private fears and anxieties of maturation and responsibility found expression in the classroom, at the Pit, and in the dean's office.

Television critics, scholars, and industry personnel have for some time now regarded the genre of situation comedy and the confinement of blacks to it as a kind of racial balkanization of commercial television. At the beginning of each new season, television critics note the absence of blacks in significant roles in nighttime drama, daytime soaps, even game shows. Critics of television's racially balkanized world correctly call for the industry to tell stories about black life in all aspects of the medium. I share this general concern, and join with their call. However, the effective and, I think, quite remarkable negotiation of the genre of situation comedy by *Frank's Place, Roc,* and *A Different World* suggests another way to think about black presence in television. Perhaps it is not so much the genre of situation comedy that is the prison house of aesthetic and cultural confinement for African Americans, but the conventions that structure and define all representations within the genre. By moving characters and stories out of the domestic family, at least for blacks, and into the spheres of neighborhood, work, community, and voluntary associations, more complex and diverse representations are possible.[5]

Rethinking and, more important, offering shows within the genre of situation comedy located across a wider range of settings and situations might also force television makers, scholars, and critics beyond simplistic and binary comparisons of drama and situation comedy. As *The Days and Nights of Molly Dodd, Roseanne, Hill Street Blues, Roc,* and *Frank's Place* all demonstrate, it is quite possible to mix, even experiment with, conventions from different genres to construct and represent the lives and experiences of people from different cultures and social locations. My call is not simply for a move to the public sphere (or, more accurately, television's construction of some notion of the public sphere) as an answer to the racial balkanization of commercial television. Rather, I want to suggest that in a show such as *A Different World* we have representations of black lives and experiences that effectively explore different ways of telling stories.

Themes

If the producers of *A Different World* had remained content with organizing episodes around the usual timeworn television themes of romance and social relationships, it would have been just another television show with black leading characters. However, the show imaginatively used the dominant conventions of the genre to saturate its televisual world with blackness—African American cultural and social practices, perspectives, codes, assumptions, and styles. By doing so, it ostensibly constructed a perspective from which to examine a broad range of issues of immediate relevance to African Americans. By taking up questions of racial conflict between blacks and whites, corporate investment in South Africa, sexual harassment, AIDS, date rape, violence against women, and affirmative action, *A Different World* examined crucial themes and topics, and in the process repositioned, even privileged, African American viewers and addressed them in terms of this constructed world of African American culture.

Whatever one thinks of *A Different World*'s claim on blackness, it so permeates the show that African American perspectives do much more than serve as the symbolic marker of difference while laboring ultimately to affirm the hegemony of a normative and unnamed whiteness. In *A Different World,* blackness labors as the subject of complex questions and issues facing all people, especially African Americans. Blackness operates as a specific perspective from which to speak, act, and see the world.

For example, separate episodes examined the issue of violence against women (first airdate July 9, 1992) and sexual harassment (January 30, 1992). In both episodes, black women were the objects of male aggression and violations. Both episodes were careful to construct stories that primarily involved women, yet they included men in the discussions, sanctions, and collective responsibility for the prevention of such violations. Certainly, both of these issues are of importance to all women and men, but they are also issues with a particular history, resonance, and urgency for black women and men. By staging such complex questions through the experiences of African American students at Hillman, these episodes spoke to the broad concerns and relevance of these questions for all people and to the particular ways they affect black middle-class men and women in the university. It was this ability to articulate the multiple positions of race, class, and gender simultaneously that distinguished *A Different World*'s treatment of these issues.

Various complex dimensions of gender were among the most consistently addressed themes in the series. Indeed, the show seemed especially sensitive to the roles of women, the construction of black masculinity, and power relations between men and women. In fact, *A Different World* was one of the few shows about blacks that consistently staged serious explorations of contemporary social issues from the perspectives of its leading female characters. For example, an episode that first aired February 15, 1990, explored the issue of corporate investment in South Africa and revolved primarily around Kim, the premed student, who had to choose between giving up a scholarship because of her principled opposition to apartheid and her practical need for the scholarship to complete her education. An episode on AIDS (January 16, 1992), which guest-starred Whoopi Goldberg, was told from the perspective of a female student and featured an informative Q and A scene that addressed myths and facts about AIDS. An-

other episode examined student encounters with class and racial prejudice and was structured around Whitley and Freddie (January 25,
1990).

Two of the episodes in particular, the one on sexual harassment and
the one on violence against women, mentioned above, illustrate *A Different World*'s intervention into contemporary African American discourses on questions of race and gender. Both episodes can be read as
dialogues about the epidemic levels of violence against black women
as well as the silence, complicity, and responsibility of black men in
such acts. By making this an issue facing black men and women, and
not just a woman's private troubles, the show engaged blackness from
the perspective of black women to explore the issue and thus to make
claims. Similarly, the episode on sexual harassment was clearly an intervention into the Thomas-Hill controversy. Again, from the televisual world of black life constructed on the show, the writers and producers took the opportunity to comment, from the perspective of
black women, on the issue of sexual harassment. In this particular episode, it is Whitley who, when confronted with sexual advances from a
black male colleague, first ignores the advances, then makes adjustments in her behavior and dress, and finally tries to bring the problem
to the attention of her (white) male boss. We experience Whitley's ambivalence, frustration, and fear as she tries to convince her friends, em-
ployers, and the audience of her violation. Of course, Dwayne and her
friends support her and attempt to help, but in the end it is Whitley
who finally convinces her boss to take action.

It would be a bit too easy to see this episode simply as an instance of
going for easy ratings points by taking advantage of a hot topic. The
show consistently dealt with controversial issues, and this particular
episode was no exception, but rather one of many episodes that addressed issues of gender. To their credit, the writers of *A Different World*
seemed equally mindful and consistent in their attention to questions
of masculinity. Ron, Dwayne, and some of the minor male characters
were constantly used to anchor B narratives that exposed their often
sexist (Ron hatched a scheme to enlist female Hillman students to participate in a phone dating service) and sometimes playful antics (Ron
hatched a scheme to sell black cosmetics to Hillman's female students).

On the question of black masculinity, two episodes come immediately to mind. One, which first aired on November 9, 1989, revolves
around the character of Ron, who gets romantically involved with a
woman who is a single parent. In the course of the relationship, Ron
becomes very attached to his girlfriend and her child, so attached, in
fact, that he considers marriage. The tension heightens and the subsequent narrative crisis is staged when Ron has to make up his mind

about the relationship and his commitment to it. He must consider whether he is financially and emotionally capable of taking on this responsibility, whether he is the object of a matchmaking game, and whether or not to end the relationship.

The second story line concerning masculinity appears in the episode about sexual harassment described above (first aired January 30, 1992). It is especially poignant because of its position as a minor story in the harassment episode and because it involves that quintessential sign of masculinity, the military. Colonel Taylor, head of campus ROTC and math instructor, is alarmed to discover that his son, Terrence (played by Cory Tyler), plans to major in dance. He discourages Terrence because, according to the colonel's military-derived notion of masculinity, dance is simply not "manly" enough. However, after attending a physically demanding rehearsal with Terrence and seeing how accomplished and committed he is to dance, Colonel Taylor is transformed. He changes his mind (grows) about his conceptions of masculinity, his son, and dance. The transformed colonel supports his son's choice and celebrates his son's gifts.

I find it refreshing that these kinds of stories involving African American characters have appeared at all on television. But even more remarkable is the way that A Different World wove them together narratively to provide points of entry for commentary, critique, and perspective on such issues as gender, masculinity, and even, on occasion, feminism. Because they did not exist in isolation or appear outside the show's constructed claims on blackness, they represented constant dialogues, of a sort, with issues within the show, between this and other shows, and issues outside of television.

This dialogic quality and some attempt to represent diversity within blackness were also evident in A Different World's representation of other complex social issues of immediate concern to African Americans. Debates over corporate investment in South Africa, the academic credibility and legitimacy of black colleges, and the salience of affirmative action were all the subjects of separate episodes. Instead of going for the easy option of representing a monolithic and totalized blackness, these episodes explored such concerns by constructing them in terms of different experiences, interests, histories, and positions within blackness.

A useful illustration of this complexity can be seen in an episode that first aired on January 12, 1990. This episode grapples with the social competitiveness and academic credibility of historically black colleges. The A story revolves around the reunion of Dwyane Wayne and a high school friend. Whereas Dwayne had decided on Hillman College, his friend had elected to attend the University of Pennsylvania. Crisis is introduced in the narrative when Dwayne's friend belittles Dwayne's college roommate, Ron (because of his entrepreneurial ventures), and when he makes cracks about Hillman's academic credibility. The friend actually encourages Dwayne to transfer to Penn, where, according to his lights, Dwayne would get a more competitive education and join a circle of influential friends. This tension and the subsequent conflict it introduces lead to a strain in Dwayne's friendship with Ron and to Dwayne's having doubts about his education and experience at Hillman. After conferring with Whitley (who in turn relays a story about the Hillman tradition in her family), Dwayne does some research on Hillman graduation rates, academic accreditation, graduate job placement, and student scores on professional exams. The episode ends on the basketball court in a kind of masculine sparring match between Dwayne and his friend from Penn. There they shoot buckets and compare information about the quality of education at Hillman and Ivy League schools. With the friend and the unknowing audience situated in the same subject position, Dwayne demonstrates that Hillman is academically competitive on all levels with Penn. Ultimately, Dwayne decides against transferring. The friend departs with the words, "Stay in touch." Dwayne replies, "No, *you* stay in touch," underscoring the fact that, of the many valuable things offered by historically black colleges, foremost is a sense of connection to community and blackness.

Operating at a number of levels—class, community, tradition, and friendship—this particular episode is especially insightful in the way it constructs, joins, and responds to constant questions about the salience and quality of education at black colleges. At a time when enrollments at historically black colleges are at an all-time high, the episode answers claims about the quality of education and preparation at historically black colleges. At yet another level, this episode represents a metaphorical intervention into the broader debates about class divisions and tensions within the African American community, tensions that are increasingly out in the open as more and more black college graduates enter the middle class by way of elite educations at Ivy League universities. By constructing Dwayne and his friend as students of similar ability and promise, the writers carefully avoid a simplistic privileging of one kind of education over the other. At the same time, the construction of these two characters effectively symbolizes issues of class and difference among black students.[6] Without indicting or blaming elite white colleges or judging the black students who attend them, the episode raises questions about the isolation, mobility aspirations, and relationship of all black university students to notions of community and culture. In a small way, this mirrors the central issues in the policy, social, and cultural debates about class divisions within black communities and the responsibility of the black middle class to the black poor and the restoration of moral and civic order.

The boundaries of A *Different World*'s dialogue with contemporary social issues were by no means circumscribed by the issues I have noted so far. In a particularly moving episode, first aired January 10, 1991, the show also ventured an examination of the military buildup leading to the Gulf War, leaving the audience, especially African Americans, to ponder the disproportionate numbers of black men involved in three major institutions—prison, the military, and the university. Yet another episode, first aired January 16, 1990, examined the heat, anger, and conflict between black and white males. Here the writers framed the conflict and tensions almost entirely in masculine terms, staging the action at a football game, where Ron's car is vandalized with the word *nigger* written on it. (Significantly, Hillman's football team had played in the game, beating a nearby predominantly white college.) This episode was used to represent the exaggerated and false perceptions blacks and white have of each other, perceptions that can lead to suspicion, hostility, and conflict. An episode that first aired April 5, 1991, even ventured into the debate over arts funding and the power of funding institutions (the state) to censor materials it considers offensive. In its final season, A *Different World* devoted two episodes to an exploration of some of the issues, conflicts, and tensions that surrounded the Los Angeles riots (Braxton 1992a), a move equaled in bravery only by the courage the program displayed in tackling the issue of apartheid in South Africa.

For me, some of the most memorable and moving episodes of the series were less explicitly about staking out defensible positions on social issues such as race, gender, and community, even though they spoke rather profoundly to public debates about these issues. For this reason I note, in particular, episodes that dealt with questions of identity and color coding (December 5, 1991), the tradition of African American community and struggle (February 8, 1990), and the episode, described above, about investment in South Africa and the personal struggle to find the courage and strength to defend one's convictions. The power of these episodes and the issues they explored rests in the subtle ways A *Different World* attempted to speak directly to black audiences, from a place of blackness.

As I indicated previously, the episode on corporate investment in South Africa is organized around the discovery that one of the major contributors to a campus scholarship fund also maintained financial investments in South Africa. The dramatic tension of the story revolves around a campus divestment movement that urges the administration and the student body to support a move to drop the scholar-ship fund unless the contributor agrees to divest South African holdings. Kim, the premed student, is caught in the middle of this de-bate. As one of the students supported by the scholarship monies, she must decide either to forgo her scholarship and jeopardize her educa-tion or to keep her scholarship and violate the political position sup-ported by many of the students at Hillman. The narrative action cul-minates with a scene at a campus meeting with various Hillman students, including Whitley, Freddie, Kim, Ron, and Dwayne, articu-lating different positions on the issue of divestiture.

Bringing this story to television was a remarkable achievement in itself. Fales pointed out to me that it was the one episode about which NBC was concerned enough to ask for a "minor" adjustment in the script. The network apparently was concerned that the episode stated as fact the claim that reforms in South Africa would come from eco-nomic pressure. NBC asked that this claim be presented not as fact but as a possibility, and the producers complied.

Fales also noted that the writers had the members of the cast, in-cluding a black South African actor, improvise their own statements on the subject of divestiture. One of the most memorable moments in the episode is a speech made by the black South African, who spoke about the connection between South African struggles against apart-heid and African American struggles for equality and the fact that each student had make up his or her own mind. It is not so much the im-provised statements or the range of political positions enunciated in this scene that I find interesting, as the fact that this episode represents an honest and rare attempt by a television show to present the com-plex issues facing the divestiture movement, particularly for African American students. I am also struck by the show's courageous effort to make an explicit political and social connection between struggles in the United States and those in South Africa. Finally, I was most im-pressed by the fact that the producers and writers made the effort to represent the voice of a black South African student.

The episode on identity and color coding is equally resonant for me in the sense that it is a rare acknowledgment, in television anyway, of the historic and harmful injuries of class and color casting within blackness. Through the characters of Kim, Mr. Gaines, and Whitley, the episode effectively challenges totalizing and narrow notions of blackness by inserting difference into contemporary and historic dis-courses. By revealing the deep injuries and pain visited on Kim because of her dark complexion, the narrative quite aggressively recuperates and repositions Kim (especially vis-à-vis fairer-skinned characters such as Whitley and Freddie), with her dark skin, as a personification of beauty. The show reaches this point by way of a brief but insightful (again, for television) tour through the history of color coding, privilege, and subordination within blackness on the basis of skin color. Now, of course, this recuperation might just as easily be read, as E. Francis White (1990) cautions us not to, as an enactment of the politics of simple reversals, where one vector of subordination (color casting) is replaced by yet another (the objectification of women and the glorification of the African goddess of beauty). I recognize the consequences of such a move within the cultural politics of blackness; nevertheless, I do want to credit the show's use of commercial television to engage this issue.

The final episode I would like to discuss that might be emblematic of *A Different World*'s strategic use of television to reposition and construct African American claims on blackness involves a fairly conventional narrative. The main narrative of the episode finds Freddie in a fairly routine story about career choices. Freddie, the embodiment of both a posthippie sensibility and contemporary political correctness, finds it difficult to conform to the requirements of a weekend career counseling seminar organized to help prepare students for careers after Hillman. Instead of dressing up, conducting a mock recruiting interview, and performing in a way that will ensure her placement with an employer or graduate school, Freddie refuses to cooperate. (Phylicia Rashad, in her role as Clair Huxtable, guest stars as the successful Hillman graduate who volunteers to run the career counseling seminar.) Far more interesting is the B story in this episode, which finds Freddie and a group of students on an archaeological dig at one of the campus buildings. There they discover relics that appear to be evidence that Hillman College was one of the stops on the historic Underground Railroad. Where the main story explores the ambivalences and pressures of career choices, the minor narrative examines the rewards and discoveries of maintaining one's vigilance in the face of pressure. The episode culminates in a moving scene with Clair Huxtable and Freddie in the basement of the building, reflecting on the horrors of slavery, the heroism of black people, especially the women who were part of the Underground Railroad, and the tradition of black colleges. In the end, it is Freddie who holds out for a career choice that she will find interesting and that will make, in her words, "a contribution" to black people. This was indeed an unusual moment in commercial network television representations of African Americans. Here was an instance where the writers and producers effectively used the structure of television to tell a story, from the perspective of black female characters, that has, perhaps with the exception of *Roots*, effectively remained absent from television.

It's a Different World, but Is It Black?

If *A Different World* contributed anything to commercial television's construction and representation of African Americans and subsequent claims on the sign of blackness, it was that it managed to tell different stories about African Americans. It managed to do so from some of the interior and exterior spaces of African American life, and it managed to articulate, in some instances, and critically engage, in others, many of the salient issues confronting African Americans. Certainly, some of the conditions that enabled this ability to tell such stories from within the conventional boundaries and practices of network television were the show's structural relationship to *The Cosby Show* and the support of NBC.[7] As important, the show's vision and representation of African American life were also shaped by the gender, ethnic, and racial mix of its production team, cast, and crew, and the kinds of stories they collectively had to tell.

But these important contributions could not and did not break completely with the conventional practices and traditional constraints to which they were flexibly but firmly tethered. For example, in only rare instances (e.g., the episodes on sexual harassment, violence against women, AIDS) did *A Different World* ever move beyond the confines of a liberal commitment to tell all (usually two) sides of an issue and leave it to viewers to make up their own minds. Perhaps with the exception of the episode on South Africa, economic and political inequalities were framed as various kinds of misunderstanding, ignorance, and lack of experience with different groups and communities. Only on issues of gender and inequality was the show consistent in its representation and critique.

The show was most uncompromising in its construction and representation of blackness with respect to questions of difference and diversity within African American life and culture. On issues of gender, social class, background, color casting, popular culture, history, and even style, the program presented complex and diverse representations of African Americans. Yet even while working from these obvious strengths, *A Different World* was itself deeply enmeshed in what Mark Crispin Miller (1990a) calls cinematic and televisual happy endings. Marriage proposals, weddings, African queens, graduations, and childbirth were all staples taken from the different world of black lives on television. Although the show managed to avoid the zero-sum game of universalism versus difference within blackness, it nevertheless depended on liberal visions and happy endings to achieve its remarkable success. This strategy, and the practices on which it depends, does not detract from the show's modest corrective to television's representation of blacks. *A Different World* was not about getting it right, or even about getting it accurate. It was about creating a space for this slice of black life in the weekly clutter of network television. It was about giving actors, producers, directors, and writers with vision a chance to work, to tell their stories. In the end, the real joy of *A Different World* was the weekly televisual ride into this black world, the small pleasures it afforded, the identification it invited, and the memories of black college life it activated for me.

7   Frank's Place: Possibilities, Limitations, and Legacies

There is great drama in our lives, in our past, in our culture and in our Africanisms. I'd like to see more of that portrayed.

Rosalind Cash, an actress who appeared on Frank's Place

If *A Different World* effectively worked from the center of commercial television to construct and represent the complexity and diversity of African American life, *Frank's Place,* and later *Roc,* achieved similar results by stretching and recoding the conventions of situation comedy. *Frank's Place* achieved this departure precisely because African American culture and black American subjectivity were central to the show's content, aesthetic organization, setting, narrative, characters, and assumptions (Childs 1984).

In *Frank's Place* we see an attempt to rewrite and reposition African American culture and black subjectivities. By *rewriting* and *repositioning,* I refer to the strategy of appropriating (or reappropriating) existing formal, organizational, and aesthetic elements in the commercial culture in general and television in particular and refashioning them into different representations. These different representations often serve as alternatives to (and occasionally critique) the dominant forms of existing culture (Foster 1985; Williams 1977).

Television representations of blacks in *Frank's Place* activated African American perspectives that were historically experienced on television, through absence, silence, and invisibility. Because the televisual reality is dominated by "normative" representations of white middle-class subjectivities and perspectives, blacks and other communities of color have had to create and fill in the televisual spaces where African American representations might otherwise fit. For various sectors of the African American community, *Frank's Place* worked through affirmation rather than silence. And it was not just the fact that the show featured blacks at the level of character and setting. The show achieved this affirmative stance through its complex treatments of social class, gender, region, and tradition, all of which were rooted in an African American point of view.

In commercial television culture, where assumptions and representations of African Americans continue to operate largely within the limits of assimilationist and pluralist discourse, I regard *Frank's Place,* then, as a moment of displacement, an attempt to push the limits of existing television discourses about blacks. The representations on *Frank's Place* were expressions of the most recent struggles over the representations of race in general and blackness in particular.

The Social Production of *Frank's Place*

Frank's Place aired on CBS during the 1987–88 television season. The series was produced by co-executive producers Hugh Wilson and Tim Reid for Viacom Studios.[1] Reid and Wilson had developed a friendship and working relationship during their time on *WKRP in Cincinnati,* which Wilson produced and in which Reid starred; that collaboration and friendship led to the development of *Frank's Place* (Campbell and Reeves 1990).

The concept for the show was developed by Wilson, Reid, and the former CBS Television head of entertainment, Kim LeMasters. CBS had experienced a drop in ratings the previous season, and was willing to experiment a little and take a chance with an innovative show such as *Frank's Place.* Moreover, network executives were familiar with Wilson's record as a producer/writer/director and Reid's work in the successful series *WKRP in Cincinnati* and *Simon & Simon.* Indeed, Reid and Wilson were able to arrange a hands-off deal with CBS in most areas of the development and production of the series. This unusual amount of control afforded Wilson and Reid the opportunity to develop *Frank's Place* with minimal interference from network executives. It was an important element in the innovative (and risky) character of the show. One other manifestation of the control the producer had was that Wilson and Reid were able to make good on their commitment to hire a multiracial crew.

The central premise of the show was this: Frank Parrish (played by Reid), a professor of Renaissance history from Boston, inherited a New Orleans restaurant (Chez Louisiane) from his father. Parrish knew little about New Orleans and even less about managing a restaurant. Over the course of the series, we, along with Parrish, learned the nuances of managing a restaurant as well as various aspects of the New Orleans black community. The primary characters in the show included the staff at the restaurant: Miss Marie (played by Frances E. Williams), the "waitress emeritus," an elderly black woman; Big Arthur (Tony Burton), the black chef, and his white assistant, Shorty (Don Yesso); Anna-May (Francesca P. Roberts), a middle-aged black waitress; and Tiger (Charles Lampkin), the elderly black bartender, and his assistant, Cool Charles (William Thomas, Jr.), also black. The regular cast also included members of the local community: Mrs. Bertha Griffin-Lamour (Virginia Capers), a black funeral home director, and her daughter Hanna (Daphne Maxwell Reid); the Reverend Deal (Lincoln Kilpatrick), a colorful local black minister; and Bubba Weinberger (Robert Harper), a white lawyer.

Once the concept of the show was set, Wilson and Reid, as the producers and writers of *A Different World* had done with black colleges, took several trips to New Orleans to get a feel for the ambience and texture of life in that city. On these trips both Reid and Wilson visited with members of the local black community. They were especially interested in getting an interior sense of New Orleans from members of the black business community. Wilson likened their activities on these trips to those of oral historians.

After setting the story concept, Wilson established a certain look for the show, which he then allowed to dictate the writing, editing, and dramatic approaches. As producer, writer, and director, Wilson wanted to get as much of New Orleans on the television screen as he possibly could. This required that Wilson, also a film director, get away from the existing conventions of television direction, camera work, and lighting (Barker 1985).[2] As a result, he developed a self-consciously cinematic look for the show: shooting with film instead of videotape; treating the main camera as the major narrative voice, rather than using three cameras to achieve this as is usually done in television situation comedies; using a faster and crisper editing technique; eschewing the use of a studio audience's response augmented with sweeteners or a laugh track; and using original music (Barker 1985). To achieve the look that he and Reid wanted, Wilson was especially meticulous about lighting the show. He hired an award-winning film cinematographer—William A. Fraker—to shoot the pilot, and then worked to have the lighting on subsequent episodes approximate the look of the pilot. This look provided one of the consistent and defining qualities for the series.

The production schedule was even dictated by the look and feel that Wilson and Reid were trying to achieve. Thus, as Wilson described it, "We had to start shooting at seven o'clock in the morning. By then the lights were on. We just shot it film style. We'd rehearse it, shoot it, and shoot it out of order so they [the network] couldn't send anybody over. There was no run-through to see, and so consequently we were left totally free."[3] So, in addition to achieving the look of the show, this proved to be a clever strategy for maintaining control over the show's production.

Achieving the look and feel that Wilson and Reid wanted was an expensive proposition by television standards for half-hour situation comedies. *Frank's Place* cost $650,000 an episode to produce.[4] According to Wilson, the producers began the series at a deficit, because CBS paid Viacom only $425,000 to produce the show. In retrospect, Wilson believes that in part the commercial failure of the show, at least in terms of lack of network support and unwillingness to ride out the storm of early low ratings, was the result of the cost involved. At some point in the season, CBS executives decided that the costs and risks of producing *Frank's Place* were too high, and they decided "to cut their losses."[5]

Wilson and his production team's commitment to creating a different kind of show was evident not only in the aesthetic look and texture of the show's content, but also in the social relations of production used to make *Frank's Place*. The crew was multiracial and composed of both men and women. More important, the entire production team served an important function in monitoring the pulse of the show. The most immediate place (and impact) for the collaborative style that defined the show (especially with respect to the representations of black cultural perspectives) occurred among the writers, the crew, and the actors. In order for this collaborative relationship to work, Reid knew going in that it had to be based on shared power and respect:

> I didn't want to do a half hour of silliness. . . . It's not enough anymore for a black to be able to play parts written for whites. . . . Too often I've seen talented blacks gain some power, only to lose it because they are afraid that they won't be hired again if they write their kind of stories. . . . Hugh knew that the only way I'd do another half-hour show was if I had some control over it. (Buchalter 1988:8–9)

Wilson and Reid assembled a team of four writers, two of whom had previously worked with Wilson on other projects. For a short period there was one female on the team, although she did not work out. The fourth team member was Samm-Art Williams, the only black writer who wrote regularly for the show.

As described by Wilson, the writing for the show was truly collaborative, except that as chief writer he exercised final authority to shape a story:

> We would discuss these stories in a group. And we would talk and talk. And sometimes we would talk about a story for days and then decide to abandon it. But then if we had something we liked, whoever the writer was who had that assignment would then write an outline and we would all read the outline. And then talk that to death. Then the writer would write a draft and sometimes a second draft. Then he would give it to me and I would write the third draft. That's why the shows sort of have a singularity of viewpoint. Because they all, with the exception of one show, would come through my final filter.[6]

They did occasionally take scripts from outside the writing staff, but even these had to go through this process of refinement and collaboration by Wilson and his team.[7]

Finally, two important personal and biographical points about Wilson and Reid's role ought to be emphasized, as they specifically concern cultural sensibilities that appeared on *Frank's Place*. Both Reid and Wilson are southerners. Because Wilson grew up, was educated, and worked in the South (where he also participated in the civil rights movement), he (like Reid) remained sensitive to southern race relations as well as to the sensibilities that define African American culture there. Second, working with Tim Reid and other black members of the crew, Wilson not only trusted their input and their sensibilities (and sought them out), but seems to have been able to use his own position as a southern white male effectively to gauge the show's representations of black southern life and culture. This willingness to collaborate on such matters is important, especially in the production and presentation of black life in commercial television.

Critically, *Frank's Place* received rave reviews. It was hailed by television critics and the public as innovative and refreshing television. Because of the absence of a laugh track, the lack of traditional resolutions at the end of each episode, and the show's blending of comedy and drama, *Frank's Place* was referred to by many critics and industry observers as a "dramedy" (Campbell and Reeves 1990).[8] Unfortunately, the show failed to receive sufficient ratings throughout its run and was eventually canceled by CBS.[9] The final episode aired October

1, 1988. In January 1990, Black Entertainment Television began broadcasting all twenty-two episodes of *Frank's Place.*

The Place of *Frank's Place* in Television Discourses about Race

> I think blacks are looked upon in this country in a very peculiar way. . . . I don't think we are taken seriously as a group that has something to say in film or theater. . . . I think we're more apt to be accepted musically and in comedy.
>
> *Rosalind Cash*

Socially and aesthetically, the distinctive character of *Frank's Place* derived from a variety of historical, generic, and aesthetic elements: situation comedy, the workplace family, American racial memory, shows about region and location, and the tradition of black situation comedy. In *Frank's Place,* African American culture was central to the lives of the characters and the structure of the show. As I will discuss in the next section, this was the cultural and historical ground upon which the show operated. In this respect *Frank's Place* was different from other programs that form part of its lineage, including *The Cosby Show.* At the same time, *Frank's Place* must be read against these shows, their familiarity, advances, and silences (Gates 1989).

In addition to the history of black television shows, *Frank's Place* also drew on and remained in dialogue with the lineage of shows about place.[10] The culture and location of New Orleans were central to the show's identity. In *Frank's Place,* food, language, setting, dress, and music were used collectively to establish the centrality of black New Orleans to the theme and feel of the show.

Frank's Place also owed much of its formal character to a previous generation of television programs about the workplace and those that used comedy and drama innovatively in the half-hour format (Taylor 1989). Susan Harris's *Soap* and Norman Lear's *Mary Hartman, Mary Hartman* are often cited as the forerunners of the innovative use of comedy and drama in the comedic format, as well as the use of endings that lack resolution (Barker 1985; Feuer 1986; Newcomb and Alley 1983). The workplace family on *Frank's Place* was also similar to those found on *The Mary Tyler Moore Show, M*A*S*H, Barney Miller,* and *Cheers* (Feur 1987; Taylor 1989).

Frank's Place, then, formed part of the continuing strategy of interruption, adjustment, and appropriation in television representations of blackness. In terms of the discourse of Reaganism, it momentarily transformed and occasionally challenged dominant representations of black Americans in commercial network television.

Recoding African American Culture in *Frank's Place*

> In my neighborhood I saw people who I respected: the shopkeeper, the butcher, the cobbler . . . the man who used to come through and sharpen knives. . . . I never saw that on the screen.
>
> *Rosalind Cash*

What African American cultural sensibilities and practices are present in *Frank's Place*? First, compared with assimilationist and pluralist television discourses about blackness, the series was distinguished by its explicit recognition and presentation of the habits, practices, manners, nuances, and outlooks of black Americans located in New Orleans. In subtle matters of language, dress, sense of place, relationship to time, pace, and body movements (especially in nonverbal communication), the show expressed a distinct sensibility or "structure of feeling" (Williams 1977).

Consider the following scene from one episode: A group of white male New York corporate executives enter Chez Louisiane ("the Chez") for a late-night dinner meeting. They are dressed in business suits that signal their social class and professional status. They present themselves with the manner and demeanor of urban businessmen—formal, reserved, controlled. In a relaxed but deliberate manner, a young black waiter slowly approaches the table. In the process of taking the businessmen's orders, he strikes up a conversation. "Y'all from New York City?" he asks. "Yes," one of them replies. The waiter continues, "Thought so. My brother lives up there but he don't like it much." "How come?" asks one of the businessmen. "Because some dude knocked out his eye, that's how come," answers the waiter, who then goes on to disclose more details of the incident, its location, and so on to his surprised patrons.

This exchange is significant because it points up the contrast in language, pace, detail, and relationship to public talk between the white northern businessmen and the southern black man. Reading this scene from a white middle-class view, one might regard the waiter's behavior as slovenly, even rude. As a black American born and raised in the South, I see his behavior, in contrast to the public formality and reserve of the white professional businessmen, as black and southern. The young man does not think about his warrant to offer or solicit private information from these complete strangers. Rather, public talk is an assumed part of the folkways of the community where he lives. The businessmen are in the Chez and in New Orleans, which is the young black man's turf. They may be made uncomfortable by the exchange, but he is not.

As I have argued, in the content and structure of *Frank's Place,* in its setting, approach to production, organization of the cast, themes addressed (voodoo, jazz, basketball recruitment, homelessness), lie the elements and expressions of a distinctive African American orientation. Formally, viewers are positioned through the setting, the script, camera placement, editing, and coding to understand the show from the point of view of black New Orleans residents. We *must* negotiate the world of *Frank's Place* through the experiences of black subjects. In this sense the show is not simply didactic nor does it merely offer a voyeuristic tour of black experiences that disempowers or exoticizes black subjects.

Because *Frank's Place* explicitly operated from an African American subject position, the multiracial cast (and viewing audience) remained grounded in assumptions and perspectives that structured an African American reality. To make sense of and appreciate the show, viewers (especially whites and others outside of this specific cultural milieu) could not simply operate outside of the "structure of feeling" that defined the show. The white members of the cast, Shorty (the cook) and Bubba (the lawyer), participated as full members of this community. In language, habits, and assumptions they actively participated in the cultural definitions and sensibilities that ordered the world of *Frank's Place*.[11]

The show's setting also expressed elements of an African American structure of feeling. The historical and social significance of New Orleans in the American past (slavery) and the origins of black American music were represented and repeatedly reinforced through the musical and visual montage that opened the show. This montage worked viscerally to establish New Orleans as a specific cultural and social location and African Americans as a significant cultural community.[12] The tightly edited collection of sepia-toned stills of New Orleans life included scenes of riverboats, the Mississippi River, Louis Armstrong, the Preservation Hall Jazz Band, the French Quarter, and Congo Square. These scenes moved rapidly across the screen to the strains of Louis Armstrong's classic recording of "Do You Know What It Means to Miss New Orleans?" The combined effect was to place the viewer aurally and visually into the experience of black New Orleans. In representing this space and place, the producers foregrounded African American New Orleans, thereby situating the program's location and identity within a particular African American formation. *Frank's Place* is not just Anywhere, USA, populated by anonymous folk, but black New Orleans, with its own particular history and story.

Food was also central to the program's identity. The cuisine featured was Creole (rather than the French Canadian-derived cajun, which enjoyed a period of trendy culinary popularity in the mid-1980s). The centrality of food to the show and its location within African American culture was revealed in a telling scene in an episode (described below) on African musicians and jazz: Upon their arrival at the Chez, a group of touring African musicians are treated to dinner. After dinner, the guests are given a tour of the kitchen and are introduced to the staff. Immediate rapport and cultural commonality is established between the musicians and the staff of the Chez through their discussions (and lessons) about food, especially those they have in common. In the dialogue between the two groups, the symbolic connections (and distinctions) between Africans and African Americans are established.

Also central to the explicit establishment of the show's preferred cultural point of view were nuances about the people and socioeconomic characteristics of the community. Indeed, I think it is significant that the restaurant was a small black business located in a black working-class community (rather than in the French Quarter) and frequented mainly by blacks. The complex class character of the program was explored in an early episode: Frank asks Tiger, the bartender, about the absence of local restaurant patrons during the middle of the week, and Tiger tells him, "These are all working people in our neighborhood, they don't go out to dinner on weeknights. White folks are afraid to come down here after dark." Here is a simple and clear observation rendered from the viewpoint of a working member of a community who knows his customers and his neighborhood.

By highlighting aspects of working-class life in New Orleans, the show moved a considerable distance from other programs contained by "normative" middle-class cultural sensibilities.[13] With its serious, ironic, and humorous explorations of issues such as drug abuse, sports, voodoo, middle-class status, and homelessness, *Frank's Place* tilted toward a more noble and serious representation of black working-class experience. The aspirations, pressures, joys, and troubles of waiters, cooks, and regular folk were represented with integrity rather than with the derision, exaggeration, and marginalization that too often are found in other television representations of blacks and working-class people. Finally, although set in a working-class context, the show moved among various class positions and experiences even as it addressed tensions among them.[14]

What distinguished the uses of cuisine, language, and music in *Frank's Place* from those found in other programs with similar themes and contributed to their status as expressions of an African American "structure of feeling"? These elements were the subjects of various episodes and, more significant, they consistently provided the context and setting for action. In at least one episode each, food and music were dominant themes. Formally, music was used, as it has been used conventionally in television, to begin and end each episode as well as to suggest emotion, cue action, and segue from scene to scene. The show's particular use of black popular musical forms such as blues, jazz, and rhythm and blues reproduced the central role of music in African American culture. Music was a constant in the show—it was always there, whether formally as a background device, on the jukebox as entertainment, or as the subject of an episode.

What is more, *Frank's Place* was one of the few series on commercial network television (along with *The Cosby Show*) that actively used blues and jazz performed by original artists in settings like those found in black communities. Reid and Wilson's commitment to presenting original music by Louis Armstrong, Lightnin' Hopkins, Jimmy Reed, Slim Gaillard, Slam Stewart, B. B. King, Muddy Waters, and Dizzy Gillespie represents a rare moment when commercial network television treated African American music as a cultural resource and the African American musician as a cultural hero.

Aside from these formal uses, black music was also the major motif of at least one episode. Written by novelist, playwright, and screenwriter Samm-Art Williams, this episode brought members of an African music and dance troupe to the Chez. During their New Orleans visit, one of the troupe's members (Adele), a master African musician and devout jazz lover, discovers that Dizzy Gillespie is scheduled to perform in town. As the narrative develops it is revealed that Adele is so enamored of jazz that he plans to defect to the United States in order to play here professionally.

Viewed against marginalization and trivialization of things African by the dominant commercial media, this was an unusual moment in American commercial network television representations of blacks. I find this representation especially interesting because the narrative is underwritten by a recognition of the hybrid relationship between the musics, cultures, foods, and customs of African Americans and Africans.[15] The representation of Adele's desire to play jazz with Dizzy Gillespie is especially significant in this regard. By structuring the story around Adele's desire to play with Gillespie, the narrative stages and enacts this syncretic understanding of the historic dialogue between black Caribbean, African, and American traditions. And this relationship is of course realized in the fact that Gillespie was the first major black jazz man to incorporate African and Afro-Caribbean influences into his music (Gillespie and Fraser 1979).[16]

At the level of narrative content, *Frank's Place,* like *A Different World,* explored an extraordinary range of themes—homelessness, greed and exploitation, basketball recruitment, voodoo, music, and personal relationships, to name a few. The program's critical appeal and aesthetic innovation owed much to this rich thematic range. Aside from the explicit representations of African American culture, the jazz episode stands out for its attempt at cross-cultural dialogue and the location of living African American cultural practices (food, music, dance) at the center of the narrative.

An episode about the college recruitment of a black high school All-American basketball player (Calvin) addressed issues—sports, education, masculinity—"relevant" to significant segments within black communities. The show examined the aspirations and complicated connections between Calvin and a white middle-aged recruiter named Chick, exploring the stakes, excesses, confusion, exploitation, and competition involved in the recruitment of black high school athletes. By using humor and irony to focus on the exploitation and absurdity of the athletic recruitment game, the episode called attention to the need for community resources to help Calvin (and countless others like him) through this process, the politics of recruiting, the balance between academics and public relations, excessive hype and reliable information, and the destiny of young black athletes.

The narrative, organized as a montage, follows Calvin's initial recruitment through the announcement of his selection of a college. The visual montage (risky for the genre of situation comedy) is presented from the vantage points of the various people (and interests) involved in the recruitment process—the athlete (Calvin), the adviser (Frank), the coach, the recruiter (Chick), and the athlete's mother. By moving from one perspective to another, we learn the motives of the various people involved. From the varying angles of these different interests we come to appreciate the enormous pressures, frustrations, and risks of exploitation that young black athletes like Calvin face.[17]

This episode is unusually explicit about the racial exploitation and arrogance that accompany the circus atmosphere of college athletic recruitment. In this exchange between two elderly black women, Calvin's mother and Miss Marie (one of the major characters in the show), notice the sense of personal and cultural violation felt by these women at the hands of insensitive white male recruiters:

CALVIN'S MOTHER: Some [recruiters] just write, but others, they

> call my house all hours of the day and night.
> They drive by my house.

MISS MARIE: And they even come by the church.

CALVIN'S MOTHER: Yeah! All these white men dropping money
in the collection plate so I can see.

This exchange reveals the clash of cultures and the different assumptions that order each world. Viewers are forced to choose sides, with those who identify and sympathize with these women quickly becoming suspicious of the recruiters and impatient with the process. Emotionally, the suspicion, impatience, and identification with the plight of these elderly women constitute an articulation of the episode's critique of the recruitment process, especially the precarious terms on which decisions about the futures of black youngsters rest.

A number of other qualities from this episode suggest its operation and location within black American cultural perspectives. As Calvin's adviser, Frank, the middle-class former university professor, represents many of the concerns of a black parent about to send a young adult to college—ratio of students to faculty, ratio of blacks to whites, school population, background of the students, graduation rates for black athletes. Significantly, Frank also mentions "the small, all-black college" as an option for Calvin. Although much of this seems lost on Calvin, I suspect it was not lost on black viewers, especially those for whom historically black colleges remain a major route to higher education.[18]

When taken together these explicit articulations of concerns relevant to black Americans reveal elements of African American experiences that are usually silent and absent in American commercial network television. It is not enough that such concerns are explicitly mentioned, however; it is in the specific selection, organization, and use of these elements that their legitimacy and resonance operate.

Frank's Place and the Limits of Television Representation of African American Culture

Although Frank's Place's rewriting of African American representations in commercial network television offered alternatives to dominant representations, there are limits even to this most hopeful set of representations. As with A Different World, after all, the series operated within the slippery and contested terrain of commercial television. Therefore, even this welcome corrective did not constitute a complete break (Foster 1985; Taylor 1988). As Frank's Place pressed the limits of dramatic and comedic television representations of black Americans, it illustrated the hegemonic strategies of containment operating in the commercial television system. Thus, although it challenged conventional aesthetic and generic boundaries and offered new ways to represent aspects of black life in the United States, *Frank's Place* did not survive in the high-stakes world of commercial popularity.

In addition to its muted commercial appeal, the show's critical insights were often contained and limited. For example, in its incisive critique of high school basketball recruitment, it was not clear where the critique was directed—the college recruitment system, urban public schools that produce students like Calvin, parents, individual recruiters, individual coaches, or students. And in an episode on homelessness, a sympathetic and insightful portrait of a homeless person is drawn, but the question of homelessness as a complex social problem remains essentially Frank's moral problem.

Within this structure of containment the character of Frank is important. It was usually Frank who expressed critical insight and moral outrage. He expressed these responses in a variety of ways—by looking away from Reverend Deal's indiscretions in disgust, by sanctioning Cool Charles for his errant drug dealings, by judging Bubba's need to mislead his family into thinking that he and Frank are involved in a homosexual relationship to get out of a difficult situation. Frank, the sophisticated but naive college professor, represents the critique and strategies for change. (Consistent with the conventions of character development in commercial television, Frank was not infallible; he too suffered loss, disappointment, and bad judgment. See Fiske 1987.)

Significantly, the show was also contained by the social and cultural limitations of a social order in which racism, social inequality, and deep suspicions of cultural differences remain. (And here I would include constraints, e.g., sexuality, within black social formations.) *Frank's Place* required its audience to engage directly the issue of cultural difference. The show also demanded competence, patience, and engagement to produce pleasure and maintain interest. The narrative structure, thematic approach, and cinematic look of the show disturbed the normal television experience. Given the institutional and market structure of commercial network television at the time, *Frank's Place* may have required too much work; it may have asked too much of an audience for which African American culture remained a fuzzy and distant experience. In this sense the show's commercial failure shaped the focus on black audiences at the same time it pushed the networks and their program suppliers toward more conventional shows featuring blacks.

The commercial failure of *Frank's Place* resecured the center of the genre of situation comedy, rather than inviting explorations of the margins. It reinforced the limited terms within which the general American television audience can explore the interiors of black social and cultural life. *Frank's Place*'s daring but short life, perhaps, is the exception that proves the rule in commercial television as it concerns blacks: representations of African Americans will remain an active part of American commercial television offerings to the extent that they remain contained, nonthreatening, and familiar (Gray 1993c; White 1991).

Postscript: *Roc* and the Legacy of *Frank's Place*

It should come as no surprise that the most pleasurable and innovative program to occupy the discursive televisual space opened by *Frank's Place* found a permanent home on the upstart Fox television network. In its look, engagement, and representation of blackness, *Roc*'s relationship to its precursor is apparent, especially in the sepia-toned stills of Baltimore that open the show, the consummate acting and writing, and the rich themes it explores from the interiors of black working-class life. As on *Frank's Place,* the production credits that frame the show are accompanied by theme music that is identifiably and historically black, in this case the a cappella voices of Take Six and the Persuasions. Together, the music and the visual montage bathe Baltimore and the *Roc* cast in the rich and vibrant tones of African American life and culture. *Roc* stars Charles S. Dutton and includes an ensemble cast who worked in the Broadway stage production of August Wilson's *Fences.* The show debuted on Fox in the fall of 1991.

Roc revolves around the lives of Roc Emerson and his extended family (father, wife, brother) at home and work. Roc is a garbage collector, his wife is a nurse, his father is retired, and his brother, a musician, is often between jobs or unemployed. The show's action is staged in a variety of settings, including the workplace, the neighborhood bar, and the home.

In the middle of the second season, *Roc* changed its method of production from the usual videotaping (edited for broadcast) to live presentation (taped without edit for broadcast). This daring throwback, for situation comedy anyway, to the early days of television brings out the best in the theatrically trained ensemble, because the live format approximates the world of live theater to which they are accustomed.

On the face of it, the claim that *Roc* continues the innovations of *Frank's Place* may seem premature, if not overblown. In fact, this was precisely the response of a female African American student in my media class one quarter when I offered *Roc* as an example of television's innovative treatments of African Americans. After all, she argued rather forcefully, when there are still precious few "serious" and "positive" images of blacks on television, how could I possibly celebrate a show that revolves around a garbage collector, especially considering that this is a step backward from the two professionals depicted on *The Cosby Show*? I suppose she might have added that *Roc* departs very little from the standard television preoccupation with home-place domesticity. And, no doubt, she would have been right.

But I want to make such a claim on behalf of *Roc* in terms of its particular construction and representation of blackness, its explicit position of address from the perspective of black working-class experiences, and the range of issues and themes that it takes up. Indeed, very much in the tradition of *Frank's Place, Roc* moves quite a way toward constructing and representing the integrity, frustration, and joys of black working-class men and women who have histories, politics, conflicts, and hopes. And it does so without reducing these complexities to normative white middle-class frames of familiarity and comfort. This is the discursive televisual space opened by *Frank's Place* and formerly occupied by *Roc*.

A consideration of some of the significant themes explored in *Roc*'s first two seasons suggests that it did not shrink from confronting complex social and personal issues. Among the significant episodes of the first two seasons were those that took on questions about gender and family relationships, police harassment of black men, sexuality, community, and gangs.

Among the most memorable episodes, and those most emblematic of the show's complex rendering of issues facing many African Americans, are two that addressed gangs and sexuality, respectively. The episode on gangs aired March 29, 1992, and guest-starred rapper Tone Loc as one of *Roc*'s neighbors. The episode directly engaged the question of how a black working-class community responds to the presence of drug dealers in their neighborhood. Without resorting to sentimentality or utopian happy endings, the episode pondered questions of collective and individual responsibility; the effectiveness of strategies such as violence, negotiation, and confrontation; and the frustration, pain, and ambivalence of living in such an untenable situation. When the drug dealers appear at Roc's door essentially to call a truce, the episode culminates in a dramatic confrontation between them and Roc. After the drug dealers threaten Roc and his family, Roc responds in kind. Still, Tone Loc offers Roc the option of violence as a way of dealing with the situation. The episode ends with the drug dealers deciding to abandon the neighborhood, but, of course, their flight really ends nothing because, as the episode clearly suggests, they will simply appear in another neighborhood to terrorize another group of African American residents.

This episode is very direct in staging these complex and passionate issues in clear terms. The dealers are black youth; their brutality and exploitation are not sidestepped, nor are Roc and his family's deep feelings of anger, violation, and urgency. A few seasons earlier, on *Amen,* the treatment of a similar issue culminated in a utopian happy ending, with gang members and members of the church congregation together in church, singing the praises of unity; in contrast, the *Roc* episode ends on a more sanguine and complex note. In this episode *Roc* directly confronts the feelings, situations, and limited options available to hardworking African American men and women who routinely face such threats to and encroachments on their security. Although Roc and the members of his family are clearly frightened, they refuse to be victims or victimized by such assaults on their lives and community (see Zook 1994). (A similar position was staked out in another *Roc* episode on police harassment of African American men.)

The other episode of *Roc* that clearly sets it apart from other television constructions of blackness aired on February 2, 1993. This episode, which addressed questions of race, sexuality, and masculinity, guest-starred Richard Roundtree as Roc's uncle, Russell. Estranged from his family for several years, Russell turns up at Roc's house to announce his marriage and to seek the blessings of Roc's family, especially Roc's father, Russell's brother. The dramatic tension is established when Russell announces that he is gay, his lover is white, and they plan to get married. This announcement sends the men in the household, especially Russell's brother (clearly a heterosexual and a race man), into a tizzy. Although it is not clear which offends them most, Roc, his brother, and especially his father are as surprised about the homosexuality as they are angered by the prospect of the interracial marriage. Whereas Roc's and his brother's anger and surprise eventually turn to ambivalence, even tolerance, Roc's father remains adamant in his anger and disapproval. At one point, Roc's father removes a photo of Malcolm X from the wall, commenting in the process that Malcolm shouldn't be subjected to such (unmanly and nonblack) behavior. Only Roc's wife shows any understanding and accepts the situation; she even suggests—insists, really—that the wedding be held at their home. In the end, as might be expected, the ceremony proceeds as planned. After many conversations and much anxiety about masculinity and sexuality, both Roc and his brother remain ambivalent but finally accept Russell's choice. At the very last minute, even Roc's father joins the ceremony, but the episode makes it clear that his change of heart is less about approval of Russell's choices than it is about his desire not to lose his brother. It is also clear that Russell will have the ceremony, with or without his brother's blessing.

I single out this episode because it is one of the few television shows about blacks, if any, that has dealt seriously with issues of sexuality, race, and masculinity from the perspective of working-class African Americans. In a stroke of brilliance, the producers cast Richard Roundtree as Russell. Roundtree, of course, is identified with the character Shaft, who, during the blaxploitation period of black cinema, represented the ultimate cinematic expression of black heterosexual virility (Guerrero 1993). By casting Roundtree as a gay black man in an interracial relationship, the producers both represented and then deconstructed black film constructions of black masculinity and heterosexuality. In this one move, they were able to mobilize and engage effectively an entire discourse of blackness, and under the full glare of television's spotlight at that.

By pulling together male homosexuality and race under the sign of a heterosexual institution such as marriage, the episode also engaged multiple and intersecting assumptions about racial propriety, heterosexual normalcy, and the power relations that underwrite them. Finally, by extending her blessings and inviting the besieged couple into her home, Roc's wife plays an especially significant role. The relationships among sexuality, race, and gender are complex and are rarely, if ever, acknowledged and addressed in television constructions and representations of African Americans. That they were taken up and explored in this way on a television series about African Americans is surely notable.

In a medium such as television, program makers and networks almost inevitably turn to formulaic and predictable stories to get them through the middle years of a series run, when ideas can be difficult to generate. It is simply easier and often more efficient to rework new variations on old themes. *Frank's Place* didn't last long enough to get to this point. *In Living Color* seems to have reached it already, and as it got older (and more successful), *The Cosby Show* increasingly relied on cuter and more precocious kids for laughs and story lines. As I write this, *Roc* is completing its third and, as it turns out, final season. My sense, perhaps more accurately my hope, was that *Roc* had enough in its brief but rich past, including its genealogical relationship to *Frank's Place* and its impressive fidelity to African American life, that it would continue in production for some time, and not turn on itself and become a weak and desperate parody of itself. What I did not count on, or expect, was that, like *Frank's Place*, *Roc* would end its run prematurely because of low ratings.

8 Spectacles, Sideshows, and Irreverence: In Living Color

I want to offer the case of *In Living Color* to foreground a cultural politics of representation that uses irreverence, satire, and spectacle to engage issues of multiculturalism and diversity within blackness. I also offer the show to highlight often-disturbing questions about the effects of such strategies for black cultural politics. I want to link the range of meanings activated by the show (and the response it generates) to broad social, cultural, and political discourses about race, sexuality, class, and gender.[1] I suggest ultimately that *In Living Color* discursively enacts a cultural politics of representation that settles around a position of ambivalence. For some, this ambivalence contests hegemonic assumptions and representations of race in general and blacks in particular in the American social order; for others, it simply perpetuates troubling images of blacks (Barlow and Dates 1990; Schulman 1992).

For many critics and admirers alike, the popular appeal and commercial success of *In Living Color* stem from its ability to appeal to audiences across a very broad gulf of racial, class, gender, and sexual difference. Indeed, the show's creator, its producer, a former black male writer, scholars, and critics seem to agree that it is the show's transgressive use of the trope of race that allows it to reconfigure audiences that are differently positioned socially. If this crossover appeal is the source of celebration, it is also the source of considerable angst and criticism. In the end, it is this constant negotiation and rearticulation that account for the show's often biting satire and its ambivalence. Both are essential for the show's commercial appeal, its cultural resonance, and its effects.

What is the show ambivalent about? It is ambivalent about representations of blackness that often come at the expense of the black working class and the poor; it is sometimes ambivalent about its representation of black difference even as it critiques white racism; it is ambivalent about gayness in the black community even when it satirizes effeminate black gay men; and it is ambivalent about black women as it reverses the terms of power in and of gender relations. Attributing this ambivalence to the disciplining power of television's commercial imperatives, Schulman (1992) puts the matter quite clearly with the suggestion that the show's "ambiguity gives it bimodal appeal—a quality deemed all-important in a commercial medium for whom the aggregate minority viewing audience is insufficient in itself to garner the kinds of ratings that yield substantial revenue" (p. 2). Dates and Barlow (1990) also indicate that sophisticated black urban viewers have cultivated a tolerance of this ambivalence, given that they too very much enjoy the show.

Ambiguity is most clearly expressed in the show's mobilization and representation, perhaps even critique, of historic stereotypes of African Americans and its parody of images of the "black underclass" with characters such as Frenchy, Anton, Benita Betrell, and the Homeboys. Even though these and other continuing characters are represented through parody and satire, the very presence of these characters (as well as the multiracial cast) set in African American contexts constantly forces viewers to jockey for a "reading position": Are these representations merely instances of inside jokes, to which African Americans have some exclusive claims? Are the show's representations harmless fun? Are the representations (and the organizations and people responsible for them) simply complicit in perpetuating stereotypical and ultimately derogatory images of African Americans? Are these representations so spectacular and exaggerated that in the end they inevitably expose and criticize the absurdity of all forms of bigotry?

Because the show's representations, the viewers and subject positions they organize, and social discourses in which they are embedded all have differently structured histories and power relations, the available social positions from which to make sense of the show are not equivalent in some pluralist sense. Schulman (1992:3) suggests, correctly I think, that the presence and assumed power of the white viewer are important to the show's representations. Within television's own discourse some viewing positions are simply more socially privileged, more economically valuable, more culturally legitimate than others. Hence, whether the images of race, gender, and sexuality in the show are complicitous with domination, critical of it, or just harmless fun rests not so much with the images and representations alone, but with the ways these images, especially the historic and contemporary meanings they carry and understandings they express, are aligned and realigned with the discourses examined in chapters 2 and 3.

In Living Color, then, requires or depends on differently positioned audiences, social and cultural discourses, and television itself for its meanings. In the end, the show's representations and the meanings they organize are inherently neither progressive nor reactionary; instead, they are potentially both, depending on how they are taken up, by whom, and under what social conditions. I am especially interested in how the representations on *In Living Color* articulate, disarticulate, and rearticulate the social location and cultural meanings of blackness in terms of black popular discourses, Reaganism, and the vectors of sexuality, gender, and class. Because *In Living Color*'s cultural significance and political potential rest with its articulations of different discourses and social positions, the show is necessarily full of contradictions.

In Living Color's social contradictions and political ambivalence on issues of sexuality, gender, race, and social class have as much to do with the fact that these issues are the focus of contention and debate in the social and cultural arena as with the producer's intentions.[2] And as such, they are grist for the ever-voracious television mill. Therefore, in considering its cultural politics, we might approach the show in terms of the ways it interrupts and reconfigures key images (masculinity, class, morality) in the chain of associations that organize the representations and cultural meanings of "blackness" and the social construction of blacks in U.S. society (Hall 1989; Mercer 1992).

I want, therefore, to consider the show and the representations it offers as an intervention in television constructions of blackness, an intervention that, at its best, disturbs existing regimes of representation of blackness and, at its worst, provides the cultural terms through which racial subordination is legitimated and reproduced. The show might be approached as a kind of cultural forum or site within which a kind of collective public pondering might take place (Newcomb and Hirsch 1983), pondering, that is, of the various ways of engaging, representing, even contesting race in American popular culture. This view of television as negotiated space—that is, for struggling over meanings—is conceptually rooted in the claim that television occupies a central space in practices of everyday life where important social encounters and cultural transformations are possible (Fiske 1989; Fiske and Hartley 1978; Lipsitz 1990b; Newcomb 1984). Thus, it is not so much television's specific treatment or approach to a particular topic that I want to privilege analytically as the social role and cultural ritual that commercial television performs in constructing a public site within which and over which struggles and negotiations over meanings occur (Fiske 1989; Newcomb and Hirsch 1983).

The Social Production of Race

Because *In Living Color* formally depends on a complex ensemble of black cultural practices—music, media images, dance, language, dress, style, urban youth culture—it realigns and balances different racially organized subject positions. Some of the show's appeal (and distinction from programs that are assimilationist and pluralist) rests with its, often troubling, rendering and interrogation of the complex relations and locations of black life. I have in mind here the intersections of sexuality, social class, gender, status, mobility, region, and age. Most often these positions and the tensions they signal are expressed through parody, satire, and irony.

It should come as no surprise that Fox is the television network on which *In Living Color* is aired; Fox also provides production facilities for the show (Braxton 1990). As the newest network in an industry facing declining network television viewers, Fox was in a position to take a programming risk with a show like *In Living Color*. Given the dramatic changes at the networks noted in chapter 4, Fox established its competitive position with a repertoire of low-cost and occasionally innovative programming. Executives at Fox (who were drawn from other networks and film studios in Hollywood and New York) initially sought to challenge the aesthetic complacency and organizational hegemony of the other three networks with original programming coupled with a tightly managed, well-planned operation. But, as Block (1990a) details, this strategy was not without its problems. In its early months the network experienced program cancellations, cost overruns, internal management battles, and feuds between stars and executives, all of which initially threatened Fox's ability to establish a stable presence in the industry.[3]

The Fox Broadcasting Company debuted with a limited program schedule. With its accumulated record of risky (e.g., *The Joan Rivers Show* and later *The Arsenio Hall Show*), innovative (e.g., *The Simp-*

sons, True Colors, Married . . . with Children), and, yes, uninspired shows (e.g., the 1990 broadcast of the Academy Award ceremonies), the network was not looking to win the ratings wars or immediately displace the dominance of the big three networks. Given its modest aim of establishing an identifiable network image and a small but profitable market niche, it is understandable why Fox would take a risk with an unconventional comedy-variety show about blacks with an unproven executive producer and a largely unknown multiracial cast (Zook 1994).

Keenen Ivory Wayans attracted the attention of Fox executives with his film *I'm Gonna Git You Sucka* and his work with Robert Townsend (on Townsend's movie *Hollywood Shuffle*).[4] Wayans's production credits also included cowriter and costar of Robert Townsend's *Partners in Crime* and cowriter and coproducer of Eddie Murphy's comedy film *Raw*. His foray into television as an executive producer also coincided with increased industry interest in black television directors, writers, and producers (and audiences). Like *A Different World* and *Fresh Prince of Bel Air, In Living Color* benefited from network television's attempt to capitalize on the commercial success of black youth culture, especially the popularity of rap and black cinema. The modest success of Wayans's own film and the successes of Spike Lee, the Hudlin brothers, John Singleton, and Robert Townsend helped generate television interest in the aesthetic and market potentials of shows about blacks.

This climate, together with the title of executive producer, gave Wayans control over all aspects of *In Living Color,* especially in hiring writers, selecting materials, assembling the cast and production crew, and generally defining the direction and look of the show. During its first two seasons, *In Living Color*'s nine-member cast included two whites (Kelly Coffield and James Carrey) and seven blacks (David Alan Grier, Tommy Davidson, Crystal Keymah, Damon Wayans, Kim Wayans, Shawn Wayans, and Keenen Ivory Wayans). Wayans also assembled a multiracial production team that included Paul Miller, a veteran director from *Saturday Night Live;* Tamara Rawitt, the show's producer, who previously ran Eddie Murphy's production company; and Franklyn Ajaye, a veteran stand-up comedian and comedy writer (Braxton 1990:88). These conditions and Fox's position as an unproven network entity provided Wayans with considerable creative control over his show.

In addition to production and casting, Wayans's defining vision is also evidenced, for example, by the high profile of rap music (from the most acceptable to the most offensive) on the show, the ability to get controversial materials past the network censors, and, perhaps most important, an irreverent approach that includes the willingness to satirize almost anything, especially controversial events and public personalities.

As in his film *I'm Gonna Git You Sucka,* parody is at the heart of Wayans's approach. He told one reporter, "You know, the thing is that parody for black people is a new thing. . . . it's hard for black people to understand that you're just making fun of them. If you're in the limelight, you become fair game. Whatever is public, is public. But a lot of people take it personal" (quoted in R. E. Childs 1992:64). The show's producer, Tamara Rawitt, shares Wayans's commitment to parody and satire, putting the matter of its use in somewhat more political terms: "The humor can work on a very subliminal level, and it is saying a lot of unsayable things. . . . However prevalent racism is, it's still a taboo topic. But through comedy, we're cleverly allowing certain things to come through. We're saying it still exists, and it has to be eradicated before progress can be made" (Braxton 1990:88).

Along with these organizational and institutional conditions of production, *In Living Color*'s appearance on commercial network television was enabled by a number of related social circumstances. In television the commercial success and dominance of *The Cosby Show* in the 1980s and the aesthetic impact of *Frank's Place* (and the public outcry stimulated by its cancellation) are two of the more obvious ones. I would also note the influence on *In Living Color* of such comedy-variety shows as *Saturday Night Live* and *SCTV* (*Second City Television*).[5] SCTV and especially the long-running *Saturday Night Live* revitalized and helped maintain the commercial and aesthetic vitality of the genre and within it the use of impersonation, parody, and satire as vehicles for social commentary and the exploration of topical issues. What is significant about *In Living Color*'s initial success as well is its use of the genre and its strategies of representation to explore African American social and cultural life.[6]

As I have suggested, *In Living Color* was also enabled by and linked to a rich storehouse of political and social discourses. I include here hotly contested intellectual and political debates among African Americans, especially the reemergence of various strains of nationalism (including the cultural force of the Nation of Islam in the symbolism and aesthetics of rap and hip-hop); debates over multiculturalism, affirmative action, and political correctness on college campuses; debates about gender relations, feminism, and sexuality; and contentions over the agenda and direction of black political strategies and aspirations. Jesse Jackson's presidential candidacy, Louis Farrakhan's musings on the state of black America, the rise of new conservative voices in the black community, and the Senate confirmation hearings on Clarence Thomas's nomination to the U.S. Supreme Court were all, at one time or another, the subject of sketches on the show.

The Politics of Representation

In Living Color is not only inserted in hotly contested discourses about blackness; through television itself, it constitutes part of these discourses. That is to say, these discourses, especially their circulation in commercial culture through a show such as *In Living Color,* provide a space within which the voracious (and of late floundering) commercial network television industry can address themes of African American life in the United States. *In Living Color's* register and appeal as a form of popular commercial culture, then, do not rest just with its treatment of a given topic or its formal and aesthetic strategies of representation, but with the way these treatments configure, draw on, and reconfigure within the representational space of television the kinds of issues and debates circulating in the society.

Indeed, it is precisely the show's position within these debates and its representation of such debates that have fueled some of the controversy surrounding the show, especially during its first year. At the center of the controversy is the question of the show's politics, especially its responsibility in constructing and representing images of blacks. Disturbing questions about *In Living Color* have been raised by viewers, scholars, journalists, even members of the show's writing staff. The most visible and outspoken of these has been Franklyn Ajaye, one of the show's black writers during its first season. Although the show's producer has described the writing process as "highly communal and open," she also has admitted that "once in a while, there might be someone who doesn't have a true cultural perspective of the black experience" (Braxton 1990:88). Ajaye's problems, however, have not been with the show's lack of commitment to an African American cultural perspective, but with the show's conception and representation of that experience—in other words, its cultural politics. Ajaye has voiced these concerns publicly. In one interview, for example, he claimed that

> whites for the most part like the show, but there's more ambivalence about it in the black community. They [blacks] would say, "Hey I like some of it, but I wish they wouldn't do this, or I wish they wouldn't do that." They think it's a good, a clever show, but they have a problem with some of the images. These were people in the 35–40 range, and I told them the show was not conceived with them in mind. It's aimed at viewers 14–25. (quoted in Braxton 1990:87)

Although he has been careful to couch his concerns and disagreements in creative terms that do not indict the show or its creators, Ajaye has remained steadfast. As he put it, "This whole urban rap thing needs to be pulled back some. . . . [The] ghetto is being glorified, and there's nothing good about the ghetto except getting out of one" (Braxton 1991:4). Given *In Living Color*'s target audience, Ajaye seemed most disturbed by the show's refusal to, at the very least, stake out a clear position with respect to the images it constructs. He believes that the show, and its producers and writers, have some responsibility to "instruct and guide" viewers. He attempted to offer some such guidance in a sketch that featured Tommy Davidson as a young black urban b-boy (rapper) who wound up on the endangered species list. The politically astute Ajaye included a line in the sketch explaining that young black males were endangered because of "homeboy poaching" ("They were being killed for their sneakers," he explained to a *Los Angeles Times* reporter; see Braxton 1990:88), but the line was dropped because the producers thought that it was too serious and too depressing for the sketch. According to press reports, Ajaye and the show's producers mutually agreed to a parting of the ways because Ajaye felt that he could not consistently and responsibly generate the kind of youth-based humor that is the staple of the show.[7]

In ways chillingly reminiscent of the *Amos 'n' Andy* controversy in the 1950s, Ajaye's public statements about *In Living Color* struck a nerve among black middle-class professionals, educators, and critics. In fact, his public statements generated enough attention that Wayans felt it important to respond to criticism about the show's images and its aims. Wayans told *Los Angeles Times* television reporter Greg Braxton: "If you have a black point of view, you're damned if you show the bad side and you're damned if you don't. We have the same diversity as any other show. We don't dwell on the homeboys for 30 minutes. We also have black professionals, people in suits" (quoted in Braxton 1990:87). When talking to people who ask him to present more positive role models, Wayans said, "I ask them what they view as positive? And how do you do a positive parody? People expect miracles in the wrong places. This show isn't going to change the world. It may have an effect, but the only thing that can change the world is the government, and the government controls the media" (p. 87). Wayans's comments here seem surprisingly apolitical, even naive, for one who created and produced such a controversial show.

To be sure, there are political lines that *In Living Color* draws, and there are stances that it takes, but the meanings the show organizes and registers are *relational*. They do not inhere in the text, and they are socially constructed, not politically determined. The politics that are enacted are therefore deeply conflicted and often contradictory. *In Living Color*'s politics range from *critical* (e.g., a sketch that parodied credit card commercials and featured a black man who could get a credit card, but who then found the card did not shield him from the suspicions and racism encountered daily by middle-class blacks) to *ambivalent* (e.g., the collection of sketches called "Men on . . . ") to *transgressive* (e.g., the various sketches featuring Homey the Clown, Anton the homeless man, and Handi-man, a physically challenged superhero) to *irreverent* (e.g., sketches featuring underclass black women gossips, Rick James, Louis Farrakhan, Arsenio Hall, Oprah Winfrey, Marion Barry, Jesse Jackson). In fact, for all its biting humor, the show still maintains a *utopian* vision. It leaves viewers "with an affirmation, a sense that there are signs that someday . . . there will be a time when prejudice [will be] obsolete, a time when at night it might be safe to walk down the street" (Schulman 1992:5).

Seen from the vantage point of the various discourses that enable *In Living Color* and in which it is positioned, a wide range of themes are figured. Among the most significant are *sexuality* (e.g., the "Men on . . . " sketches, sketches featuring Prince), *masculinity and gender relations* (e.g., sketches about a female animal trainer who trains men and advises women on how best to control [black] men in relationships), *racism* (e.g., sketches that make white guilt the focus of humor), *racial identity* (e.g., sketches featuring the Brothers Brothers, Tom and Tom), *social class* (e.g., sketches featuring Homey the Clown, Frenchy, Anton, the black café, Cephus and Reesy, Benita Betrell, two black talent agents from Funky Finger Productions in Compton), *nationalism and politics* (e.g., sketches about Jesse Jackson, Louis Farrakhan), and *black popular culture* (e.g., sketches on Arsenio Hall, Prince, Oprah, Vanilla Ice; the presence of rap music and the Fly Girls).

Aesthetically, *In Living Color* reorganizes specific images, themes, and events from America's racial past as well as contemporary African American cultural and social practices to distinguish itself from other television shows. In fact, in her inventory of the show's strategies of representation Schulman (1992:4) claims that the show depends on historical and contemporary stereotypes, white spectatorship, idealized visions of a multiracial order, and role reversals for its humor, modes of address, and cultural meanings.

And of course *In Living Color*'s strategy of representation relies heavily on rap music and hip-hop sensibilities. Rap and hip-hop are used deliberately but quite strategically in the program to generate identifications across racial lines. From the angle of the television industry, this strategic use of rap is also a useful marketing strategy for appealing to and reconfiguring different audiences in terms of race, gender, and age. Other television shows, notably *The Arsenio Hall Show*, *Where I Live*, and *Fresh Prince of Bel Air*, have used similar strategies, as has a great deal of television and radio advertising.

But I do not want to downplay the extent to which *In Living Color* is supremely televisual and therefore at the very center of contemporary commercial media and popular culture. In other words, attention to issues of sexuality, class, race, gender, masculinity, and so on are figured in terms of television itself. That is to say, these issues serve as vehicles for commenting on the medium of television itself—advertising (e.g., the credit card commercial parody), variety shows (e.g., the Brothers Brothers), home shopping networks (e.g., the Homeboy Shopping Network), science fiction/action adventure programs (e.g., *Star Trek*), talk shows (e.g., Oprah Winfrey's and Arsenio Hall's shows), PBS (e.g., "Men on . . . "), and television news (e.g., the Rodney King beating). In an ironic twist, many of the show's sketches offer commentary on commercial television's own exclusions, exaggerations, and complicity in the construction and representation of blackness. This critical performance and intervention has been illustrated nicely in sketches parodying recent credit card commercials and the PBS staple *This Old House*.

The sketch that parodied the signature style of certain credit card television commercials playing widely at the time the sketch was aired used the popular advertising convention of the individual testimonial to construct the experience of what, on the face of it, seemed to be a typical credit card customer. In this instance, however, the customer, played by David Alan Grier, was a black middle-class professional male whose very blackness and maleness generated suspicion and harassment each time he attempted to use his "prized" "Equity Express" card. These "routine troubles" were presumably provoked because this customer was a black male and, as such, a signifier for suspicion and danger.

In a parody of PBS's *This Old House*, Anton (Damon Wayans), a homeless black man, instructed the audience on the complexities of constructing shelter out of cardboard. Representations in the sketch satirized the well-known series in which a host and remodeling expert instructs (white) middle-class homeowners in the challenges and joys of restoring old houses. In both the commercial and *This Old House* sketches, commonsense assumptions about citizenship, property, and social class were parodied, and hence the ironic juxtaposition of class and race with familiar tropes of middle-class homeownership and unemployed homelessness was made explicit. Politically, these images are especially effective because they disturb the presumed separation of these discourses. In effect, they are reconfigured and politicized by their relocation to the same discursive space.

Sketches such as those described above call attention to assumptions about race and class as the basis for idealized representations. In other words, because African Americans seldom, if ever, appear in such televisual spaces as credit card commercials or home remodeling programs, In Living Color's staging (through parody and irony) foregrounds these cultural forums, calling attention to their exclusion of blacks and the normalization of class (middle class) and race (white). As Schulman (1992) notes, these sketches indicate that, at its critical best,

> In Living Color does not offer a plausible picture of American society as open and pluralistic. Nor does it, taken as a whole, suggest that the American Dream is accessible to people of color. Ironically, its subtext seems to be that whether individual African Americans are "deficient" or "gifted" has mattered little to white society, which has historically viewed them as "all alike." (p. 5)

In addition to In Living Color's engagement of race, class, and television in these sketches, the show also represents different subject positions within blackness. This diversity within blackness is most often represented through the trope of social class, although one would also have to include gender, sexuality, and race.

The Politics of Ambivalence: Race, Class, Gender, and Sexuality

It is precisely the show's preoccupation with these themes of difference, and the disturbances they produce within but also outside blackness, that interests me. Therefore, I want to consider how In Living Color achieves that disturbance through its representation of culture (African American traditions and practices, language, dress, music, body), its formal strategies (humor, satire, parody), its multiple subject positions (gender, social class, race), and its themes (sexuality, racism, ethnicity, stereotypes). The potential to politicize its disturbances, to articulate and disarticulate dominant assumptions about race, gender, and class relations, is at the heart of the show's critical possibilities. I use the words potential and possibilities here quite deliberately, for, as I have noted, the show's disturbance is often ambivalent and, at times, even reactionary.

Within the broad landscape of commercial network television, where dominant representations of blacks have been deployed through invisibility, trivialization, and exaggeration, the leading edge of *In Living Color*'s critical engagement and commentary continues to be race. That is to say, *In Living Color* frames issues primarily, though not exclusively, in racial terms, and by so doing acknowledges the continuing salience of race and racism as a major feature of American society. Yet, at the same time, and at the very least, the show also acknowledges many of the internal tensions (class, status, gender, and sexuality) within blackness. At least some part of the show's ambivalence stems from its negotiation between a "racialized (black) point of view" and the desire to challenge this position by acknowledging difference (class, gender, and sexuality) within blackness.[8]

Central to *In Living Color*'s treatment of race is its construction and engagement of whiteness. Whether in relation to liberal guilt, assumptions about (white) feminine beauty, or the normalization of racist absurdities, whiteness is a consistent object of ridicule, satire, and commentary. This satire is often staged through a kind of racial role reversal, where, as in the continuing character of the white fire marshal, white foolishness simply replaces black foolishness. This reversal of roles is more often than not ineffective as a critical politics because the meanings of these reversed images for blacks and whites alike are organized by racialized relations of power. Occasionally, sketches that parody white liberal guilt or white fear of black criminality actually name and engage the dynamics of white privilege and power in relationship to blacks (Braxton 1991; Schulman 1992). In any case, it is the show's willingness to construct and parody whiteness explicitly from the angle of blacks that makes its disturbances all the more unsettling.

Because the leading and most compelling edge of the show's critique is race, its explorations of sexuality, class, and gender often do not occupy the same discursive space as race. Therefore, when deployed in television through representational strategies such as satire and parody, the discursive privileging of race also has the effect of trivializing internal differences and complexities based on class, gender, and sexuality, even as it names these.

Take one of the show's most popular and most controversial collections of sketches, "Men on . . . ." These often hilarious sketches feature two black gay men who provide weekly commentaries on film, literature, travel, art, and other topics. Antoine (Damon Wayans) and Blaine (David Alan Grier) are stereotypically dressed in delicate fabrics with bright colors. In their reviews and commentaries the pair cleverly deconstruct everyday language while transforming heterosexual allusions and assumptions into wordplay on homoerotic desire. By way of taste, gesture, manner, and language they construct and perform effeminate sensibilities. At the most literal level, of course, these performances are carefully designed to satirize cross-dressers and stereotypes of black drag queens and (at the risk of a stretch) perhaps even to comment on issues of masculinity among black males.

Discursively, however, especially given the pervasiveness of homophobia within the black community, one must go further; that is, one might just as easily read the sketches as a trivialization of gay men. The sketches may even reaffirm masculine heterosexual power (and hostility) in relationship to, if not gay men, then growing interrogations and critiques of masculinity by black feminists, lesbians, and gay men. The "Men on . . . " sketch that ended the 1990–91 season is illustrative. In this sketch, Antoine took a hit on the head (in a device reminiscent of the Melvin and Mario Van Peebles film *Identity Crisis*), after which he experienced a loss of memory, including the fact that he is gay. Antoine's memory loss produced a crisis for Blaine, who was faced with Antoine's new heterosexual identity and the prospect that Antoine might never recover his "true" identity. Identity was clearly in play here, because it was represented as socially constructed and one that Blaine preferred to claim in terms of gayness. But such play and performance are very much the point, because audiences are also mindful that it is black heterosexual men who perform these roles.

This sketch and others featuring Antoine and Blaine activate and engage crucial debates about identity, sexuality, and desire within the discourse of blackness. Although the sketches are not specifically about black gay men, the body, dress, language, and gesture are deliberately organized to construct and convey something about the characters' identities. Moreover, and perhaps this helps to account for their resonance, these parodies and the strategies of representations on which they depend join historical contemporary debates and representations in the black community about homophobia, black gay men, masculinity, sexuality, and drag queens (Riggs 1991b). With the increasing visibility and authority of black gay and lesbian voices, heterosexual and nationalist claims on blackness are no doubt being contested. A generous reading of the "Men on . . . " sketches follows the idea of television as the site of various kinds of contests and struggles over meaning. Hence, what we may be experiencing through the parodies in these sketches is a kind of public acknowledgment, contestation, and renegotiation of blackness, especially the specific terms in which masculinity, sexuality, desire, and identity have been figured in commercial culture. Again, however, these representations are anchored by the politics of ambivalence, because the particular discursive space within which the contestation of sexuality occurs in the show is still mediated by the privileged position that black heterosexual masculinity enjoys.

Even though race and masculinity remain privileged in relationship to gayness, the show nevertheless acknowledges multiple subject positions (and the tensions between them) within the African American experience. Whatever one thinks of *In Living Color* and its particular treatment of black gay men, the reading of its cultural politics must not simply stop at or remain within the closed system of the text.

A similar ambivalence is apparent in *In Living Color*'s treatment of social class, especially its rendering of the urban underclass. (The show's repertoire also includes sketches that represent issues of class by way of black middle-class professionals, or what Wayans calls "people in suits.") I have in mind the various sketches that use specific caricatures and settings to signify the urban underclass—the Homeboy Shopping Network, Frenchy (a caricature of Rick James), the questionable brothers from Funky Finger Productions in Compton, the workers in a black café, and the female gossip Benita Betrell. As is true for the characters in the "Men on . . . " sketches, the class position of these characters is signaled through detailed and often exaggerated attention to *taste and style* (pink leather, cheap wine, sneakers, hair curlers, jerri curls), *gesture, body,* and *talk* (gossip, nonstop talk, inappropriate words) of the characters. Take, for instance, the characters in the Homeboy Shopping Network sketches. Usually, two black youth appear selling (stolen?) goods from the back of their van. Their bodies are draped in baggy clothes and oversized gold-toned chains; with their caps askew, they gesticulate wildly, moving their bodies in dips and sweeps that accent, freeze, and dramatize the rhythm and meaning of their b-boy lingo. Their goods—an ATM, radios, watches, posters of Michael Jackson and Ronald Reagan—are all consumer commodities that are valued more as badges of living large in the American dream than for their utility or practicality.

As with the case of sexuality, these representations of class differences are deliberately constructed to generate and articulate identifications through race, class, and generation. The issue of positionality (both spectator and characters) is especially important here because, at best, the sketches produce ambivalence. To be sure, even ambivalence might be regarded as an improvement over representations of the black poor usually found in television news, crime shows, policy debates, and films that either objectify the black poor or construct them as victims. *In Living Color*'s ambivalence seems to trivialize and disempower the black poor at the same time it clearly acknowledges them. That is to say, Frenchy, the Homeboys, and the other characters do appear in their own worlds; they authorize their own words and they make little apology for their circumstance.

To its credit, *In Living Color* takes the circumstances and perspectives of the black poor (both on and off the screen) seriously enough to represent them, even if only in parody and satire. After all, Wayans, Ajaye, and Rawitt have repeatedly emphasized to the press the show's commitment to a black perspective (Braxton 1990, 1991; R. E. Childs 1992). For many black viewers this is the point of *In Living Color's* humor and appeal. On the other hand, for viewers positioned differently by class, ethnicity, gender, and race, the black poor can just as easily become objects of derision. Where comedians such as Richard Pryor and Franklyn Ajaye have used satire and parody strategically to take viewers inside the worlds of the black poor and disenfranchised in order to criticize racism and class inequality and to stake out their relationship to and claims on these worlds, the sketches in *In Living Color* seem to stop short.[9]

What is most troubling to me about *In Living Color's* parody is not so much its humor, but its use of that humor in the service of ambivalence. For a segment of the black community on which so many different kinds of claims are made, including uncritical nationalist celebrations and racist demonizations, this ambivalence makes it hard to construct a critical space from which to speak, especially because it so effectively and cleverly organizes several different social positions. In the end, I fear that the hegemonic balance tilts far too dramatically and decidedly in the direction of objectification and derision. For all their high jinks, clever deconstructive turns, and transgressive hipness, *In Living Color's* sketches about the black poor more often than not seem simply to chump out, leaving the black poor exposed and positioned as television objects of middle-class amusement and fascination. Much like the homeless character, Anton, the black poor appear as amusing social incompetents with whom few can or should identify and for whom most have little if any feelings. But I suppose that is the point—it is, after all, parody. This remains, nevertheless, a disturbing feature of the show.

In Living Color's rendering of gender also seems to produce much the same kind of troubling ambivalence that I have been describing with respect to sexuality and social class. The show's most disturbing treatments of gender reproduce a racial and sexual division of labor in which black women, especially their bodies, are the explicit objects of satire and derision by black men. This marginalization is most apparent in sketches where women are explicitly figured—sketches that refer to women (especially black women) as "bitches" and sketches featuring waitresses in a working-class café, black beauty contestants, parodies of Oprah Winfrey (especially her weight), the working-class stage mother (which again foregrounds issues of weight and size), the "ugly" woman (played by a man) who wants but cannot get a man, and, yes, the Fly Girls. All of these representations seem to depend on trivialization, hostility, and exaggeration for their humor. Of course, with the presence of the Fly Girls one cannot help but notice the preoccupation with black female bodies and body parts as measures of feminine beauty and intelligence. One also cannot escape the degree to which black men, with the possible exception of the "Men on . . . " sketches, are immune from representations that focus so exclusively on the body as expressions of masculine appeal and social competence. To be fair, some sketches explicitly acknowledge some of the rich and complex dimensions of gender relations. In addition to having a number of talented women in the cast, the show regularly features sketches that challenge masculine assumptions and power over women (e.g., parodies of Sharazaad Ali).

In these representations of gender, sexuality, and social class, audiences are variously positioned to laugh at and occasionally with these representations. For the most part, however, viewers can hardly take any of them seriously. After all, because *In Living Color* deals in parody, these are not characters we want to get to know or to care about as human beings with complexity and dignity. (The possible exception is Homey the Clown, a frustrated and rather mean-spirited character to whom some viewers have become attached.) Again, as Wayans has tried to make clear, this is the point. These are jokes! But this identification, this getting the jokes, is, for me, still politically unsettling. Although *In Living Color*'s parodies and its strategy of caricature do not always add up to cultural critique, the show has effectively made commercial television and popular culture a site over which and within which cultural debates and contests over meanings occur.

Conclusions

In Living Color's thematic focus and its strategies of representation in no way ensure radical, even progressive, claims on blackness and representations of African Americans. The production of any kind of critical cultural politics in commercial network television cannot rest with a single series, episode, sketch, or character. The show's ability to move beyond its important but momentary effect of disrupting hegemonic representations of blackness remains at best ambivalent and contingent. But I regard even this momentary and often troubling disruption as important. *In Living Color*, like *Frank's Place, Roc,* and *A Different World,* cumulatively disturbs and interrupts television's own discourse, a discourse that is still too insular, self-referential, and complacent on questions of race and ethnicity. And, of course, even in a program such as *In Living Color,* television's power to normalize, trivialize, and routinize is ever present. In fact, *In Living Color* has so quickly moved to the stage of routinization that its transgressive edge has long since disappeared. Moreover, during the 1992–93 season Wayans actually left the show as executive producer because of creative and scheduling differences with Fox. Hence, I deliberately characterize the show's contributions to diverse representations of blackness with conditional terms such as *contingent* and *ambivalent.*

I continue to believe that the cultural force of *In Living Color* can be realized where there are other active practices and discourses that critique, empower, frame, and authorize its constructions and representations of African Americans. In the absence of other cultural practices and social movements aimed at transforming social relations of power both in and over representation, then, one might well be tempted (correctly, I think) to read *In Living Color* as mere distraction, as appropriated images and representations that have been softened and displaced though comedic conventions and tolerated as harmless television entertainment that resecures the dominant terms of power. Or, in a slight variation, the show might be seen as simply providing an "authentic" black view of the world from within the sacred and privileged territory of blackness.

There are, to be sure, problems that complicate the meanings of the show and the critical cultural potential it might hold as popular culture—its use of humor, its staging of and privileging of race (as well as middle-class heterosexual dominance) as the leading edge of its critique. The attempt to represent race relations and the diversity within blackness is one of the qualities that distinguishes *In Living Color* from other representations of blacks on commercial television. The show's strategies of representation, ambivalent positions, and location within commercial network television require not just dismissal, but complex and nuanced readings. Part of *In Living Color*'s rich potential has always been its transgressive and irreverent stance, but a cultural politics based on irreverence and transgression is tricky. What the show signifies in its representations of race gender, class, and sexuality is necessarily contingent and indeterminate. For some, the show's strategies of representation produce critical insights; for others, especially those African Americans who complained to writer Franklyn Ajaye, they produce representations that are dangerous and embarrassing. In the end, the show's meanings depend on how it organizes its audiences and negotiates the discourses, debates, and circumstances that enable and constantly reposition it within the larger society.

9   Jammin' on the One! Some Reflections on the Politics of Black Popular Culture

We live in a consumer culture where we seem to have unlimited choices in how we construct ourselves in the realm of public life. In a media-saturated consumer culture such as the United States one can, momentarily at least, locate a person or group socially through personal style—hair, dress, tastes, music, movements, and talk. Through personal (and collective) style we endlessly invent and re-invent, position and reposition ourselves in public life.

Although feminist scholars have gone to some length to point out the oppressive and denigrating impact of consumer culture on women and young girls, the body, nevertheless, seems to reign as the preeminent site for the expression of individual imagination and collective cultural identity. From the demarcation of gang territory through the use of dress, colors, and hand signs to radical rejections (and celebrations) of beauty myths through markings, tattoos, and mutilation, obsessions with the body in places like Los Angeles, Miami, and San Francisco have transformed the body into a hyperspace of identity. We use adornment and inscription to camouflage, even parody, our social locations in a world of increasing social control, surveillance, and social inequality. At the same time the body has become a major site for individual and collective expression of identity, the (re)organization and circulation of identities, including the literal bodies on which they hang, constitute a major enterprise of modern consumer culture industries, including fashion, health and fitness, music, and advertising.

By emphasizing the dual nature of this process of self-construction and representation and the role of consumer culture in its production and circulation, I want to foreground the constructed and contested nature of black expressive youth culture and the politics of culture it enacts. Often the expressive styles of black youth labor to reproduce, in commercial culture at least, the terms and processes of marginalization, control, and domination; but just as often the expressive styles of black youth serve as points of intervention and struggle over claims about black youth (Lipsitz 1994).

As one important terrain for the representation and circulation of black youth style, the media, especially television, music video, popular music, and film, operate as sites and resources through which and with which black youth construct, invent, and situate themselves in public spaces. I regard black youth styles as an expressive attempt by these youth to reposition themselves and in the process reconfigure and disrupt those political, cultural, and moral discourses that constantly police, contain, and otherwise discipline them (Lipsitz 1994; Rose 1994).

By framing the representation of black youth in terms of the relations among various systems of meaning (moral, cultural, political and commercial), representation (media and consumer culture), and subsequent struggles over them, I want to situate black youth subjectivities at the center of popular cultural analysis.[1] Any cursory examination of contemporary music, video, television, and advertising would suggest that such a repositioning is historically warranted and, furthermore, consistent with Cornel West's (1993) reminder that we are experiencing the African Americanization of American popular culture. Such a repositioning also necessarily reconfigures the center, especially in terms of the politics of representation.

Indeed, given the level of saturation of the media with representations of blackness, the mediascape can no longer be characterized accurately using terms such as *invisibility*. Rather, we might well describe ours as a moment of "hyperblackness." The emphasis on struggles or contests over representations in the media highlights the need for a look at the complexity and vitality of black youth culture, especially the important discursive role it plays in enacting and reconfiguring claims on and representations of blackness in the media. My argument, then, is that, multiply structured as they are by social class, education, gender, and region, black youth cultures and the social positions they articulate and mobilize can never be completely marginalized, appropriated, and absorbed. Rather, as enacted through black expressive forms, black youth subjectivities are constantly produced, made, and remade.

Within the mediascape of contemporary consumer culture, black youth constantly use the body, self-adornment, movement, language, and music to construct and locate themselves socially and culturally. These, I believe, are the sites of some of the most complex and imaginative practices in black popular culture. These constructions of identity within and through commercial popular culture also represent significant and strategic interventions and cultural struggles in a world that is, for black youth, often hostile and suspicious. Although the various constitutive elements of black youth style often operate within separate discursive spaces, they also constitute a certain kind of coherence. It is a coherence, as Dick Hebdige (1979) shows in the case of British youth, that forms a kind of bricolage constructed of elements, traditions, refuse, and practices of contemporary culture.

Using the case of contemporary rap music, Tricia Rose (1994) and Robin D. G. Kelley (1994) show, for example, how the musical practices of black youth signify meanings within the context of social locations and circumstances that often deny, block, and negatively sanction access by black youth to the material and status rewards offered by U.S. society. Rose (1994) carefully details how black (and latino) youth in the Bronx combine technology, oral traditions, vernacular language, dance, and graffiti writing to construct complex counterrepresentations. The elements that came to be called hip-hop and rap emerged in the midst of the fiscal and social crisis of New York City in the late 1970s that produced massive social and economic dislocation for large numbers of black and latino youth. Kelley (1994) brilliantly connects the emergence (and appeal) of the genre of gangsta rap in Los Angeles to the structural deindustrialization and subsequent social reconfiguration of Los Angeles. These structural changes and social processes (ethnic and racial dislocation, competition and territorialization expressed most dramatically in the form of gangs), together with the cultural impress of Hollywood's image machine, Kelley suggests, help to explain and contextualize the salience, glorification, and centrality of the figure of the outlaw and the gangsta in the Los Angeles rap scene.

Both Kelley and Rose are extraordinarily careful not to use factors like social context or cultural significance to explain away or excuse the nihilism, violence, misogyny, and homophobia so often associated with black male youth culture. Instead, by carefully attending to the complex relationship of cultural and social forces at play in producing these practices, both are able to grapple with the complex and contra-dictory character of rap as a leading edge of African American youth culture. Their exemplary analyses of black popular culture avoid a zero-sum (dismissal/celebration) approach to popular culture, espe-cially rap.

The terms, representations, and claims operating in the ensemble of inscriptions that characterize black youth culture, then, are socially situated and culturally produced. It is in this continual process of cul-tural invention that we can glimpse something about how individuals, groups, and communities struggle against and reproduce forms of domination in their attempt to make a world for themselves.[2]

I take as my major texts for this exploration the representations of urban black youth found in mass media and popular culture as they circulate through the mass entertainment system of American com-mercial television.[3] Following the theorizations of Rose and Kelley, I focus on this dynamic process of cultural invention by African Ameri-can youth to highlight their claims on blackness and their engagement with such media forms as music, video, advertising, and television.

Jammin' on the One! Elements of Black Youth Popular Style

Black youth styles are expressed through a number of distinct but re-lated forms that constitute an ensemble of cultural practices. The ex-pression of black youth styles, articulated through body, hair, lan-guage, music, and dress, produces a dynamic dialogue (Lipsitz 1990b) with African American cultural traditions, a coherence that Paul Gil-roy (1991a, 1993), following Amiri Baraka (1991), has aptly de-scribed as "the changing same." Negotiating between discourses of blackness as a fixed or absolute essence and blackness as a radical so-cial construction, Gilroy sees blackness as a socially situated produc-tion that is constantly invented and reinvented from tradition. Using popular music as his analytic trope, Gilroy accepts the existence of dif-ferent black Atlantic Diasporic traditions, but avoids essentializing, re-ifying, or fixing them. He is critical of approaches that do, as well as of those that posit a blackness as always made anew without regard for the social locations and traditions in which they are embedded.

By theorizing blackness in this way, Gilroy forces us to see black expressive forms in different parts of the black Atlantic as related so-cial processes of invention, travel, interruption, and remaking (see also Hall 1989). Thus, for Gilroy, African American cultural expressive popular forms are not fixed, essential, and unchanging, as some cul-tural guardians of black (for Gilroy, African American) cultural tradi-tions would have it. Indeed, Gilroy's larger project and more general discussion of the black Atlantic seems heavily staked in disarticulating specific claims by African Americans from what he regards as their hegemonic status relative to blackness in the Caribbean and England.

Although I would quarrel with Gilroy's particular construction and representation of black American claims on blackness as hegemonic (together with Lipsitz's, 1990b, notion of dialogue), I do find productive his conceptualization of blackness in terms of the notion of the "changing same." This view of blackness as a cultural trope is alert to, but not blinded by, the socially constructed character and context in which different notions of blackness are made and made meaningful. African American, black Atlantic, and African traditions do survive and exist in popular forms and practices through which they are socially organized and made culturally meaningful. But they are not, as some neonationalists and Afrocentric advocates would have it, frozen in time in some original form to be preserved and revisited and resurrected as a source of authentic affirmation and guidance. Rather, traditions are differently structured, constantly invented and reinvented, appropriated, modified, and transformed within specific historical, social, and cultural conditions. This is the condition of the changing same, a condition that must be constantly situated and theorized and not assumed in the manner of either essentialism (ethnic absolutism) or radical social construction.

The use of music, dance, dress, language, and the body as sites for the articulation of certain decidedly black sensibilities is neither recent nor specific to black youth. Punks, hippies, and rastas (and before them black nationalists) have used hair, for example, as a site to express identity and identifications that distinguished them from those outside of their social formations. The point, as Lipsitz (1990b) shows with Chicanos in Los Angeles and the Mardi Gras Indians in New Orleans, is that marginalized and subordinated communities have creatively transformed and used popular cultural artifacts and practices such as music, costumes, parades, traditions, and festivals to transgress their particular locations, to express their visions, and to invent themselves. What characterizes black youth culture in the 1990s and therefore warrants careful attention is the central role of the commercial culture industry and mass media in this process. I want to try to capture some of the flavor—the dialogue and hybridity—of black youth practices and inventions, especially their circuits and manifestations of mass media and commercial culture. Hence, I want to take a closer look at two of the less obvious elements of the expressive style of black youth—hair and dance.

Without claiming that my discussion is definitive, I want to appreciate and hence foreground the fact that aurally, kinetically, and visu-

ally, rhythm emerges as the central thread that unifies contemporary
black youth culture (Rose 1989, 1994; Snead 1990). That is, rhythm
(through the play and endless reconfiguration of repetition) is imaginatively deployed and constantly recombined in the language and
wordplay of rap; in the insistent movement and expression of bodies
in contemporary popular dance; in the angles, curves, and lines of contemporary hairstyles worn by both men and women; and, of course, in
the scratches, spaces, bass lines, and grooves (especially funk) that are
so central to most contemporary black popular music.[4] Rhythm and
repetition, in other words, are common elements that organize the
multiple and syncretic practices of contemporary black youth styles.

Hair

In many public arenas (streets, shopping malls, television programs,
schools, playgrounds, movie theaters, concert halls) throughout
America's major cities, one can see a wide range of hair textures,
shapes, sizes, and colors among black youth: jerri curls, dreadlocks,
extensions, braids, parts, crowns, and intricate designs cut into the
hair. Kobena Mercer (1990) reminds us that for blacks in various locations within the black Atlantic, hair has long been one of the sites in
which black youth identity has been expressed. One's hairstyle can be
used to locate one's personal taste and cultural outlook (e.g., processes
in the 1950s, Afros in the 1960s, braids in the 1970s, jerri curls in the
1980s, extensions in the 1990s).

Mercer (1990) suggests that the endless variations in black hairstyles might be understood as a kind of inventive reworking and expression of blackness rather than as some pathological imitation of
whiteness. That is, black hair is a place where the particular sensibilities of various black cultural experiences are symbolically inscribed.
Rather than reading the expressions of black hairstyles as a kind of
internalized psychological state (e.g., assimilation) or authentic black
essence (nationalism), Mercer argues instead that they are the continual inventions and articulations of black cultural imaginations
played out on the material and symbolic surface of the body. By simply
inscribing these surfaces and spaces with various icons, shapes, and
figures, black youth literally use their bodies to construct their identities (see Bakhtin 1984).

Following Mercer, we can locate historically and socially the discourses that shape and inform these bodily inscriptions of blackness.
The contemporary hairstyles that adorn the heads of black youth engage a rich and imaginative amalgam of contemporary and historical
influences: commercial consumer culture (e.g., Batman insignias, Mer-

cedes-Benz and BMW logos, sports logos, black superstars), Africa and Afrocentricity (hairstyles that reproduce and emulate crowns and various forms of headdress), urban street life (e.g., parts, geometric designs, and bald heads), middle-class entrepreneurial spirit (crew cuts, fades), the Caribbean (e.g., dreadlocks), and contemporary African American cultural and political neonationalism informed by the philosophies of Malcolm X, the Nation of Islam, and the Black Panther Party (e.g., Afros, fades, boxes, jerri curls).

These shifting hairstyles incorporate elements from different historical and contemporary periods that are constantly reinvented and reassembled to produce new forms and meanings. Thus, although the figure of Michael Jordan, a Batman insignia, or the logo of BMW cut into the hair of a black male may explicitly suggest identification with materialist aspirations of a hedonistic consumer culture, it might just as easily indicate the fertile imagination of black youth playing with a storehouse of readily available images and meanings from commercial consumer culture. (For an interesting theoretical elaboration of this point, see Sawchuk 1988). The use of parody, irony, and, yes, irreverence (in this case toward the body and commercial culture) as both affirmation and spectacle should not be lost. (Think, for example, of NBA star Dennis Rodman, whose hair color changed in one season from red to blond, or sitcom star Sinbad, who once sported a blond "do.") It shows, I believe, active intervention, appropriation, and participation in an environment dominated by consumer commodities that have displaced, taken over, and now compete with values and mores that have traditionally defined and guided African American communities. Following Cornel West's concerns about rampant nihilism among black youth, I would prefer to read the centrality of consumer commodities in the iconography of black youth as an expression, rather than the cause, of the breakdown of civility and morality in the black public sphere. Perhaps we should read the inscriptions on the bodies and heads of black youth as forceful and direct expressions of the seduction and power of consumer capitalism. (After all, how different are these emblems of identity and self-expression from "buppie," "chuppie," and "yuppie" preoccupations with badges and emblems of status that come in the form of designer labels and national brands as signs of quality in consumer goods?)

Whatever political and moral conclusions one draws, in the broader discourse of representation and the politics of identity, using the body as a site of inscription and representation is simply one of a number of imaginative ways in which youth with limited resources and power not only get noticed, but express themselves in their own voices and on their own terms (Lipsitz 1994).[5]

Movement/Dance

As in the past, popular dance, performance, gesture, and pose remain among the most dynamic and expressive cultural forms through which black youth express and authorize their own subjectivity (Hazzard-Gordon 1990). Contemporary black youth continue to select, recycle, and embellish body movements from different groups and periods, inflecting them with new meanings.

Body movements, given coherence by the centrality of rhythm in the black music tradition, express the imagination and experience of life in modern urban spaces (for an interesting discussion of the vitality of such spaces, see Whyte 1989). In the video explosion of the 1980s, movement and dance in the videos of artists such as Paula Abdul, Heavy D. and the Boyz, Big Daddy Kane, Hammer, Janet Jackson, Quincy Jones, and Salt-N-Pepa expressed the authority and imagination of a generation of black youth whose preoccupation was to be noticed and taken seriously on their own terms and at almost any cost.

No doubt, many of the dance styles that turn up in contemporary black youth style have long traditions in the social and cultural rituals of various parts of Africa, the United States, Latin America, and the Caribbean. In addition to being held together and punctuated by black music, these movements are marked by polyphonic and independent movements of various body parts—legs, arms, head, and trunk. They are at once cybernetic, athletic, and erotic in their incorporation of traditional and contemporary elements.

This imaginative incorporation of aesthetic and social elements in the service of contemporary cultural invention by black youth can be seen in two popular dances from the 1980s, the cabbage patch and the running man. The running man in particular might be read as a metaphor for the urgency and velocity of life in urban America. This dance and its poignant name express the character of life in large urban areas, where black youth (especially males) are the objects of surveillance, control, and pursuit by the police, gangs, and the criminal justice system. The running man is not only an expression of the dynamism and immediacy of life in the city but also a major survival strategy for urban youth.[6]

Not at all bashful, or for that matter imaginative, about preoccupations with sex, young black men and women also incorporate suggestive and literal sexual movements and accents as central elements of popular dance styles. Bumps, grinds, and thrusts of the hips, butt, and entire lower body graphically mark the place of sensuality and the erotic in the popular music and dance of black youth.[7] As youth preoccupations with sex have become both more explicit and more intense, they have also become more central and graphic in the popular dance styles of black youth. And for many adults they have also become more disturbing and troublesome. This disturbance is not so much about the place of the erotic and the sexual in black popular culture, especially dance; black popular forms of music and dance have always erected and maintained a public place for the sensual and the erotic. Rather, both this sexual preoccupation and the disturbance it produces are made particularly meaningful in relationship to recent moral panics, the crisis of AIDS, and the epidemic rates of teen pregnancy and violence in the black community. Many policy and moral debates explicitly target popular music, music video, and dance in relation to social, cultural, and moral debates about increased violence against women, increased homophobia and gay bashing, and increased teen pregnancy (Grossberg 1992; West 1993).

For many, some of the most offensive and troubling expressions in contemporary popular music and dance are primarily, but not limited to, masculine movements and styles incorporated from sports, notably street basketball, gymnastics, and exercise culture. (Many of the celebration routines performed by black athletes in highly organized team sports, such as basketball and football, incorporate clear elements of popular black dance styles to express their individuality.)

In the culture of rap and contemporary dance, young men and women pose in defiant (and, for many, menacing) stances of authority and affirmation. These are simultaneously expressions of individual autonomy, the influence of the peer group, and distance from the culture of adult authority and control. Like rap music samples, such comportment of the body is borrowed and remixed from urban street culture, Hollywood westerns and gangster films, and the military. This sense of authority is equally present in the performance of black male jazz musicians, where the body functions as an extension of the instrument or voice. As Miles Davis and many of his critics and admirers recount in his autobiography, for musicians and listeners alike, the body, dress, and general style of many musicians, especially during the 1950s and 1960s, served as a crucial means of expressing black passion, defiance, and authority (Davis and Troupe 1992; Tate 1992).

There are some correspondences, then, among the pose of the rapper, the stance of the jazz musician, the celebration rituals of the athlete, and the popular dances of black youth. They all operate on a plane of visceral and visual expression to articulate an individual and collective body positioned in a dynamic relationship to sexual, aesthetic, and physical sensibilities rooted in African American culture.[8]

Social, Historical, and Cultural Locations of
Contemporary Black Youth Culture

In the popular American imagination, so much of which is profoundly shaped and institutionally structured by the popular media, especially television, black gangs, drug dealers, and unemployed and incorrigible blacks (especially black male youth) represent fear and menace. As I noted in chapters 2 and 3, in television news accounts and newspaper stories, blacks, especially the black poor, are presented as victims of crime, perpetrators of crime, and the objects of white fear and suspicion. Recall, for example, Ronald Reagan's construction and strategic use of the black welfare queen, the Bush administration's reliance on the image of Willie Horton, and the blanket surveillance of black neighborhoods in Boston in search of black male suspects following Charles Stewart's murder of his wife.

Even in critically celebrated films put out by Hollywood's image machine, liberal treatments of black life remain, by and large, imprisoned by and dependent on the agency of whites. Black subjectivity and agency are framed and made possible at the behest of sympathetic whites such as the contentious but benign Miss Daisy in *Driving Miss Daisy*, the ambitious but dutiful young white officer in *Glory*, and the transgressive but loyal Idgie in *Fried Green Tomatoes*.[9]

Where personal and institutional constraints are not as explicit or rigid, black subjectivities are often framed in terms of individualism and exceptionalism. Here I have in mind television and press depictions of successful blacks who are constructed as exceptional. In this assimilationist discourse of positive images, the quality of exceptionalism organizes and drives media representations of personal success (e.g., the former chair of the Joint Chiefs of Staff, General Colin Powell; New York Mayor David Dinkins; Virginia Governor Douglas Wilder; Secretary of Commerce Ron Brown; and entertainers such as Oprah Winfrey, Bill Cosby, Michael Jackson, and Janet Jackson). This black exceptionalism, marked by individuality, separates these individuals from black collectivity or community.[10]

In many of the media representations of success and achievement, blacks appear as objects rather than as the subjects of their own construction. They are, as it were, inserted into a discourse of menace or benign acceptance within a larger American discourse of individual success and assimilation. In such stories moral, cultural, and behavioral accounts dominate as explanations for the state of various depressed sectors of black America, especially the disenfranchised and the poor.

These representations of black exceptionalism leave little room for complex collective (and individual) expression of black subjectivity and imagination. They depend on the notion of role models for their appeal—either positive (in the case of individual success) or negative (in the case of collective threat). In the negative case they tend to portray poor black youth as either victims or soulless predators who, because of fatal moral and character flaws, cannot possibly transcend the limits of their condition. These youth must be carefully and continually surveyed and contained (Lipsitz 1994).

But the very same images of threat and menace that underwrite television and media representations of black youth in the news have another cultural dimension, one of titillation, adoration, celebration, and consumption (Jones 1991). There can be little doubt that the poses, stances, dances, and general body comportment of rappers that have become almost conventional in popular ad campaigns for Nike and Reebock athletic wear, Gap jeans, and Calvin Klein underwear, to name only a few, originated in the very quarters of black youth culture that signal threat and menace to civic and moral order. In other words, while holding to my claims about the social locations and political salience of contemporary black youth expression, I do think it important to foreground the centrality of black youth expression for consumer commercial culture and hence black youths' travel through and transformation in the production and consumption circuit of consumer capitalism (Frith 1988).

As these traces and signs of black youth culture percolate through the commercial mainstream by way of advertising, film, and television, they labor discursively in several directions at the same time. As consumers and producers of their media images, black youth, in the manner of organic intellectuals, seem to understand implicitly and negotiate effectively the dual nature of their representations. For example, rap artists such as Ice-T, Ice Cube, Queen Latifah, Monie Love, Public Enemy, Boogie Down Productions, and Paris cleverly use the media, especially music video, to transform and reposition images of black menace and threat into expressions of affirmation and defiance (for an application and elaboration of this argument, see Hebdige 1989). These and other black rappers effectively stage their self-authored and authorized representations under the glare of the very spotlight that is also used to commodify, survey, contain, and marginalize black youth. They do so without apology or regard for the public codes of civility or the culture of politeness with respect to race that so saturates public discourse (Hebdige 1989).

When presented at the floodlit center of American commercial culture (e.g., fashion magazines, music video, advertising, commercial network television), the expressions of black youth are transported into a media hyperspace where they are magnified into a spectacle of hyperblackness. Transformed by the electronically shaped circuit of their production and travel, once in this floodlit center this hyper-blackness is repositioned yet again, not only in relation to social dis-courses and institutions of domination and containment, but in rela-tion to commercial imperatives of spectacle, commodification, and objectification. Through the conventions, aesthetics, and structures of the concert tour, the television screen, the fashion spread, and cinema, the cultural expressions of black youth become accessible to much broader audiences. They are more available for and susceptible to transformation—including reinvention, modification, and appropria-tion. And, of course, because these very same conditions of production and circulation are also available to black youth, this same media space refracts these electronic images of blackness back to black youth, who in turn use them to engage, transform, modify, and rein-vent blackness.

This complex status of black youth style as a meaningful cultural practice *and* cultural commodity is the source of its cultural power and commercial appeal. This commodity character, and hence the poten-tial for commercial appropriation and commodification, is constantly present, especially for representations such as those in black "ghet-tocentric" (Jones 1991) cinema and television shows—for example, *In Living Color* or rap videos—that most directly and forcefully disrupt and subvert dominant constructions and representations of black youth.

Black popular practices, then, are deeply contradictory. This con-tradictory character is part of the condition of black cultural politics in commercial culture. As popular expressions and forms, including the sensibilities and subjectivities they articulate, ride the popular currents of commercial culture, they remain contested, contradictory, and con-stantly mediated by the social and political circumstances and dynam-ics that situate them.

The Cultural Politics of Black Youth Style

What is registered as counterhegemonic, reactionary, and affirmative in the complex ensemble of black youth style, then, can be analytically discerned only by situating the constituent elements socially and then reading them relationally as an ensemble. To be sure, popular repre-sentations of black youth that appear on commercial and cable televi-sion are codified and frozen. One could even argue that these repre-sentations are institutionally mediated and intentionally constructed to maximize their commercial (read crossover) appeal. Such a reading is completely warranted, given that music video and advertising are first and foremost promotional and marketing devices designed to stimulate product sales. What is more, music videos and television commercials are structured by aesthetic and organizational conventions that are shared and negotiated by record executives, art directors, agents, producers, and artists themselves. Nevertheless, in relationship to the popular media and public spaces where such practices are generated and produced, representations of black youth styles in commercial and cable television are important precisely because of their constructed and mediated nature (Frith 1988; Goodwin 1992; Grossberg 1992; Hebdige 1989).

Television (especially music videos, television ads, situation comedy, comedy-variety programs, and sports) is made up of cultural zones and social spaces of mediation, contestation, and circulation among groups that are differently positioned socially and differently organized culturally. Television is an important space for the production, expression, and circulation of contemporary black youth identity. In short, an interrogation of television constructions and representations of expressive black youth culture can shed some light on the operation of television as a social space of cultural struggle.

As a commercial space, television also represents a vital public site of cultural contestation where different claims on and representations of blackness bump up against, compete with, displace, complement, and comment on each other. Thus, black representations of youth culture exist in the same cultural space as neoconservative demonizations, commodified appropriations, and innovative explorations. Although clearly different from the street or community of origin, television is nonetheless a shared site, another place in the popular imagination where multiple representations of black youth get framed and presented. Indeed, television, especially music television and advertising, is the common place where different and differently interested claims on blackness (ethnic, racial, corporate capitalist, suburban middle-class, nationalist, assimilationist, urban poor) meet, each borrowing from the others, each using the others for its own ends, each making meanings of the others in often different, conflicting ways. Let me be clear here: I do not mean to celebrate the presence of this borrowing and exchange in some pluralist interest-group sense, but I do want to underscore the fact that these different representations and claims on blackness, including television itself, are situated and structured by shifting and unequal relations of power (including class, gender, race, and sexuality).

The representations of black youth on music television, in TV advertising, and in comedy-variety, stand-up comedy, and situation comedy programs draw viewers, significant numbers of whom are black youth themselves. Thus, by treating these electronic and mass-mediated images as "representations" rather than as real(istic) reflections of certain kinds of black youth practices, we can avoid the burden of representation that weighs so heavily on popular commentary and analysis of black images on television. In commercial media representations and refractions of blackness, there are multiple levels of self-reflexivity operating, the most dominant of which is an organizational imperative underwritten by institutional and aesthetic conventions that define and structure television as a profit-making corporate enterprise. Again, processes of both self-representation and media commodification are at work. It is the play of both commercial imperatives and cultural desires that makes television such an important site of social and cultural struggles over the sign of blackness.

Television representations of blackness and the range of possible meanings that can be made from them are not completely open. How they are constructed and positioned within social and cultural discourse is what gives them meaning and significance, not the fact of their existence alone. Just as audiences are socially organized and structured, so too are representations of black youth culture. That is to say, such representations operate in and are structured by discourses of youth and race that are hierarchically arranged. These discourses and the social and material relations of power in which they are embedded (and that they also help to reproduce) are the terms within which responses and meanings are registered and made. I think that it is possible to view identifications and meanings generated from the margins (the production of black youth styles and expressions—rap music) and at the center (advertising, fashion, and language styles that emulate black youth styles) of the culture as evidence of the differential (and hierarchically ordered) registers of social responses to black youth.

Here Stuart Hall's (1981a) notion of popular culture as a site of struggle and contestation is appropriate (see also Kelley 1992). I have claimed that it is possible to understand the popular constructions and expressions of black youth as subversive attempts on the part of black youth to open social and cultural spaces in which to express themselves. Let me be clear about this. I am not speaking of these expressions and their content as necessarily involving politics or social movements in some intentional or programmatic sense. Instead, I mean to point to the process by which these representations enact discursive struggles in cultural and social spaces (including commercial media). The impact of these cultural expressions and the effects they produce in commercial media (especially the reactions they generate among agents, organizations, and institutions of social control) suggest something of the power of these representations. Consider, for example, the campaign of the Parents' Music Resource Center to label recorded music, or the condemnations in the press by police departments, police associations, the Federal Bureau of Investigation, and the general law enforcement community as a result of Ice-T's uncensored LP *Cop Killer* and Public Enemy's video for their song "By the Time I Get to Arizona," which features staged attacks on various Arizona state officials (Gray 1989; Grossberg 1992).

That the dominant apparatus of representation (and circulation) has responded with attempts at incorporation, surveillance, marginalization, and control tells us something about the power and potency of these expressions. What the consequences of that power will be for the rearrangement of social and cultural relations and the distribution of power in society is socially and historically contingent, and therefore remains to be played out.

10 Margin (in)to Future: From a Racial Past to a "Different" Future

> Only in a place where beliefs are viewed as a kind of seasoning or taste, like a fondness for curry or the dog track, could such optimism prevail, I thought. And I soon realized, as I listened to social workers and high school teachers talk about the viability of "multiculturalism," this generous but finally unthreatening construction meant little more than the right of immigrants to eat foods from their native countries and have their art and culture appreciated. Certainly no one I talked to seemed to imagine diversity of this kind very differently than stockbrokers do when they refer to diversified portfolios. . . . Stocks and bonds, it should be recalled, do not have long histories of antipathy; Koreans and Japanese, to take just one obvious example, do.
>
> David Rief, Los Angeles: Capital of the Third World, *1991*

Competing claims on "blackness" float in and out of our cultural imaginary at a dizzying rate: black popular claims on a glorious past such as those depicted by Eddie Murphy (*Coming to America*), Michael Jackson ("Remember the Time"), Arrested Development ("Tennessee"), and Afrocentric rappers; the "United Colors of Benetton" ad campaign that celebrates racial and ethnic difference with representations of the world as a multiracial "tribe"; the motion picture *Ghost*, in which Whoopi Goldberg's character possesses special spiritual powers that are put in the service of white heterosexual love; constructions of America's racial past such as those found in *Mississippi Burning*, *I'll Fly Away*, *Eyes on the Prize*, and *Malcolm X*; and the proliferation of icons of blackness such as "X," silhouettes of Africa, and kinte cloth adorning bodies, hats, billboards, and magazine covers.

As these media representations of blackness take form, disappear, and reappear, they call up histories, effects, sentiments, and desires. In the process, they seem to generate a certain political urgency for African Americans to interrogate the past critically, locate themselves in the present, and come to terms with their desires for the future. In this moment of struggle over the sign of blackness and terms of a multicultural future it is more and more difficult to distinguish progressive political possibilities from neoliberal and conservative rewrites of the same old racial narratives.

How are we to make sense, then, of the representational strategies and politics in mass media and popular culture whose conceptual labors are put in the service of producing a new racial subject, of rewriting a strife-ridden past into a harmonized vision of possibility, a different future? What are we to make of the rapid and rapidly changing circuit of blackness that confronts us at the blink of an eye, the click of the channel changer? And what, if anything, do these different registers and constellations of "blacknesses" tell us about different and competing claims on our racial past, about our sense of the racial present, and about the desire for and possibilities of a racial future? In the rush of these various representations of blackness, what are the economies and assumptions, desires and politics that organize and underwrite them? And, perhaps most important, have the transformations and subsequent shifts in media representations of blackness really amounted to anything?

The notion of a racialized past that frames one part of this chapter's title is intended to call attention to the United States as an explicitly racialized and sexualized social formation, that is, a formation that remains structured by unequal access to and distribution of power and rewards organized along class, race, and gender lines. I also mean it to point to the discursive regimes of representation that produce and construct images of subjects and subject positions in the cultural imaginary in terms of this racialized social formation.

I mean to mark the notion of a "different" future in my title as a way of describing and interrogating the discursive adjustments, struggles, and claims that have occurred in the dominant regimes of representation as a result of the struggles of women, African Americans, gays and lesbians, latinos, and Asians. I end this book with some observations about blackness, diversity, and multiculturalism as a way of pondering the shifts in representation taking place in popular culture and media.

In popular culture and mass media representations of race, blackness has become the cultural site of a kind of discursive shift, one that constantly recodes and repositions blackness as an entrée into America's multicultural future. Despite the urgent and complex lessons about race offered by Los Angeles in 1992 or Miami and New York in the 1980s, in the 1990s blackness seems to function still as a dominant media trope for representations and debates about race. As Americans wrestle with difficult social issues such as education, welfare, crime, the family, violence, the economy, and the collective construction and representation of themselves as a multicultural, multiracial society, the trope of blackness expresses and organizes a broad range of claims, counterclaims, and meanings about the United States as a racialized social formation.

In other words, as a cultural sign "blackness" is still called upon to perform some rather amazing feats; as Toni Morrison (1992a) puts it with reference to the Hill-Thomas hearings: "What was at stake during these hearings was historic. In addition to what was taking place, something was happening. And as is almost always the case, the site of the exorcism of critical national issues was situated in the miasma of black life and inscribed on the bodies of black people" (p. x). It is the media figure of blackness that interests me here, especially the range of cultural and social work it is called upon to perform.

The figure of blackness noted by Morrison was the site of projection, demonization, repression, desire, nostalgia, spectacle, and fear. But it also labored to realign, disarticulate, and express collective and individual hope and disappointment about American life. In a *New York Times* review of several collections about the Hill-Thomas hearings, Ronald Dworkin (1992) offers us a sense of the discursive labors and double duties that blackness had to produce: "Despite Judge Thomas' own past claims that blacks must think and act as *individuals,* in the end he appealed directly to the *black community,* above the heads of the senators he was facing, claiming that community's support just because *he was black, just because he was one of them*" (p. 38; emphasis added). As Morrison and contributors to her volume, especially Wahneema Lubiano (1992) and Kimberle Crenshaw (1992), suggest, it was the discursive field of race as a site of political and cultural spectacle where, in the hearings anyway, this image of blackness operated. This field became the crucial cultural site of the shift from race to difference. Again Toni Morrison (1992a) puts the matter most directly and clearly:

> In a racialized and race conscious society, standards are changed, facts marginalized and repressed, and the willingness to air such changes, to debate them, outweighed the seemliness of a substantive hearing because the actors were black. . . . The participants were black so what could it matter? The participants were black and therefore "known," serviceable, expendable in the interests of limning out one or the other of two mutually antagonistic fabulations. Under the pressure of voyeuristic desire, fueled by mythologies that render blacks radically serviceable instruments of private dread and longing, extraordinary behavior on the part of the state could take place. (p. xviii)

By examining the stakes, processes, and narrative economies of the hearings and their representations of race and gender, Morrison and her contributors call attention to the political and cultural spaces within which the discourse of blackness operated, in this instance, to reconfigure the politics of gender and race and, within that, the representation of blackness in the social order.

With her essay "Eating the Other," from her book *Black Looks,* bell hooks (1992) has also contributed to my thinking about these issues. By marking the circuits of what she calls the "commodification of identity and difference," hooks signals the subtle shift and distinction between nostalgia and desire. She offers a way of examining the discursive labors performed by blackness in contemporary constructions and representation of the past in the present for the construction of a vision of the future.

Together with the works of hooks and Morrison, Michael Rogin's (1990) and Wahneema Lubiano's (1992) reflections on social amnesia, media spectacle, and covert operations in contemporary cultural politics provide an angle from which to examine the discursive processes of appropriation, repression, and spectacle. Together these processes enable (in our present) a vision of the future mobilized on the labors of the past. In different ways, Rogin and Lubiano effectively use the notions of spectacle, demonization, covert operations, and amnesia to show how the Reagan/Bush presidencies on the one hand and the Hill-Thomas hearings on the other created public frames of understanding.

Both Rogin and Lubiano indicate that it was the demonization of blackness—welfare queens, the aggressive black female, the menacing black male criminal—in the public sphere of media spectacle that enabled the mobilization of a counterimage of blackness—the figure of individuality, competence, exceptionalism—as difference (as opposed to "other"). In short, blackness as menace and "other" labors at the level of media and cultural spectacle (and common sense) to produce an assimilationist and pluralist discourse about blackness anchored by difference: blackness as exceptional. This neoconservative claim on blackness as exceptional in turn represses and renders covert the very sociological understandings and political struggles against inequality, racism, and marginalization that produced it in the first place.

I want to suggest, then, that in our present moment, we can interrogate media and popular cultural representations of blackness for the discursive logic and theoretical assumptions on which visions of racial possibility are socially constructed. These constructions are mobilized around rather specific and decontextualized figures of blackness as difference. Here I mean difference not so much as a historic and structural basis for inequality, subordination, and exploitation, but as an accepted but relatively insignificant feature of contemporary multi-racial societies such as that found in the United States. The discursive repression of the collective use of difference is deeply political. That is to say, the need to repress social and political uses to which racial difference has been put in American society in favor of the recognition of individual difference and celebration of universality, meritocracy, and individualism depends on the trope of blackness. The very presence of race as a marker of individual difference rather than as the basis for historic and contemporary structured social inequality transforms and translates racialized oppression into celebratory narratives about ethnic arrival, structural openness, and multicultural tolerance. Such celebrations comfort and affirm, as I have been suggesting, precisely because they are built on specific discursive strategies—selection, repression, nostalgia, desire, and spectacle—that together recycle, recombine, and rewrite narratives of racial oppression and struggle into narratives of racial difference and pluralist toleration. Among the consequences of this discursive rewriting and incorporation are the maintenance and protection of existing structures and relations of power in terms of class, racial, and gender inequality.

To explore further this concluding example of the struggle over the sign of blackness in the media, I want to map this discursive shift from racial struggle to racial difference and its (liberal) rescripting of the cultural conditions of imaginary possibility. I do so by critically interrogating three instances of media representation of blackness. Again, I regard these representations as emblematic because they illustrate and frame the discursive shifts and readjustments at work in our media present that necessarily stage cultural representations of a different racial future. First are representations that excavate or mine a racial past on which the twin operations of desire and nostalgia are enacted. Second are representations and constructions that offer blackness as mediation "among and between" whiteness, mediations that are underwritten by processes of repression and selection. And third are those representations, staged as spectacle, that disarticulate blackness from social and sociological locations as struggles over power and challenges to structured racial and gender inequality.

Blackness and the Racial Past

During the 1980s and early 1990s, Hollywood cinema and commercial television took up the recent past, exploring the American history of race relations. *Mississippi Burning, Fried Green Tomatoes, I'll Fly Away, In the Heat of the Night, Berkeley in the Sixties, The Sixties,* and *Eyes on the Prize* are all feature films, television series, and documentaries that are either set in or concerned with the recent American racial past (especially 1954–63, the period of the modern civil rights movement). What is most interesting and revealing to me about these commercial media representations is not just their periodization and subject matter, but the way in which they have deployed and positioned representations of this historical period in our imaginary present.

Again, I am plagued by the nagging question of how to make sense of these constructions and representations and the significance of their appearance in our present—not any one of them alone, but as part of a set of discursive openings that offer a way of constructing the past, representing the present, and staging the future. In spite of their specific and individual treatments, these and related bodies of work are distinguished by their attempt to grapple with a difficult and complex period of U.S. history. With the exception, perhaps, of the award-winning PBS series *Eyes on the Prize,* many of these representations, most notably *Mississippi Burning,* have been the objects of heated debate over the representation of blacks, the movement, and the state. From the perspective of both acknowledging the horrors of the period and shaping the account of it, these representations might also be seen as expressions of desire by neoliberals and conservatives alike for distance from the days of segregation and lynching; desire for new standards against which to measure progress; desire for a kind of (racial) equality that accepts the general terms, goals, and aspirations of the civil rights movement—integration and racial tolerance; and a desire to affirm the elimination of structured social inequality. By representing this historical period in the present as desire for a future rooted in lessons about racial equality learned from the past, the way is opened for a nostalgic return and discursive recuperation—a return not to the horrors of a racial past that still remain with us, but to a distant and reconfigured imaginary past. In a racialized formation such as that in the United States, which remains structured by gender and racial social inequality and exploitation, such desires and claims on the past cut more than one way.

From the angle of contemporary American racial struggle and complexity (class, gender, and ethnicity), there are, to be sure, African American claims on and reappropriations of the same period. As evidenced by the popular imagery of black youth culture noted in the previous chapter, black claims on this period privilege and then celebrate the aspirations, militance, and anger of the black nationalist and black power movements. In this struggle to lay claim to the past, which might be read as a counterdiscourse to dominant cinematic and television representations of the civil rights movement, it is Malcolm X who is the object of black youthful celebration and political desire. The commercial representation of the civil rights movement and the goals of integration and interracial cooperation seem not to have much salience for large numbers of contemporary black youth.

Prompted by David Bradley's (1992) careful and thoughtful reflections about the place of Malcolm X in the popular imaginary, I would suggest that regardless of the content of the claims over the truth status of the history, African American claims about the past are also called upon to perform a certain kind of discursive labor, a clearing of sorts into which new conditions of cultural and political possibility can also be imaged (see also Early 1992; Wood 1992). In the context of contemporary racial suspicions, social hostilities, economic dislocations, and political powerlessness, both this counterrepresentation and dominant commercial media representations find resonance. To be sure, they are expressed in different registers and articulate differently positioned segments of American society, but their cultural power is inescapable.

What interests me, moreover, is their coexistence and struggle in the same discursive media space. In this sense, all of these representations constitute claims on the past as desires, in hooks's sense, for constructing a vision of the future. It is not just the sharp differences in claims on the past that define the discursive labors of different representations of the recent past, but the way they mark and mobilize that past in the service of the present and the future. These discourses exemplify what George Lipsitz (1990b) calls struggles over the memory and countermemory, and, most important, they are registered at the site of popular and commercial culture.

Black Exceptionalism as Difference

Ghost, with its performance by Whoopi Goldberg, and *The Hand That Rocks the Cradle* are two films from the past decade or so (*Trading Places, The Shining,* and *Sister Act* also come to mind) in which blackness as difference performs a certain kind of discursive labor in the social construction of visions of the future.[1] In both films, blackness is figured as cultural and personal qualities that transcend and, from the position of dominant spectatorship established by the films, reinscribe whiteness as the normative site of everyday life. Although the films are staged from the vantage point of whites, exceptional blacks are acknowledged, even embraced. As with images of black success in television news and talk shows, this exceptional blackness has to be harnessed and ultimately placed in the service of good.

Because the "multicultural" perspectives of these films explicitly represent blackness and difference as routine facts of everyday American life, little attention is required and therefore given to noting or commenting on these qualities of difference. There is little explicit need to bring blackness into the orbit of American humanity and sociability. Because it is already marked as a sign of individual difference, the problem, rather, is to translate this difference and the exceptionalism on which it is based into a universal sign of possibility for other blacks. For whites this quality of difference and its positioning within whiteness operates to break down racial barriers and suspicion. (Think, for instance, of the social dynamic about race and blackness at work in the media's coverage and celebration of the achievements and reign of the former chair of the Joint Chiefs, General Colin Powell.)

Unlike the historic stereotypes of blackness—figured as inferiority and loyalty to whiteness—in earlier generations of Hollywood cinema (Guerrero 1993), contemporary films in the age of multiculturalism begin with the figure of blackness and difference. The struggle is not to make blackness representable so much as it is to contain it and make contemporary media representation of it part of the normative order. Thus, the labors of black images in many of these films are not about convincing us of the salience of black subject positions, but about how to make such positions serve. The black characters in *Ghost, Fried Green Tomatoes,* and *The Hand That Rocks the Cradle,* for example, rewrite and recycle traditional roles of racial difference—the obedient African slave and Native American as well as the compliant latino and Asian whose particular histories, circumstances, and desires are either erased entirely or subordinated to the film's central subjects. Ironically, the twist in these films is that difference within blackness (spirituality, musicality, humanity) is marked as a quality that, when put to use, can do a world of good. In the end, the Goldberg character in *Ghost* is both a spiritual conduit from the world of the living to that of the dead and an affirmation that the triple sites of other—blackness, spirituality, woman—are, as Morrison says, known and thus serviceable to that ultimate American fantasy—romantic love and the white heterosexual family.

Similarly, the condition of mental retardation or undying loyalty is coded as the mark of humanity and innocence and packaged in the black bodies of maids, servants, cooks, and gardeners. In *The Hand That Rocks the Cradle* and *Fried Green Tomatoes,* black bodies are the sites onto which are projected racial and sexual suspicions and knowledge/insight. In these films, black characters instinctively sense and witness evil and abuse at the hands of whites and, within the limits of their social power and location, act to stop it. In the final analy-

sis, black agency in these films is possible only at a purely metaphysi-
cal level, although physical acts of courage by blacks suggest fierce
loyalty, devotion, and caring for "their" white folk.

Because these films explicitly acknowledge difference, it is this acknowledgment that marks the place and presence of blackness, both in
the present and in the future. And of course it is this quality of difference that resolves the crisis of white familial and romantic love. These
representations are underwritten, then, by appeals to blackness, to exceptionalism, to difference. Such appeals are culturally resonant in
many quarters because they repress and then bypass the messiness of
racial conflict and struggle that is rooted in historical and contemporary relations of unequal power, social inequality, and economic exploitation. I still marvel at the lengths to which film producers and directors go to acknowledge and normalize blackness. For example,
there is an uncanny correspondence between the character played by
Cicely Tyson in *Fried Green Tomatoes* and that played by Hattie
McDaniel in *Gone with the Wind* (and even Morgan Freeman in *Driving Miss Daisy*). Both actresses offer stellar performances, to be sure.
Nevertheless, in both films, and especially *Fried Green Tomatoes,*
black women are figured as protective and loyal servants who enable
white women's humanity without ever so much as hinting about their
own lives, families, or histories. Even in celebrated contemporary films
about (white) sisterhood, such as *Fried Green Tomatoes,* this part of
the story is simply and easily repressed. Even in the film's enlightened
and complex treatment of gender, blackness is both present and absent. Black characters simply appear, completely embedded in a white
world.

Blackness as Spectacle

Consider for a moment the dominant frame that defined the national
press coverage of the Los Angeles riots—racial discourses of black and
white conflict, criminal discourses of lawlessness, economic discourses
of private property, moral discourses of irresponsibility, the public
spectacle of a city out of control. In the search for a hook or an angle
from which to cover the crisis, the national press seemed at once *para-
lyzed* by an inability to speak coherently about race and *spellbound* by
the action, the drama, the spectacle.[2] We witnessed at once the continual search for a frame (and, in the process, the selective erasure of
contemporary complexities about racial and urban politics in post-
civil rights America) and the continual intrusion of a frame—the spectacle and drama of racial conflict—that would not go away (Gooding-
Williams 1993). The fact of this incoherence together with television's

dependence on spectacle and drama (witness the proliferation of real-ity-based crime, cop, and rescue shows on commercial television) pro-duced coverage that dramatically illustrates how the political and cul-tural issue of race is both acknowledged and displaced at one and the same moment.

Next, consider the coverage of the Anita Hill-Clarence Thomas hearings. Two African Americans made claims and counterclaims about character, competence, sexuality, social class, blackness, and gender. Their blackness and the different articulations and disarticula-tions their blackness produced across and within difference, like the riots, affirmed the salience of race in the American social and cultural landscape in the context of Reaganism and at the very same time de-nied that salience. The spectacle of the hearing produced and exacer-bated deeply felt contradictions within black communities and across the borders of race, gender, and class. Although these shifting alliances revealed both the contradictions and the limitations of essentialist ap-proaches to race, like the coverage of the Los Angeles riots they were still activated and represented through the spectacle of a media system strongly driven by the demands and requirements of drama, conflict, and action. As Toni Morrison (1992a) notes, the representation and coverage of the hearings by the media were as important as the sub-stantive issues with which they were concerned.

Along with the power of these events as media spectacles, the frames that defined and anchored them, like Hollywood film, oper-ated through the strategies of repression and amnesia, which left out significant elements that shaped and produced them—in the case of Los Angeles, the presence of European, Asian, latino, and African ra-cial and ethnic groups and complex internal distinctions, conditions, and histories for each; the structural, social, and historical conditions that shaped and defined the sites of conflict, contact, and alliance; the persistence of unemployment, violence, gangs, and a pattern of urban neglect; and the historic strategies of surveillance, policing, deporta-tion, and police violence.

Left out of the coverage of the Hill-Thomas hearings were the poli-tics and relations of power along lines of class, gender, and sexuality within African American communities; the debates and conflicts be-tween black and white feminists; and the politics and relations of power within African American communities along the lines of social class. Also omitted from Thomas's own mobility story were his social and political connections to patriarchs of conservative power. Absent too were Anita Hill's own particular history, formation, and alliances. In this television spectacle, blackness operated as an empty signifier available for mobilization and use by black nationalists, liberal feminists, and conservative white males in an always ready discourse about race, gender, and sexuality.

Wahneema Lubiano's (1992) analysis of the representations and spectacle of the hearings is insightful:

> Cover stories . . . simultaneously mask and reveal political power and its manipulations. Cover stories cover or mask what they make invisible with an alternative presence, a presence that redirects our attention, that covers or makes absent what has to remain unseen if the seen is to function as the scene for a different drama. One story provides a cover that allows another story (or stories) to slink out of site. Like the covers of secret agents, cover stories are faces for other texts. They are the pretexts that obscure context, fade out subtexts and in the case of the Clarence Thomas hearings protect the texts of the powerful. (p. 324)

Television audiences who watched were treated to the spectacle of black male-female hostility, judgments about black intellectual competence, displays of white male patronage, and titillating talk about black bodies and sex.

Lubiano's account is equally applicable to media coverage of the Los Angeles riots. In the coverage of the L.A. crisis, lawlessness, family dissolution, innocent victims, model minorities, and menacing black bodies all helped keep viewers glued to their sets. The spectacle of public lawlessness and "colored" (read in the media coverage as black) rage, together with neoconservative discourses of immorality and irresponsibility, served to mobilize and redefine acceptable notions of blackness and difference. This media spectacle of racialized rage, together with repression and amnesia, cleared the way for another notion of cultural difference in general and blackness in particular. Difference and exceptionalism could be joined to acknowledge and celebrate individuality, cultural uniqueness, and membership in the "United Colors of Benetton." Such membership does not require recognition and critique of structures of power and social formations that are gendered and racialized.

Television's New Black Subjects: A Different Future?

In dominant media and popular culture we see the emergence and construction of new black subjects and subject positions. These new discursive subjects are situated in cultural and media representations of a racial order marked discursively by images that incorporate notions of blackness into the existing social, cultural, and political order without necessarily challenging and disturbing that order. As Lubiano (1992) notes, "Thomas made himself not a 'man' but an empty vessel into which the state could pour what it needed and then attempt to make all of us consume it as blackness, an ineffable blackness in order to draw attention away from what we are actually consuming: yet another narrative of state power" (p. 335).

In the framing of these representations of blackness as small, insignificant matters of difference (rather than the basis for structures and relations of power) and in the presentation of them as spectacle in the circuits of film, advertising, and television, the relationship of these constructions to what Lipsitz (1990b) calls lived histories and social struggles is safely hidden and relegated to the level of the covert. The special and unique qualities of African Americans, whether Whoopi Goldberg or Clarence Thomas or Malcolm X, can be celebrated and folded into the existing system of gender, race, and class. Daily we witness on television the transformations of racialized relations of power into entertainment and spectacle based on difference. Like so much of what happens on television, this move represents a kind of approved and sanctioned knowing and not knowing. In this rearticulation, the existing order can be affirmed, as can the new and different subject positions that it underwrites. But as African American claims and struggles within and over the representation of blackness suggest, this is only one possible articulation. Cultural struggles, including those over the representation of blackness in our *present,* help to prepare the groundwork, to create spaces for how we think about our highly charged racial *past* and possibilities for our different and yet-contested future. Commercial television is central to this cultural struggle. In the 1980s, claims and representations of African Americans were waged in the glare of television. Those representations and the cultural struggles that produced them will, no doubt, continue to shape the democratic and multiracial future of the United States.

Postscript

With the end of Reaganism and the election of Bill Clinton, the discursive claims on blackness in political debate, journalism, and culture wars entered yet another articulation. Media spectacles in the 1980s and early 1990s were crucial to this realignment—the Los Angeles riots and subsequent trials; the Anita Hill-Clarence Thomas hearings; continuing controversies over rap music; continuing press coverage of rampant violence and drugs in the inner cities; the Dan Quayle-Murphy Brown television exchanges over motherhood, family, and traditional values.

Bill Clinton certainly positioned himself and his administration to make different claims and interventions in this newly configured discourse. Clinton visited black communities and churches during his campaign for the presidency, thereby establishing a more welcoming and less hostile relationship to African Americans and questions of race.

President Clinton has appointed prominent men and women of color to key posts in his administration and has given significant speeches that explicitly address the concerns of blacks. At the same time, however, he publicly abandoned a key black female nominee—Lani Guinier—when questions about her legal writings and policy positions came under public scrutiny. Clinton backtracked on key campaign pledges, such as the promise to recognize gays and lesbians in the military. He also spent an enormous amount of cultural and political capital to ensure passage of the North American Free Trade Agreement, even though it pitted him against key sectors of his constituency, especially labor. He has repeated this pattern in his lack of a clear and firm policy on Haiti. Even with this new articulation, code words such as *crime, underclass, gangs,* and *violence* continue to stand in for blackness, marginality, and aberrant behavior. (And news reports suggest that in many ways the United States in the 1990s is more racially segregated than it was in the 1960s.)

As I was completing this book, I would often look in on the offerings in the afternoon portion of the TV schedule. The afternoons are, of course, increasingly populated with inexpensive reality-based shows, entertainment newsmagazines, and talk shows hosted by Les, Sally, Geraldo, Phil, Jenny, and Oprah. Amid the clutter and chatter about broken families, psychotic breaks, sex-change operations, and unrealized love, I found on afternoon television considerable and engaging talk, debate, and struggles over race in the United States. True, much, if not all, of this talk is thoroughly steeped in a therapeutic model of feel-good insight and individual transformation, but under the glare of the hot lights of television it is one of the few places where such conversations take place on a regular basis.

Black-oriented television shows continue to come and go on commercial network television with alarming, if not predictable, frequency, and most of the ones that survive continue to operate within the separate-but-equal television world. By spring 1994, *Roc, Sinbad,* and *South Central* had all been canceled. Arsenio Hall had also decided to call it quits. Those shows that survive continue to present safe, predictable, and familiar images of (mostly young) black Americans. Cable offerings occasionally challenge the sealed-up television worlds of blackness and whiteness with programming that explores various kinds of diversity, but many of these are still limited to music, comedy, variety, and sports.

In the rush of industry reorganization and mergers, the television networks (like the popular music industry with rap and the National Basketball Association with Magic Johnson and Michael Jordan) turned to African Americans to get through their crisis. Yet in the wake of restructuring and the formation of new players in the television game, it appears as if blacks are once again out of fashion on commercial television, except as sources of amusement, titillation, and fascination. Broad sectors of the U.S. television viewing audience, it seems, are no longer interested in the lives and experiences of African Americans.

With the cancellations of *Roc, South Central, Sinbad,* and *The Arsenio Hall Show* at the end of the 1993–94 television season, the pickings on commercial network television are, once again, pretty slim. I was particularly disappointed (and distressed) to learn of the cancellations of *Roc* and *South Central.* As direct descendants of *Frank's Place,* these two programs in particular most clearly represented for me high moments of innovative possibility and direction for black representations in commercial network television. I was prepared to rethink many of the arguments made in this book, and, most important, the cancellations troubled my initial (hopeful) conclusions. I thought that perhaps I had been too hopeful, too optimistic about the disturbances and possibilities for black cultural politics at the site of commercial culture. I worried that the cancellations of such fine programs signaled a theoretical endorsement of a more pessimistic "business as usual" reading of television and its treatment of blacks.

In the end I have resisted this impulse. I have come to realize that the social and cultural conditions that produced these moments have changed and that the conditions of the present moment may require a different kind of conversation, dialogue, challenge, and representation. Just as the presence and work of black athletes, musicians, and writers have reconfigured and redefined the very nature of sports, sounds, and stories in the social and cultural life of the United States, so too has the presence of *The Cosby Show, Frank's Place, Roc, A Different World, In Living Color,* and *South Central.* These and future representations of and claims on blackness are part of an ongoing dialogue within and across social locations and positions within and outside black communities. Black television makers, audiences, storytellers, and programming have transformed the look and feel of commercial network television. Inevitably, television programs about and representations of blacks will come and go, but I remain hopeful about the force and vitality of African American claims on the meanings, circuits, and uses of representations of blackness. I remain alert to the fact that such claims are sites of political and cultural struggle, that they are conditioned socially and are without pure political guarantees; they are, nevertheless, crucial sites and expressions of struggle.

Notes

1. Black Cultural Politics and Commercial Culture

1. This question is generated by the important work of Stuart Hall on issues of representation and articulation. See, for example, Hall (1985, 1989).

2. Reaganism and the Sign of Blackness

1. It seems to me that along with neoconservatives, black youth have also understood the centrality of media and commercial popular culture.

2. Of course, for large numbers of blacks, latinos, the poor, heterosexual women, and gays and lesbians, Reaganism represented the greatest threat to a life of hope and possibility in the United States.

3. I would like to thank David Wellman for calling my attention to the historic shifts in neoconservative claims on whiteness. See also Takagi (1993) and Wellman (1993).

4. I thank Harvey Molotch of the University of California, Santa Barbara, for his sharp insights; "culture of civility" is his term to describe civil society in the post-civil rights period.

5. Clyde Taylor (1991) and David Roediger (1991) show how similar strategies were used, especially in film and minstrelsy, in late-nineteenth- and early-twentieth-century America.

6. In October 1993, network news broadcasts covered black churches and community groups in New York City that launched a public attack on hard-core rap music and artists for the use of derisive language and degrading images of black women.

7. See Greg Tate's *Flyboy in the Buttermilk* (1992) for an interesting account of the Bush inaugural party.

8. Professor Childs offered these remarks at a campus forum held at the University of California, Santa Cruz, in the immediate aftermath of the Los Angeles riots, May 1992.

9. See Gerald Early's essays on the African American contestants and winners of Miss America contests in the 1980s in his *Tuxedo Junction* (1989).

10. In some instances, as in the short-lived Fox series *Alien Nation,* racial politics and race issues can be represented without the presence of blacks.

3. African American Discourses and the Sign of Blackness

1. Commercial television talk shows such as those hosted by Oprah Winfrey, Phil

Donahue, and Arsenio Hall, along with such public television forums as *The McNeil/ Lehrer NewsHour, Frontline,* and *P.O.V.,* as well as commercial films such as *Do the Right Thing, Boyz N the Hood,* and *Straight Out of Brooklyn,* and rap music controversies involving Ice-T, Ice Cube, N.W.A., 2 Live Crew, and others, more often than not provided the access points for routine discussions among African Americans about pressing issues of the day.

2. Of course, in this regard one of the great challenges still facing television network news remains how to make complex stories about economic crises or housing policies come to life. In the face of this persistent problem, news producers and network executives rely on entertainment conventions such as conflict, drama, and character to make complex stories intelligible and entertaining. The recent spate of simulated-reality programs based on the lives of rescue workers, cops, and drug agents simply extends this logic.

3. Delia Douglas, a graduate student in sociology at the University of California, Santa Cruz, has noted the relative silence and marginalization of black Canadians in U.S. and British cultural studies discussions of identity, blackness, and oppositional culture. I want to thank Delia for calling my attention to the vibrant and productive discussions of blackness taking place in Canada.

4. In the midst of attacks on affirmative action, suspicion and hostility between traditional departments and African American scholars, and a lucrative job market based on the academic star system, diasporic and postcolonial scholars have been especially appealing to many elite U.S. universities. Black academic stars from England, the Caribbean, Africa, and South Asia have often been sought out aggressively by elite American universities, whereas many African American scholars have not.

5. I take this particular reference to the burden of representation from Marlon Riggs's 1991 documentary, *Color Adjustment.*

6. To this list I would certainly add the novels of Ishmael Reed and Alice Walker.

7. See the recent literature now available on black cinema, for example: Cham and Andrade-Watkins (1988), *Framework* (1989); Diawara (1992a, 1992b, 1993), Pines and Willemen (1989), and Guererro (1993).

8. Of course, there are important critiques, debates, defenses, and explorations of the contradictions and tensions in rap on questions of nationalism, gender, sexuality, and race. For an examination of the best of this work, see Rose (1994), Kelley (1994), Zook (1992, 1994), and Tate (1992).

4. The Transformation of the Television Industry and the Social Production of Blackness

1. Discussions with Tommy Lott and Clyde Taylor helped shape many of the ideas in this section.

2. Other significant shows from the late 1980s and early 1990s successfully employed this targeting strategy, including *Hill Street Blues, St. Elsewhere, thirtysomething,* and *Twin Peaks.*

3. Since 1986, with the appearance and runaway success of *The Cosby Show,* no network has begun a new television season without at least one black-oriented program in its lineup.

4. At a 1990 University of California, Santa Barbara, sociology colloquium, Harvey Molotch referred to such acknowledgment as a part of the post-civil rights "culture of civility." I thank him for this insight.

5. See also Simon Frith's *Facing the Music* (1988) for a more detailed argument about the relationships among corporate sponsorship, music television, advertising, and popular music.

6. Ken Auletta (1991) exhaustively details the players, circumstances, and stakes involved in these transformations at the networks. My account and summary of the changes at the networks in this section are heavily indebted to press reports and the discussions of Auletta, Ben Block (1990a), and Huntington Williams (1989).

7. General Electric's managerial expertise and productivity lay in the areas of electronic equipment, home appliances, and heavy manufacturing, and much of its style and approach to managing the television network came from experience in these areas.

8. Two previous takeover attempts by others had been unsuccessful.

9. According to *Newsweek*, CBS fired some seven hundred people in the broadcast group in the summer of 1986, which resulted in a savings of $40–50 million. In 1986, CBS experienced the first quarterly loss in its history (Powell and Alter 1986).

10. In the most notable public fight during the entire period, Dan Rather sparred on the air with then presidential candidate George Bush. In another episode, Rather walked off the set of the *CBS Evening News,* leaving the screen blank for a short period and an embarrassed network and news division without an anchor for its prestigious evening news broadcast.

11. Using categories such as social class, ethnicity, and gender, popular culture has historically played an important role in the creation and production of its discursive object—in this case, the black audience for delivery to advertisers. These themes have been productively explored by Lipsitz (1990a), Marchand (1985), Press (1991), and Spigel (1992). Their studies are especially notable because together they illustrate the increasing refinement and logic of differentiation at work in the labors of popular culture and the media.

12. In interviews that I conducted in 1989 and 1990 with black producers, writers, and actors, almost to a person, they all reported that the television industry operates on the basis of a kind of benign racism—not explicit, seldom hostile, and deeply embedded in the tradition and culture of the business. These black industry personnel described the subtle ways in which interest in things African American is marginal to nonexistent. Sally Steenland (1987, 1989) reports data that, structurally at least, support these more qualitative assessments of the culture of television.

5. The Politics of Representation in Network Television

1. One of the very specific ways in which the presence of these limited spheres of individual influence has been expressed in the organization and production of television programs about blacks is through the use of black professionals as consultants and advisers in the development of programs featuring blacks. For an interesting discussion of this phenomenon in the cases of women, Mexican Americans, and blacks in television, see Katheryn Montgomery's *Target Prime Time* (1989).

2. See Horowitz (1989) for a detailed discussion of the role of black film executives in the production of several commercially successful films in the 1980s.

3. In some instances, black actors and actresses exert some influence on the creative vision and direction of black representations. These actors and actresses, however, do not or may not choose to receive production and writing titles (interview with Marla Gibbs, 1990; see also Zook 1994).

4. My interview data confirm observations made by Gitlin (1983), Horowitz (1989), and Steenland (1987, 1989).

5. Black studio and network executives with whom I spoke reported that black executives are concentrated at the middle levels of the management structure, where they often have the power to stop a project, but few are positioned at the very top, where they can "green-light" a project (interviews with Stanley Robertson, Dolores Morris, and Frank Dawson, 1990). See also Horowitz (1989).

6. See *Black Film Review* (1993) for a discussion of the crucial role of black filmmakers such as Oscar Micheaux in generating counterrepresentations of blacks.

7. Also, black women were big, loud, and dark, and fulfilled the role of the nurturing caretaker of the white home (e.g., *Beulah*).

8. In 1952, *Amos 'n' Andy* received an Emmy Award nomination (Ely 1991).

9. Many of the criticisms leveled at rap music and programs such as *In Living Color* have their roots in the black cultural politics of this period. Concerns about racial embarrassment, black perpetuation of stereotypes, and so on were as urgent, especially for the black middle class, then as they are now.

10. Another show from the period that followed this pattern for the social construction and representation of blackness was *Room 222*.

11. Other variety shows of the period featuring black hosts included *The Leslie Uggams Show* (1969), *The Flip Wilson Show* (1970–74), and *The New Bill Cosby Show* (1972–73).

12. In the early 1970s, *The Flip Wilson Show,* a comedy-variety show starring comedian Flip Wilson, enjoyed a four-year run. The show has been characterized as a breakthrough in commercial television because it was the first black-led variety show to rate consistently among the top-rated shows in television. This show included, among other things, the kind of black-based parody and humor that would reappear in the late 1980s with the explosion of black comedy and variety (see Kolbert 1993).

13. See Dates (1990:257) for an inventory of black-oriented miniseries that aired following the commercial success of *Roots.*

14. *The Jeffersons* originally aired in 1975 and enjoyed a ten-year run. I place the series in relationship to these other programs because of the centrality of the mobility narrative in the show. Discursively, the series is important to the shows set in poverty because it serves to reinforce (rather than simply realize) the mobility myth.

15. African American writers from 227 told me that in the culture of the industry, black-oriented programs that explicitly attempt to address issues of inequality and racism or that seem to have a didactic function are regarded as "message shows." They also suggested that from the perspective of studios and the networks, such shows are perceived as risky and difficult to bring to the screen without stirring up trouble or offending some primary constituent (e.g., producers, networks, advertisers) in the production process (interviews with writers, 1990).

16. *The Arsenio Hall Show* is similar in this respect. The chatty format is really about the class and mobility aspirations of a new generation of young blacks and whites.

17. One of the executive producers at 227 described the show as a "reality-based show about a nice middle-class black family," therefore not a show with "messages or anything of that nature." She also conceded that the primary interest of the show is comedy (interview with Irma Kalish, 1990).

18. During the 1992–93 season, shows such as *Roc* and *Where I Live* continued this approach to programs about blacks.

19. Although designed to showcase the individual stars of the show, aesthetically *The Cosby Show*'s style also moved through subtle but noticeable changes, the most remarkable being the slow evolution of the show's opening strip over successive seasons. The background setting and theme music for the show's opening moved steadily from an

empty blue screen (accompanied by jazz) background to a tropical island setting (accompanied by steel pans and Caribbean music) to a grafitti-filled wall on an urban street corner (accompanied by urban-based funk).

20. The continued circulation and availability of many of these older programs through reruns and cable are central to my claim that these programs are structured by pluralist discourses.

21. See Dates and Barlow (1990) for discussion of the formation, operation, and impact of black media organizations and black participation in mass media in the United States.

22. See Fregoso (1990a:264). The special issue of *Cultural Studies* published in October 1990 represents an important intervention by Chicana/o scholars on the issue of identity, racial politics, and cultural representation (Chabram and Fregoso 1990). See also Hall (1988).

23. Paul Gilroy (1991b) has written rather persuasively about the cultural impress of blacks in England on the normative notions of what it means to be British, especially black and British. George Lipsitz (1990a) makes a similar argument.

6. It's a Different World Where You Come From

1. The observations and analysis in this chapter are based on interviews with Susan Fales, screenings of episodes of *A Different World* from fall 1989 to spring 1992, and observations at a taping of one episode in spring 1990. All statements attributed to Fales are from my interviews with her in spring 1990.

2. Though the writers included a diverse mix of people from different gender, ethnic, and racial backgrounds, Fales admitted that they all attended predominantly white colleges and universities.

3. This issue was a particularly sensitive one for experienced black writers on shows that came to be regarded as black message shows. Several black writers on these shows were especially troubled by this label, particularly given that their stories were not appreciated, they seldom got the chance to do other material, their work was not recognized, and the fact that there is so much mediocrity and cultural gatekeeping in the industry. This impression is certainly driven home by a recent Writers Guild report on the status of minority writers in the guild and in the industry (Bielby and Bielby, 1989b; see also Bielby and Bielby 1989a; Steenland 1989).

4. As happened with *The Cosby Show,* this focus on the black middle-class style and its circulation through television invites criticism about the commodity character and function of the show. Hence, the place of black style in the show is seen by such critics not just as an expression of blackness but also as a sales pitch for the reduction of black style to commodity. In my view, this critical observation is not without merit, but though it is obviously true in some respects, the show also inhabited the public spaces of television to make claims on blackness and black youth culture that have been heretofore absent. After all, commercial television itself is the quintessential space of commodification.

5. Other shows, such as *Amen, Homeroom,* and *Out All Night,* have been set in more public places. *Amen* is typical of what happened to all of these shows—they quickly retreated into home-place domesticity. Although *Amen* was ostensibly set in the black church, the show's dominant narrative and subsequently its humor came to depend on activities and relationships in the home.

6. In my interview with her, Fales noted that most of the writers on *A Different World* were graduates of predominantly white, often elite, universities.

7. Indeed, I have often wondered whether *A Different World* was the vehicle through which its creator, Bill Cosby, could get some of his more explicit political and social concerns aired on television without risking his own image and considerable power as a corporate pitchman and best-selling author.

7. Frank's Place

1. Most of the information in this section was taken from a day-long seminar and discussion with *Frank's Place* coexecutive producer Hugh Wilson. The seminar was held in New Orleans, Louisiana, in November 1988. Many of the details of the production of the show are more fully reported and developed in Campbell and Reeves (1990). For a different reading, see White (1991) and Reeves and Campbell (1989).

2. Wilson's best-known and most commercially successful film was *Police Academy.*

3. Wilson made these remarks during the seminar discussion described in note 1, above.

4. Even this figure seems modest compared with the reported $1 million per episode cost of *The Cosby Show.* See Lippman (1990).

5. In the course of its twelve-month run, *Frank's Place* was bounced around the CBS schedule constantly, occupying six different time slots on four different nights.

6. Wilson made these remarks during the seminar discussion described in note 1, above.

7. It is not surprising that Wilson used this approach, given that he honed his writing and directing skills at MTM studios, where this approach was widely used.

8. Some observers in the television industry attribute the commercial failure of *Frank's Place* to its blurring of these genres and its failure to develop a clear identity.

9. The cancellation of *Frank's Place* prompted widespread protests and letter-writing campaigns on the part of organizations such as the National Urban League and the NAACP.

10. Other notable programs with a strong sense of place have included *Dallas* (Texas), *Newhart* (Vermont), *The Andy Griffith Show* (North Carolina), *Designing Women* (Atlanta), and *Spencer for Hire* and *St. Elsewhere* (Boston).

11. This universe of African American cultural sensibilities is rare in commercial television; one other site where such representation occurs is music videos.

12. My observations on this point are indebted to Rosa Linda Fregoso (1990b), who offers a similar analysis about the use of music to establish cultural location and significance in Chicano film.

13. See White (1991) for an interesting discussion of what she sees as a move away from the hegemony of this "normative" power toward an "indifference" that appears in the guise of diversity. See also my response to White in Gray (1993b).

14. One episode explored color caste and class conflicts within the southern black experience. In this episode, Frank was faced with the difficult task of choosing between two black fraternal organizations that were distinguished by class background and skin color. A similar theme was, of course, at the center of Spike Lee's *School Daze.*

15. The presentation of music was also significant because of the space in the program given to both traditional African music and dance and American jazz. Musicians and dancers performed in traditional African costumes. (A further affirmation of the close relationship between Africans and African Americans was expressed by Hanna's mother, who, during the performance by the African troupe, explained to Tiger [and the audience] the origins of various costumes and the symbolism of the instruments.)

16. In the 1950s, Gillespie hired the Cuban drummer Chano Pozo to play in his band.

17. For example, as a family acquaintance and adviser, Frank is interested in securing the best academic environment for Calvin; Calvin's mother, who is both proud and tired, wants Calvin to make the right decision and for the circus to end; Calvin's high school coach wants a university coaching position; Chick, the university recruiter, wants a successful basketball program and to compete in the final four at the NCAA basketball tournament; Calvin wants "to wear number 17, to play on national television, to start [his] freshman year, and a twelve million dollar NBA contract." In contrast to the collective pressures on Calvin and the interests of those around him, Calvin's aspirations seem simple, albeit poorly prioritized. Against the background of his eighth-grade reading ability and weak high school preparation, his goals seem out of reach.

18. *The Cosby Show* must also be credited with introducing references to historically black colleges into the plots and narratives of situation comedy. Cliff and Clair Huxtable talked about having attended Hillman, a fictitious black college, and their daughter Denise also decided to go there. Filmmaker Spike Lee's influence on this issue should not be lost; his successful musical *School Daze* was set in a southern black college.

8. Spectacles, Sideshows, and Irreverence

1. In the context of this discussion I use the term *enabled* in a very particular way: to specify the potential articulations of television texts with the expression of issues, debates, and moods operating in the society; to identify established traditions and practices; and to identify frames, perspectives, and positions operating in the social construction of meanings.

2. Here I am invoking a notion of popularity at odds with a market or industrial approach based on the numbers of viewers. Rather, this notion of popularity is rooted in the identification and mobilization of identifications and practices in discourse. See Fregoso (1990a), Hall (1981b), Fiske (1989), and Lipsitz (1990b).

3. For an interesting account of some of the conflicts, largess, jealousies, and mismanagement at Fox in its early years, see Block (1990a).

4. Executives at Fox also hired filmmaker James L. Brooks to produce *The Simpsons* (Brooks also had a great deal of television experience, having won several Emmys for writing and producing *The Mary Tyler Moore Show*) and Topper Carew to produce *Homeroom*.

5. Among some of the forerunners in this genre I would include *The Steve Allen Show, Your Show of Shows, The Ernie Kovacs Show, The Flip Wilson Show,* and the short-lived *Richard Pryor Show*.

6. During its first season, *In Living Color* won an Emmy for outstanding variety, music, or comedy program.

7. Ajaye moved on to another comedy-variety television show about blacks, Fox's short-lived *Townsend Television*.

8. Of course, this stance always has the potential to reinscribe and privilege a particular (nationalist) construction of blackness that is rooted in the position of the black middle-class male heterosexual.

9. I would like to thank Clyde Taylor for calling my attention to this dimension of the show's humor.

9. Jammin' on the One!

1. This notion of cultural struggle implies, at the very least, the existence of access to various forms of power and the ability to implement them. Given the material con-

straints on black youth and their access to various forms and expressions of power, the location of struggles over meaning at the site of culture is of particular interest. The attempt of black youth to assert subjectivity and authority through the use of the body, language, music, dance, and so on represents an important moment and an attempt to bring a measure of equality to their unequal access and relationship to various quarters of the dominant culture. I thank Teshome Gabriel for bringing this point to my attention.

2. The observations in this section have greatly benefited from my discussions with Rosa Linda Fregoso.

3. In particular, my observations are drawn from representations found on Black Entertainment Television (*Video Soul, Rap City*) and MTV (*Yo! MTV Raps*).

4. This unity is detectable in the music of rap culture, the fusions and collaborations of Miles Davis and Quincy Jones, the dynamism of Janet Jackson and her calls for unity of the rhythm nation, and in Public Enemy's anthem, "Fight the Power." It is also expressed in the dance movement of Pee-wee Herman and the running man, and in verbal expressions such as "Jammin' on the one."

5. Like musical tastes, hairstyles represent one of the earliest and most important expressions available to youth for separating and distancing themselves from adult authority, institutional control, and social practices where they do not have a great deal of power, space, or voice.

6. I want to thank Rosa Linda Fregoso for pointing out the dual significance of this dance and its name. One of my students further complicated my reading of this dance by pointing out that it meant one thing prior to the commercial success and adoption of it by M. C. Hammer and Vanilla Ice and something quite different afterward. My thanks to Ryan Monihan for this important insight.

7. For an interesting and often amusing discussion of the institutional policing of the contemporary body by the state, see Kroker and Kroker (1988). See also Bakhtin (1984) and Hebdige (1989).

8. These expressions are not limited to the world of popular music performance or athletics. They are also expressed in the performance of the black minister and in the detectable leaks in the formal presentation and demeanor of the Wall Street banker or the college professor. I also think that traces of the kind I have described constitute one of the ways in which inscriptions of black cultural sensibilities are expressed in commercial television. Obviously, what is detectable as an expression of African American sensibilities has less to do with biology (black skin) than with performance and presentation through language and the body. Examples of these kinds of leaks and expressions can be seen in the character of Thelma on the series *Amen*. For an interesting discussion of this topic, see comments by South African pianist Abdullah Ibrahim (Dollar Brand) in a video titled *A Brother with Perfect Timing*.

9. Lisa Kennedy and bell hooks, among others, have recently made similar observations about black films. They charge that in black films the subjectivities of women are contained by black men (*Do The Right Thing*) and that the subjectivities of darker, working-class segments of the black community are subordinated and marginal to those of fairer and middle-class blacks (*House Party*). For more complete elaboration, see Kennedy (1990) and Wallace (1992a).

10. Another illustration of this set of discourses can be seen in two stories that appeared in the March 7, 1990, issue of the *Los Angeles Times*. One story, which appeared with a large photo, was a racial uplift story about the successful crossover of black radio (i.e., urban contemporary). The piece detailed the rise and successful bridging of black and white markets by black radio stations and programmers in major U.S. markets. (In the photo that accompanied the story, a respectable black businessman appeared in a

tailored business suit.) To the immediate right of this story was another story about black music. This one, what I would call a problem story, reported the details of a Florida state investigation into a Miami-based rap group accused of presenting suggestive, pornographic, and otherwise unacceptable lyrics in their music. Headlined "2 Live Crew, Nasty as They Wanna Be," the piece detailed the intentions of a Florida state legislator who pushed to have the group's lyrics monitored and if necessary labeled as pornographic because they offend public sensibilities (*Los Angeles Times,* March 7, 1990, F1).

10. Margin (in)to Future

1. *Demolition Man,* released in 1993 and starring Wesley Snipes, is another interesting example that comes to mind.

2. I want to thank Rosa Linda Fregoso and Dana Takagi, who both insisted on the unreadability of contemporary racial politics in Los Angeles in the language of a pre-civil rights discourse. See also Gooding-Williams (1993).

References

Allen, Jonathan. 1986. "The Struggle for the Soul of CBS News." *Newsweek,* September 15, 52.

Allen, Robert, ed. 1987. *Channels of Discourse: Television and Contemporary Criticism.* Chapel Hill: University of North Carolina Press.

Asante, Molefi K. 1990. *Afrocentricity: The Theory of Social Change,* 2d ed. Trenton, N.J.: Africa World.

Atkins, David, and Barry Litman. 1986. "Network TV Programming: Economics, Audiences, and the Ratings Game, 1971–1986." *Journal of Communications* 36 (Summer): 32–50.

Auletta, Ken. 1991. *Three Blind Mice: How the TV Networks Lost Their Way.* New York: Random House.

_____. 1983. *The Underclass.* New York: Random House.

Baker, Houston. 1991. "Hybridity, the Rap Race, and Pedagogy for the 1990s." Pp. 197–209 in Andrew Ross and Constance Penley (eds.) *Technoculture.* Minneapolis: University of Minnesota Press.

_____. 1984. *Blues, Ideology and Afro-American Literature: A Vernacular Theory.* Chicago: University of Chicago Press.

Baker, Katheryn. 1988. "Prime Time Viewing Down—Nielson." *Boston Globe,* January 7, 38.

Bakhtin, Mikhail. 1984. *Rabelais and His World.* Bloomington: Indiana University Press.

Baraka, Amiri. 1991. "The Changing Same (R&B and New Black Music)." Pp. 186–209 in Amiri Baraka, *The Leroi Jones/Amiri Baraka Reader.* New York: Thunder's Mouth.

Barker, David. 1985. "Television Production Techniques as Communication." *Critical Studies in Mass Communication* 2: 234–46.

Bernstein, Sharon. 1990. " 'Generations' Draws Blacks Despite Ratings" *Los Angeles Times,* March 26, F1, F9.

Berube, Michael. 1991. "Public Image Limited: Political Correctness and the Media's Big Lie." *Village Voice,* June 8, 31–37.

Bielby, William T., and Denise D. Bielby. 1989a. "From Market to Hierarchy: Industrial Change and the Employment Relation in Television Production." Paper presented at the annual meeting of the American Sociological Association, San Francisco.

_____. 1989b. *The 1989 Hollywood Writer's Report: Unequal Access, Unequal Pay.* West Hollywood, Calif.: Writers Guild of America, West.

Bierbaum, Tom. 1990. "Net's Struggle to Stem Viewer Loss Falls Flat." *Variety,* April 18, P1.

Black Film Review. 1993. The History of Black Film [special issue]. Vol. 7, no. 4.

Block, Ben. 1990a. *Outfoxed: Marvin Davis, Barry Diller, Rupert Murdoch, Joan Rivers, and the Inside Story of America's Fourth Television Network.* New York: St. Martin's.

———. 1990b. "Twenty-First Century Fox." *Channels,* January, 36–40.

Bloom, Allan. 1987. *The Closing of the American Mind.* New York: Touchstone.

Bobo, Jacqueline. 1991. "Black Women in Fiction and Non-Fiction: Images of Power and Powerlessness." *Wide Angle* 13, nos. 3–4: 72–81.

———. 1988. *"The Color Purple:* Black Women as Cultural Readers." Pp. 90–109 in E. Deidre Pribram (ed.) *Female Spectators: Looking at Film and Television.* London: Verso.

Bobo, Jacqueline, and E. Seiter. 1991. "Black Feminism and Media Criticism: The Women of Brewster Place." *Screen* 32: 3.

Bradley, David. 1992. "Malcolm Myth Making." *Transition* 56: 20–48.

Braxton, Greg. 1992a. "A 'Different' Take on the L.A. Riots." *Los Angeles Times,* August 13, F1, F9.

———. 1992b. "Sights, Sounds and Stereotypes." *Los Angeles Times,* October 11.

———. 1992c. "Where More Isn't Much Better." *Los Angeles Times,* October 4, Calendar, 3, 82, 84.

———. 1991. "To Him Rap's No Laughing Matter." *Los Angeles Times,* July 14, Calendar, 4, 82, 84.

———. 1990. "Hip-hop TV's Leading Edge." *Los Angeles Times,* November 4, Calendar, 9, 87–88.

Buchalter, Gail. 1988. "I Want to Do More Than Just Survive." *Parade,* August 21, 8–9.

Burns, Gary, and Robert Thompson. 1989. *Television Studies: Textual Analysis.* New York: Praeger.

Butler, Cheryl B. 1991. *"The Color Purple* Controversy: Black Woman Spectatorship." In Manthia Diawara (ed.) Black Cinema [special issue]. *Wide Angle* 13, nos. 3–4: 62–72.

Butsch, Richard. 1990. "Home Video and Corporate Plans: Capital's Limited Power to Manipulate Leisure." Pp. 215–35 in Richard Butsch (ed.) *For Fun and Profit: The Transformation of Leisure into Consumption.* Philadelphia: Temple University Press.

Campbell, Richard. 1991. *60 Minutes and the News: A Mythology for Middle America.* Urbana: University of Illinois Press.

Campbell, Richard, and Jimmie Reeves. 1990. "Television Authors: The Case of Hugh Wilson." Pp. 1–15 in Gary Burns and Robert J. Thompson (eds.) *Television Studies: Authorship.* New York: Praeger.

———. 1989a. "Covering the Homeless: The Joyce Brown Story." *Critical Studies in Mass Communication* 6: 21–42.

———. 1989b. "TV News Narration and Common Sense: Updating the Soviet Threat." *Journal of Film and Video* 42, nos. 2–3: 58–74.

Carby, Hazel. 1987. *Reconstructing Womanhood: The Emergence of the Afro-American Woman Novelist.* New York: Oxford University Press.

———. 1986. "It Jus Be's Dat Way Sometime: The Sexual Politics of Women's Blues." *Radical America* 20, no. 4: 9–22.

Carey, James W. 1989. *Communication as Culture: Essays on Media and Society.* Boston: Unwin Hyman.

———, ed. 1988. *Media, Myths, and Narratives: Television and the Press.* Newbury Park, Calif.: Sage.

Carter, Bill. 1990. "Nervous TV Networks Are Trying the Untried." *New York Times,* September 6, C15, C18.

Chabram, Angie C., and Rosa Linda Fregoso, eds., 1990. Chicana/o Cultural Representations: Reframing Alternative Critical Discourses [special issue]. *Cultural Studies* 4 (October).

Cham, Mbye B., and Claire Andrade-Watkins, eds. 1988. *Black Frames: Critical Perspectives on Independent Black Cinema.* Cambridge: MIT Press.

Childs, John Brown. 1992. "Preparing for the Big One." *Z Magazine,* July/August, 56–58.

———. 1984. "Afro-American Intellectuals and the People's Culture." *Theory and Society* 13: 69–90.

Childs, Ronald E. 1992. "Keenen Ivory Wayans: Tops Ratings Color His Success." *Ebony Man,* March, 62–65.

Christian, Barbara. 1988. "The Race for Theory." *Feminist Studies* 14, no. 1: 69–79.

Christon, Lawrence. 1989. "The World According to the Cos." *Los Angeles Times,* December 10, Calendar, 6, 45–47.

Clark, Stuart Alan. 1991. "Fear of a Black Planet." *Socialist Review* 21, nos. 3–4: 37–41.

Collins, Patricia Hill. 1990. *Black Feminist Thought: Knowledge, Consciousness and the Politics of Empowerment.* New York: Routledge.

———. 1989. "A Comparison of Two Works on Black Family Life." *Signs* 14: 875–84.

Cooper, Michael Barry. 1989. "Big Daddy Hall's New Jack Chit Chat." *Village Voice,* May 23, 27–31.

Cox, Meg. 1989. "Is NBC Putting Ratings before Taste?" *Wall Street Journal,* April 11, B1.

Crenshaw, Kimberle. 1992. "Whose Story Is It Anyway? Feminist and Anti-Racist Appropriations of Anita Hill." Pp. 402–41 in Toni Morrison (ed.) *Race-ing Justice, Engendering Power: Essays on Anita Hill, Clarence Thomas, and the Construction of Social Reality.* New York: Pantheon.

———. 1991. "Beyond Racism and Misogyny: Black Feminism and 2 Live Crew." *Boston Review* 16 (December): 6–33.

———. 1989. "Demarginalizing the Intersection of Race and Sex: A Black Feminist Critique of Anti-Discrimination Doctrine, Feminist Theory, and Anti-Racist Politics." *University of Chicago Legal Forum:* 139–67.

Cripps, Thomas. 1983. *"Amos 'n' Andy* and the Debate over American Racial Integration." Pp. 33–54 in John E. O'Connor (ed.) *American History, American Television: Interpreting the Video Past.* New York: Frederick Ungar.

Czitrom, Daniel. 1982. *Media and the American Mind: From Morse to McLuhan.* Chapel Hill: University of North Carolina Press.

Dart, Bob. 1992. "Yes, TV Can Make You a Jerk." *San Francisco Chronicle,* February 26, D3, D5.

Dates, Jannette. 1990. "Commercial Television." Pp. 253–303 in Jannette Dates and William Barlow (eds.) *Split Image: African Americans in the Mass Media.* Washington, D.C.: Howard University Press.

Dates, Jannette, and William Barlow, eds. 1990. *Split Image: African Americans in the Mass Media.* Washington, D.C.: Howard University Press.

Davis, Miles, and Quincy Troupe. 1992. *Miles: The Autobiography.* New York: Simon & Schuster.

Diawara, Manthia, ed. 1993. *Black American Cinema.* New York: Routledge.

———, ed. 1992a. Black Cinema [special issue]. *Wide Angle* 13, nos. 3–4.

———. 1992b "Cinema Studies, the Strong Thought and Black Film." In Manthia Diawara (ed.) Black Cinema [special issue]. *Wide Angle* 13, nos. 3–4: 4–11.

Di Leonardo, Micaela. 1992. "Boyz on the Hood." *The Nation,* August 17–24, 178–86.

Downing, John. 1988. "The Cosby Show and American Racial Discourse." Pp. 46–74 in G. Smitherman-Donaldson and T. A. Van Dijk (eds.) *Discourse and Discrimination.* Detroit: Wayne State University Press.

D'Souza, Dinesh. 1992. *Illiberal Education: The Politics of Race and Sex on Campus.* New York: Free Press.

Du Brow, Rick. 1990. "Can Jeff Sagansky Steer CBS Back into the TV Limelight?" *Los Angeles Times,* January 13, F12.

Duster, Troy. 1985. "Social Implications of the New Black Urban Underclass." In C. Carson and M. McLeod (eds.) *Poverty with a Human Face.* San Francisco: Public Media Center.

Dworkin, Ronald. 1992. "One Year Later, the Debate Goes On." *New York Times Book Review,* October 25, 1, 33, 38–39.

Dyson, Michael. 1989. "Bill Cosby and the Politics of Race." *Z Magazine,* September, 26–30.

Early, Gerald. 1992. "Their Malcolm, My Problem: On the Abuses of Afrocentrism and Black Anger." *Harper's,* December, 62.

———. 1989. *Tuxedo Junction.* Hopewell, N.J.: Ecco.

Easton, Nina J. 1991. "Good News/Bad News of the New Black Cinema." *Los Angeles Times,* June 16, Calendar, 5–6, 86–87.

Edsall, Thomas. 1984. *The New Politics of Inequality.* New York: W. W. Norton.

Edsall, Thomas B., and Mary D. Edsall. 1991. *Chain Reaction: The Impact of Race, Rights, and Taxes on American Politics.* New York: W. W. Norton.

Ehrenreich, Barbara. 1990. *Fear of Falling: The Inner Life of the Middle Class.* New York: HarperCollins.

Ely, Melvin Patrick. 1991. *The Adventures of Amos 'n' Andy: A Social History of an American Phenomenon.* New York: Free Press.

Epstein, Barbara. 1991. "Political Correctness and Collective Powerlessness." *Socialist Review* 21, nos. 3–4: 13–37.

Fabrikant, Geraldine. 1992. "For NBC, Hard Times and Miscues." *New York Times,* December 13, sec. 3, pp. 1, 6.

Farley, Reynolds. 1984. *Blacks and Whites: Narrowing the Gap.* Cambridge: Harvard University Press.

Farley, Reynolds, and Walter Allen. 1987. *The Color Line and the Quality of Life in America.* New York: Russell Sage Foundation.

Ferguson, Russell, et al., eds., 1990. *Out There: Marginalization and Contemporary Cultures.* Cambridge: MIT Press.

Feuer, Jane. 1987. "The MTM Style." Pp. 52–84 in Horace Newcomb (ed.) *Television: The Critical View.* 4th ed. New York: Oxford University Press.

———. 1986 "Narrative Form in American Network Television." In Colin McCabe (ed.) *High Theory/Low Culture: Analyzing Popular Television and Film.* New York: St. Martin's.

Finke, Nikki, and Diane Haithman. 1989. "Life in the TV Pressure Cooker." *Los Angeles Times,* March 23, sec. 6, pp. 1, 10.

Fiske, John. 1989. *Understanding Popular Culture.* Winchester, Mass.: Unwin Hyman.

———. 1987. *Television Culture.* London: Methuen.

Fiske, John, and John Hartley. 1978. *Reading Television.* London: Methuen.

Foster, Hal. 1985. *Recodings: Art, Spectacle, and Cultural Politics.* Port Townsend, Wash.: Bay.

Framework. 1989. Third Scenario: Theory and the Politics of Location [special issue]. Vol. 36.

Frazier, E. Franklin. 1957. *Black Bourgeoisie: The Rise of a New Middle Class.* New York: Free Press.

Fregoso, Rosa Linda. 1993. *The Bronze Screen: Chicana and Chicano Film Culture.* Minneapolis: University of Minnesota Press.

———. 1990a. *"Born in East L.A.:* Chicano Cinema and the Politics of Representation." In Angie C. Chabram and Rosa Linda Fregoso (eds.) Chicana/o Cultural Representations: Reframing Alternative Critical Discourses [special issue]. *Cultural Studies* 4 (October): 264–81.

———. 1990b. "Hyperidity in Chicano Cinema." Paper presented at the meeting of the International Association for the Study of Popular Music, New Orleans, May.

Frith, Simon, ed. 1988. *Facing the Music: Pantheon Guide to Popular Culture.* New York: Pantheon.

Fuller, Linda K. 1992. *The Cosby Show: Audiences, Impact, and Implication.* Westport, Conn.: Greenwood.

Gans, Herbert. 1979. *Deciding What's News: A Study of the CBS Evening News, NBC Nightly News, Newsweek, and Time.* New York: Pantheon.

Garfinkel, Perry. 1988. "Frank's Place: The Restaurant as Life Stage." *New York Times,* February 17, C1.

Gates, David. 1990. "Decoding Rap Music." *Newsweek,* March 19, 60–63.

Gates, Henry Louis, Jr. 1992a. "Black Demagogues and Pseudo-Scholars." *New York Times,* July 20, A15.

———. 1992b. *Loose Canons: Notes on the Culture Wars.* New York: Oxford University Press.

———. 1989. "TV's Black World Turns—but Stays Unreal." *New York Times,* November 12, Arts and Leisure, 1, 40.

———. 1987. "What's in a Name? Some Meanings of Blackness." *Dissent* (Fall): 487–95.

Garofalo, Reebee, ed. 1992. *Rockin' the Boat: Mass Music and Mass Movements.* Boston: South End.

George, Lynell. 1993. "Brave New World: Grayboys, Funky Aztecs, and Honorary Homegirls." *Los Angeles Times Magazine,* January 17, 14.

George, Nelson. 1992. *Buppies, B-Boys, Baps, and Bohos: Notes on Post Soul Black Culture.* New York: HarperCollins.

Gillespie, Dizzy, and Al Fraser. 1979. *To Be or Not to Bop: Memoirs of Dizzy Gillespie.* Garden City, N.Y.: Doubleday.

Gilroy, Paul. 1993. *The Black Atlantic: Modernity and Double Consciousness.* Cambridge: Harvard University Press.

———. 1992. "Cultural Studies and Ethnic Absolutism." Pp. 187–99 in Lawrence Grossberg, Cary Nelson, and Paula A. Treichler (eds.) *Cultural Studies.* New York: Routledge.

———. 1991a. "Sounds Authentic: Black Music, Ethnicity, and the Challenge of a 'Changing Same.' " *Black Music Research Journal* 11, no. 2: 111–36.

———. 1991b. *There Ain't No Black in the Union Jack: The Cultural Politics of Race and Nation.* Chicago: University of Chicago Press.

———. 1990. "One Nation under a Groove: The Cultural Politics of Race and Racism in Britain." Pp. 263–82 in David T. Goldberg (ed.) *The Anatomy of Racism.* Minneapolis: University of Minnesota Press.

Gitlin, Todd. 1990. "Down the Tubes." P. 49 in Mark Crispin Miller (ed.) *Seeing through Movies.* Pantheon: New York.

———. 1986. *Watching Television.* New York: Pantheon.

———. 1983. *Inside Prime Time.* New York: Pantheon.

Glasgow, Douglas. 1981. *The Black Underclass: Poverty, Unemployment and the Entrapment of Ghetto Youth.* New York: Vintage.

Goldberg, David T., ed. 1990. *The Anatomy of Racism.* Minneapolis: University of Minnesota Press.

Goldman, Kevin. 1991. "ABC and a Producer Who Gets Big Bucks Hit a Rough Patch."
    Wall Street Journal, October 29, A1, A8.
Goldstein, Patrick. 1991. "His New Hood Is Hollywood." *Los Angeles Times,* July 7,
    Calendar, 6–7, 22.
Goldstein, Richard. 1991. "The Politics of Political Correctness." *Village Voice,* June
    18, 39–41.
Gooding-Williams, Robert, ed. 1993. *Reading Rodney King—Reading Urban Uprising.*
    New York: Routledge.
Goodwin, Andrew. 1992. *Dancing in the Distraction Factory: Music Television and
    Popular Culture.* Minneapolis: University of Minnesota Press.
Gray, Herman. 1993a. "African American Political Desire and the Seductions of Con-
    temporary Cultural Politics." *Cultural Studies* 7: 364–74.
_____. 1993b "Black and White and in Color." *American Quarterly* 45: 467–72.
_____. 1993c. "The Endless Slide of Difference." *Critical Studies in Mass Communi-
    cation* 10: 190–97.
_____. 1991. "Oppositional Readings, Mainstream Writing: A Review of *Split Image:
    African Americans in the Media." Journal of Communication* 41, no. 4: 145–47.
_____. 1989. "Television, Black Americans and the American Dream." *Critical Studies
    in Mass Communication* 6: 376–87.
_____. 1986. "Television and the New Black Man: Black Male Images in Prime Time
    Situation Comedy." *Media, Culture and Society* 8: 223–43.
Greenly, Andrew. "Today's Morality Play: The Sitcom." *New York Times,* May 17, Arts
    and Leisure, 1, 40.
Grossberg, Lawrence. 1992. *We Gotta Get Outta This Place: Popular Conservatism
    and Postmodern Culture.* New York: Routledge.
Guerrero, Ed. 1993. *Framing Blackness: The African American Image in Film.* Philadel-
    phia: Temple University Press.
Gunther, Marc. 1990. "Black Producers Add a Fresh Nuance." *New York Times,* Au-
    gust 26, Arts and Leisure, 25, 31.
Hacker, Andrew. 1992. *Two Nations: Black and White, Separate, Hostile, Unequal.*
    New York: Charles Scribner's Sons.
Haithman, Diane. 1990. "NBC President Pleads for Easing of Constraints." *Los Ange-
    les Times,* January 17, F9.
_____. 1989. "Generations in Black and White." *Los Angeles Times,* March 27, sec. 6,
    pp. 1, 8.
Hall, Stuart. 1992a. "Cultural Studies and Its Theoretical Legacies." Pp. 277–95 in
    Lawrence Grossberg, Cary Nelson, and Paula A. Triechler (eds.) *Cultural Studies.*
    New York: Routledge.
_____. 1992b. "What Is This 'Black' in Black Popular Culture?" Pp. 21–37 in Michelle
    Wallace, *Black Popular Culture: A Project by Michelle Wallace* (Gina Dent, ed.). Se-
    attle: Bay.
_____. 1990. "The Emergence of Cultural Studies and the Crisis of the Humanities."
    October 53: 11–25.
_____. 1989. "Cultural Identity and Cinematic Representation." *Framework* 36: 68–82.
_____. 1988. "Toad in the Garden: Thatcher among the Theorists." In Cary Nelson
    and Lawrence Grossberg (eds.) *Marxism and the Interpretation of Culture.* Urbana:
    University of Illinois Press.
_____. 1986. "On Postmodernism and Articulation." *Journal of Communication In-
    quiry* 10, no. 2: 45–60.
_____. 1985. "Signification, Representation, Ideology: Althusser and the Post-Struc-
    turalist Debates." *Critical Studies in Mass Communication* 2: 91–114.

_____. 1981a. "Notes on Deconstructing the Popular." In Raphael Samuel (ed.) *People's History and Socialist Theory*. London: Routledge & Kegan Paul.

_____. 1981b. "Whites of Their Eyes: Racist Ideology and the Media." In George Bridges and Rosalind Brunt (eds.) *Silver Linings*. London: Lawrence & Wishart.

_____. 1980. "Encoding/Decoding." In S. Hall et al. (eds.) *Culture, Media, Language*. London: Hutchinson.

Hampton, Henry. 1989. "The Camera Lens as Two-Edged Sword." *New York Times*, January 15, H29, H37.

Hazzard-Gordon, Katrina. 1990. *Jookin': The Rise of Dance Formations in African American Culture*. Philadelphia: Temple University Press.

Hebdige, Dick. 1988. *Hiding in the Light: On Images and Things*. London: Comedia.

_____. 1979. *Subculture: The Meaning of Style*. London: Methuen.

Hoberman, J. 1991. *Vulgar Modernism: Writings on Movies and Other Media*. Philadelphia: Temple University Press.

hooks, bell. 1992. *Black Looks: Race and Representation*. Boston: South End.

Horowitz, Jay. 1989. "Hollywood's Dirty Little Secret." *Premiere*, March, 56, 59–64.

Hughes, Robert. 1992 "The Fraying of America." *Time*, February 3, 44–49.

Institute for the Study of Social Change. 1992. *Diversity Report*. Berkeley: University of California.

Jameson, Fredric. 1979. "Reification and Utopia in Mass Culture." *Social Text* 1: 130–48.

Jhally, Sut, and Justin Lewis. 1992. *Enlightened Racism: The Cosby Show, Audiences, and the Myth of the American Dream*. Boulder, Colo.: Westview.

Johnson, Haynes. 1991. *Sleepwalking through History: America through the Reagan Years*. New York: W. W. Norton.

Johnson, James H., and Melvin Oliver. 1991. "Economic Restructuring and Black Male Joblessness in U.S. Metropolitan Areas." *Urban Geography* 12: 542–62.

_____. 1989. "Inter-Ethnic Minority Conflict in Urban America: The Effects of Economic and Social Dislocations." *Urban Geography* 10: 449–63.

Jones, Jacquie. 1991. "The New Ghetto Aesthetic." In Manthia Diawara (ed.) Black Cinema [special issue]. *Wide Angle* 13, nos. 3–4: 32–44.

Kaplan, Peter W. 1986. "Dads Who Know Best." *Esquire*, June, 167–69.

Katz, Michael. 1989. *The Undeserving Poor: From the War on Poverty to the War on Welfare*. New York: Pantheon.

Kelley, Robin D. G. 1994. "Kickin Reality, Kickin Ballistics: The Cultural Politics of Gangsta Rap in Postindustrial Los Angeles." In Eric Perkins (ed.) *Droppin' Science: Critical Essays on Rap Music and Hip Hop Culture*. Philadephia: Temple University Press.

_____. 1992. "Notes on Deconstructing 'the Folk.' " *American Historical Review* 97: 1400–1406.

Kellner, Douglas. 1990. *Television and the Crisis of Democracy*. Boulder, Colo.: Westview.

Kennedy, Lisa. 1990. "Wack House: *House Party* Is Business as Usual." *Village Voice*, March 13, 67.

Keyes, Cheryl. 1984. "Verbal Art Performance in Rap Music: The Conversation of the 80s." *Folklore Forum* 17: 143–52.

Kilson, Martin. 1981. "Black Social Classes and Intergenerational Poverty." *Public Interest* 64: 58–78.

Kimball, Roger. 1990. *Tenured Radicals: How Politics Has Corrupted Our Higher Education*. New York: Harper & Row.

Koch, Neal. 1990. "West Coast Time." *Channels*, February, 45.

Kolbert, Elizabeth. 1993. "From 'Beulah' to Oprah: The Evolution of Black Images on TV." *New York Times*, January 15, B4.

Kroker, Arthur, and Marilouise Kroker, eds. 1988. *Body Invaders: Panic Sex in America.* New York: St. Martin's.

Landry, Bart. 1987. *The New Black Middle Class.* Berkeley: University of California Press.

Lemman, Nicholas. 1984. "The Culture of Poverty." *Atlantic,* September, 26.

Lester, Julius. 1991. "The Unkindness of Strangers." *Transition* 53: 79–86.

Lippman, John. 1990. "Cosby Makers Ask NBC for a $1 Million Bonus." *Los Angeles Times,* March 22, A1.

Lipsitz, George. 1994. "We Know What Time It Is: Race, Class, and Youth in the Nineties." Pp. 15–29 in Andrew Ross and Tricia Rose (eds.) *Microphone Fiends: Youth, Music, and Youth Culture.* New York: Routledge.

——. 1990a. "Listening to Learn and Learning to Listen: Popular Culture, Cultural Theory, and American Studies." *American Quarterly* 42: 615–37.

——. 1990b. *Time Passages: Collective Memory and American Popular Culture.* Minneapolis: University of Minnesota Press.

Lorde, Audre. 1990. "Age, Race, Class, and Sex: Women Redefining Difference." Pp. 281–89 in Russell Ferguson et al. (eds.) *Out There: Maginalization and Contemporary Cultures.* Cambridge: MIT Press.

Los Angeles Times. 1990. "FCC Considering Ending Cable TV Monopolies." *Los Angeles Times,* January 12, D2.

Loury, Glenn C. 1985a. "Beyond Civil Rights." *New Republic,* October 7, 22–25.

——. 1985b. "The Moral Quandary of the Black Community." *Public Interest* 79: 9–22.

Lubiano, Wahneema. 1992. "Black Ladies, Welfare Queens, and State Minstrels: Ideological War by Narrative Means." Pp. 323–64 in Toni Morrison (ed.) *Race-ing Justice, En-gendering Power: Essays on Anita Hill, Clarence Thomas, and the Construction of Social Reality.* New York: Pantheon.

MacDonald, J. Fred. 1983. *Blacks and White TV: Afro-Americans in Television since 1948.* Chicago: Nelson-Hall.

Marchand, Roland. 1985. *Advertising the American Dream: Making Way for Modernity, 1920–1940.* Berkeley: University of California Press.

Mathews, Jack. 1990. "What Pathe Is Getting for $1 Billion MGM Buyout." *Los Angeles Times,* March 8, F1, F4.

Marable, Manning. 1991. *Race, Reform, and Rebellion: The Second Reconstruction in Black America, 1945–1990.* 2d ed. Jackson: University of Mississippi Press.

Marriott, Michael. 1993. "Harsh Rap Lyrics Provoke Black Backlash." *New York Times,* August 15, sec. 1, p. 16.

McCain, Nina. 1986. "The Significance of Cosby." *Boston Globe,* February 20, Living/ Arts, 69–70.

McClaurin-Allen, Irma. 1987. "Working: The Black Actress in the Twentieth Century: Interview with Rosalind Cash." *Contributions in Black Studies: A Journal of African and Afro-American Studies* 8: 67–77.

McDowell, Deborah E. 1987. "The Changing Same: Generational Connections and Black Women Novelists." *New Literary History: A Journal of Theory and Interpretation* 18: 281–302.

Meechan, Eileen. 1990. "Why We Don't Count: The Commodity Audience." In P. Mellencamp (ed.) *The Logics of Television: Essays in Cultural Criticism.* Bloomington: Indiana University Press.

Mellencamp, Patricia, ed. 1990. *The Logics of Television: Essays in Cultural Criticism.* Bloomington: Indiana University Press.

Mercer, Kobena. 1992. " '1968': Periodizing Postmodern Politics and Identity." Pp. 424–50 in Lawrence Grossberg, Cary Nelson, and Paula A. Treichler (eds.) *Cultural Studies*. New York: Routledge.

———. 1990. "Black Hair/Style Politics." Pp. 247–65 in Russell Ferguson et al. (eds.) *Out There: Marginalization and Contemporary Cultures*. Cambridge: MIT Press.

Michaelson, Judith. 1991. "TV Adjusts Its Mirror." *Los Angeles Times*, September 22, Calendar, 5, 78–80.

Miller, Judith. 1992. "The Republicans: Can They Get It Together?" *New York Times Magazine*, August 16, 18.

Miller, Mark Crispin. 1990a. "End of Story." Pp. 186–247 in Mark Crispin Miller (ed.) *Seeing through Movies*. New York: Pantheon.

———, ed. 1990b. *Seeing through Movies*. New York: Pantheon.

———. 1988. "Cosby Knows Best." In Mark Crispin Miller (ed.) *Boxed In: The Culture of TV*. Evanston, Ill.: Northwestern University Press.

———. 1986. "Dads and Their Discontents." *Village Voice*, November 25, 45–47.

Montgomery, Katheryn. 1989. *Target Prime Time*. New York: Oxford University Press.

Morley, David. 1986. *Family Television: Cultural Power and Domestic Leisure*. London: Comedia.

Morrison, Toni. 1992a. "Introduction: Friday on the Potomac." In Toni Morrison (ed.) *Race-ing Justice, En-gendering Power: Essays on Anita Hill, Clarence Thomas, and the Construction of Social Reality*. New York: Pantheon.

———. 1992b. *Playing in the Dark: Whiteness and the Literary Imagination*. Cambridge: Harvard University Press.

Moyers, Bill. 1986. "Taking CBS News to Task." *Newsweek*, September 15, 53.

Murray, Charles. 1984. *Losing Ground: American Social Policy, 1950–1980*. New York: Basic Books.

Nasar, Sylvia. 1992. "The Rich Get Richer, but Never the Same Way Twice." *New York Times*, August 16, sec. 1, p. 3.

New York Times. 1987. "Writers Guild Contends Producers Practice Bias." June 24, sec. 1.

Newcomb, Horace. 1984. "On the Dialogic Aspects of Mass Communication." *Critical Studies in Mass Communication* 1: 34–50.

Newcomb, Horace, and Robert S. Alley. 1983. *The Producer's Medium: Conversations with Creators of American TV*. New York: Oxford University Press.

Newcomb, Horace, and Paul Hirsch. 1983. "Television as a Cultural Forum: Implications for Research." *Quarterly Review of Film Studies* 8 (Summer): 45–55.

Newsweek. 1991. "Was Cleopatra Black?" September 23, 42–52.

———. 1990. "Taking Offense." December 24, 48–55.

Nicholson, David. 1992. "The Director with Tongue Untied." *Washington Post*, June 15, C1, C4.

Njeri, Itabari. 1993. "The Menace of Nihilism." *Los Angeles Times Magazine*, August 29, 33.

———. 1989. "Fresh Talk." *Los Angeles Times Magazine*, April 16, 10–18, 48–50.

Normant, Lynn. 1985. "The Cosby Show: The Real Life Drama behind Hit TV Show about a Black Family." *Ebony*, April, 27–34.

O'Connor, John E., ed. 1983. *American History, American Television: Interpreting the Video Past*. New York: Frederick Ungar.

O'Connor, John J. 1992. "Still Trapped in a Vast Wasteland." *New York Times*, December 13, sec. 2, pp. 1, 31.

———. 1991. "Blacks on TV: Scrambled Signals." *New York Times*, October 27, sec. 2, pp. 1, 36.

———. 1990. "On TV Less Separate, More Equal." *New York Times,* April 29, sec. 2, pp. 1, 35.
Omi, Michael. 1989. "*In Living Color:* Race and American Culture." Pp. 111–23 in Sut Jhally and I. Angus (eds.) *Cultural Politics in Contemporary America.* New York: Routledge.
Omi, Michael, and Howard Winant. 1993. "The Los Angeles 'Race Riot' and Contemporary U.S. Politics." In Robert Gooding-Williams (ed.) *Reading Rodney King—Reading Urban Uprising.* New York: Routledge.
———. 1986. *Racial Formation in the United States: From the 1960s to the 1980s.* New York: Routledge.
Phillips, Kevin. 1991. *The Politics of Rich and Poor: Wealth and the American Electorate in the Reagan Aftermath.* New York: Harper Perennial.
Pines, Jim, and Paul Willemen. 1989. *Questions of Third Cinema.* London: British Film Institute.
Powell, Bill, and Jonathan Alter. 1986. "Civil War at CBS." *Newsweek,* September 15, 46–50.
Press, Andrea. 1991. *Women Watching Television: Gender, Class, and Generation in the American Television Experience.* Philadelphia: University of Pennsylvania Press.
Real, Michael. 1991. "Bill Cosby and Reading Ethnicity." Pp. 58–84 in Leah R. Vande Berg and Lawrence A. Wenner (eds.) *Television Criticism: Approaches and Applications.* London: Longman.
Reed, Adolph. 1991a. "The Rise of Louis Farrakhan: Parts 1/2." *The Nation,* January 21/28, 51–56/86–92.
———. 1991b. "The Underclass as Myth and Symbol: The Poverty of Discourse about Poverty." *Radical America* 24, no. 1: 21–43.
———. 1988. "The Liberal Technocrat." *The Nation,* February 6, 167–70.
Reed, Adolph, and Julian Bond. 1991. "Equality: Why We Can't Wait." *The Nation,* February 9, 733–37.
Reeves, Jimmie. 1988. "Rewriting Newhart: A Dialogic Analysis." *Wide Angle* 10, no. 1: 76–91.
Reeves, Jimmie, and Richard Campbell. 1994. *Cracked Coverage: Television News, the Anti-Cocaine Crusade, and the Reagan Legacy.* Durham, N.C.: Duke University Press.
———. 1989. "Misplacing *Frank's Place:* Do You Know What It Means to Miss New Orleans?" *Television Quarterly* 24, no. 1: 45–60.
Reid, Mark. 1993. *Redefining Black Film.* Berkeley: University of California Press.
Ressner, Jeffrey. 1990. "Off-Color TV." *Rolling Stone,* August 23, 50.
Rief, David. 1991. *Los Angeles: Capital of the Third World.* New York: Touchstone.
Riggs, Marlon. 1991a. *Color Adjustment* (film). San Francisco: California Newsreel.
———. 1991b. "Confessions of a Snap Queen." In Valerie Smith, C. Billops, and A. Griffin (eds.) [Special issue]. *Black American Literature Forum* 25, no. 2.
Roediger, David R. 1991. *The Wages of Whiteness: Race and the Making of the American Working Class.* London: Verso.
Rogin, Michael. 1990. "Make My Day! Spectacle as Amnesia in Imperial Politics." *Representations* (Winter): 99–124.
———. 1987. *Ronald Reagan: The Movie.* Berkeley: University of California Press.
Rose, Tricia. 1994. *Black Noise: Rap Music and Black Culture in Contemporary America.* Middletown, Conn.: Wesleyan University Press.
———. 1990. "Never Trust a Big Butt and a Smile." *Camera Obscura* 23: 109–31.
———. 1989. "Orality and Technology: Rap Music and Afro-American Cultural Resistance." *Popular Music and Society* 13, no. 4: 35–41.

Rosentiel, Thomas B. 1989. "TV News: Is Seeing Believing?" *Los Angeles Times,* November 5, A1.

Sawchuk, Kim. 1988. "A Tale of Inscription/Fashion Statements." Pp. 60–77 in Arthur Kroker and Marilouise Kroker (eds.) *Body Invaders: Panic Sex in America.* New York: St. Martin's.

Schulman, Norma M. 1992. "Laughing Across the Color Line: *In Living Color.*" *Journal of Popular Film and Television* 1 (Spring): 2–8.

Siegel, Ed. 1989a. "The Networks Go Ethnic." *Boston Globe,* September 16, Living/Arts, 7, 14.

———. 1989b. "Season of Slim Pickings." *Boston Globe,* July 13, Living/Arts, 69, 74.

Smith, Valerie, C. Billops, and A. Griffin, eds. 1991. [Special issue]. *Black American Literature Forum* 25, no. 2.

Snead, James A. 1990. "On Repetition in Black Culture." In Russell Ferguson et al. *Out There: Marginalization and Contemporary Cultures.* Cambridge: MIT Press.

Sowell, Thomas. 1984. *Civil Rights: Rhetoric or Reality?* New York: William Morrow.

———. 1983. *The Economics of Politics and Race.* New York: William Morrow.

———. 1981. *Ethnic America: A History.* New York: Basic Books.

Spigel, Lynn. 1992. *Make Room for TV: Television and the Family Ideal in Postwar America.* Chicago: University of Chicago Press.

Stamets, Bill. 1992. "Marlon Riggs: In His Own Image." *In These Times,* April 22, 5–6.

Steele, Shelby. 1990. *The Content of Our Character.* New York: St. Martin's.

Steenland, Sally. 1989. *Unequal Picture: Black, Hispanic, Asian, and Native American Characters on Television.* Washington, D.C.: National Commission on Working Women.

———. 1987. *Prime Time Power: Women Producers, Writers, and Directors in TV.* Washington, D.C.: National Commission on Working Women.

Steinfels, Peter. 1979. *The Neo-Conservatives: The Men Who Are Changing America's Politics.* New York: Simon & Schuster.

Takagi, Dana. 1993. *Retreat from Race: Asian Admissions and Racial Politics.* New Brunswick, N.J.: Rutgers University Press.

Tartikoff, Brandon. 1992. *The Last Great Ride.* New York: Turtle Bay.

Tate, Greg. 1992. *Flyboy in the Buttermilk: Essays on Contemporary America.* New York: Simon & Schuster.

Taylor, Clyde. Forthcoming. *Breaking the Aesthetic Contract.* Minneapolis: University of Minnesota Press.

———. 1991. "The Rebirth of the Aesthetic in Cinema." In Manthia Diawara (ed.) Black Cinema [special issue]. *Wide Angle* 13, nos. 3–4, 12–30.

———. 1988. "We Don't Need Another Hero: Anti-Thesis on Aesthetics." Pp. 80–85 in Mbye B. Cham and Claire Andrade-Watkins (eds.) *Black Frames: Critical Perspectives on Independent Black Cinema.* Cambridge: MIT Press.

Taylor, Ella. 1989. *Prime-Time Families: Television Culture in Postwar America.* Berkeley: University of California Press.

Torres, Richard. 1990. "Prime Time Apartheid." *City Sun,* February 28–March 6, 10.

Turner, Patricia A. 1994. *Ceramic Uncles and Celluloid Mammies.* Garden City, N.Y.: Anchor.

Vianello, Robert. 1984. "The Rise of the Telefilm and the Network's Hegemony over the Motion Picture Industry." *Quarterly Review of Film Studies* 9: 204–18.

Wallace, Michelle. 1992a. *Black Popular Culture: A Project by Michelle Wallace* (Gina Dent, ed.). Seattle: Bay.

———. 1992b. "Negative Images: Toward a Black Feminist Cultural Criticism." Pp. 654–72 in Lawrence Grossberg, Cary Nelson, and Paula Treichler (eds.) *Cultural Studies*. New York: Routledge.

———. 1990a. *Invisibility Blues: From Pop to Theory*. London: Verso.

———. 1990b. "Modernism, Postmodernism, and the Problem of the Visual in Afro-American Culture." Pp. 39–51 in Russell Ferguson et al. (eds.) *Out There: Marginalization and Contemporary Cultures*. Cambridge: MIT Press.

Washington, Erwin. 1989. "Why? And What Can Be Done?" *Crisis Magazine*, 96, no. 6: 34–42.

Waters, Harry F., and Janet Huck. 1988. "TV's New Racial Hue." *Newsweek*, January 25, 52–54.

Wellman, David T. 1993. *Portraits of White Racism*. 2d ed. New York: Cambridge University Press.

West, Cornel. 1993. *Race Matters*. Boston: Beacon.

———. 1992a. "Learning to Talk of Race." *New York Times Sunday Magazine*, August 2, 24.

———. 1992b. "The Postmodern Crisis of the Black Intellectual." Pp. 689–706 in Lawrence Grossberg, Cary Nelson, and Paula A. Treichler (eds.) *Cultural Studies*. New York: Routledge.

———. 1990. "The New Cultural Politics of Difference." Pp. 19–39 in Russell Ferguson et al. (eds.) *Out There: Marginalization and Contemporary Cultures*. Cambridge: MIT Press.

White, E. Francis. 1990. "Africa on My Mind: Gender, Counter Discourse, and African-American Nationalism." *Journal of Women's History* 2, no. 1: 73–97.

White, Mimi. 1991. "What's the Difference? Frank's Place in Television." In Manthia Diawara (ed.) Black Cinema [special issue]. *Wide Angle* 13, nos. 3–4: 82–96.

Whyte, William H. 1989. *City: Rediscovering Its Center*. Garden City, N.Y.: Doubleday.

Williams, Huntington. 1989. *Beyond Control: ABC and the Fate of the Networks*. New York: Atheneum.

Williams, Patricia J. 1991. *The Alchemy of Race and Rights: Diary of a Law Professor*. Cambridge: Harvard University Press.

Williams, Raymond. 1977. *Marxism and Literature*. New York: Oxford University Press.

Williams, Walter. 1982. *The State against Blacks*. New York: McGraw-Hill.

Willis, Susan. 1991. *A Primer for Everyday Life*. New York: Routledge.

Wilson, Hugh. 1988. "Observations on the Meaning of *Frank's Place*." Presented at the seminar on *Frank's Place* at the annual meeting of the Speech Communication Association, New Orleans.

Wilson, William J. 1987. *The Truly Disadvantaged: The Inner City, the Underclass, and Public Policy*. Chicago: University of Chicago Press.

———. 1980. *The Declining Significance of Race: Blacks and Changing American Institutions*. 2d ed. Chicago: University of Chicago Press.

Winston, Michael R. 1982. "Racial Consciousness and the Evolution of Mass Communication in the United States." *Daedalus* 111: 171–82.

Wood, Joe. 1992. *Malcolm X: In Our Own Image*. New York: St. Martin's.

Zook, Kristal Brent. 1994. "How I Became the Prince of a Town Called Bel Air: Nationalist Desire in Black Television." Doctoral dissertation, University of California, Santa Cruz.

———. 1992. "Reconstructions of Nationalist Thought in Black Music and Culture." Pp. 255–66 in Reebee Garofalo (ed.) *Rockin' the Boat: Mass Music and Mass Movements*. Boston: South End.

Index

Compiled by Robin Jackson

Herman Gray teaches cultural studies, popular culture, mass media, and African American culture in the Sociology Board at the University of California, Santa Cruz. He is on the editorial boards of *Cultural Studies, Critical Studies in Mass Communication,* and *Communication Research,* and is also a member of the board of directors of Signifyin' Works, an independent film company begun by Marlon Riggs. He participated in the making of Riggs's independent documentary film about the history of black representations in television, *Color Adjustment.*